GOD'S LAST AND ONLY HOPE

God's Last and Only Hope

THE FRAGMENTATION OF THE
SOUTHERN BAPTIST CONVENTION

Bill J. Leonard

William B. Eerdmans Publishing Company
Grand Rapids, Michigan

Copyright © 1990 by Wm. B. Eerdmans Publishing Co.
255 Jefferson Ave. S.E., Grand Rapids, Mich. 49503

Printed in the United States of America

Library of Congress Cataloging-in-Publication Data

Leonard, Bill.
    God's last and only hope: the fragmentation of the Southern Baptist Convention /
Bill J. Leonard.
        p.   cm.
    Includes bibliographical references.
    ISBN 0-8028-0498-5
    1. Southern Baptist Convention—History—20th century. 2. Baptists—United
States—History—20th century. 3. Church controversies—Baptists—History—20th
century. 4. Fundamentalism. I. Title.
BX6462.3.L46   1990
286′.132—dc20
                                                                        90-35591
                                                                            CIP

To
Candyce C. Leonard
and
Stephanie E. Leonard
women—family—friends

I am more tremendously convinced than ever that the last hope, the fairest hope, the only hope for evangelizing this world on New Testament principles is the Southern Baptist people represented in that Convention. I mean no unkindness to anybody on earth, but if you call that bigotry then make the most of it.

Levi Elder Barton
June 29, 1948

Contents

Preface

IN 1922, J. FRANK NORRIS, THE PASTOR OF FIRST BAPTIST CHURCH, FORT Worth, Texas, wrote, "That thing you call the denomination, that machine, . . . destroys the initiative of the individual and makes him a cog in the wheel. . . . It's wholly contrary to the New Testament."[1] Ten years later, T. T. Martin, one of the Southern Baptist Convention's best-known evangelists, wrote that "Pastor J. Frank Norris and those lining up with him are now organizing 'Fundamentalist' Baptist churches in different cities, and it is spreading." Martin warned that Norris and his followers had caused "the wreckage of the influence of God's ministers of the Gospel; the injuring of the work of pastors and churches; the tearing down of institutions; the turning of thousands and scores of thousands from the co-operative work of Baptists."[2] Martin, a staunch conservative, declared that it was time for Southern Baptists to activate the "Paul-with-Peter policy," withstanding Norris "to the face because he was to be blamed" (Gal. 2:11).[3] Throughout most of this century, Southern Baptists of various types have been "withstanding" each other over issues of theology and denominational relationships. In 1990, that confrontation continues with greater intensity than ever before.

Controversy and schism have characterized American religious history since the colonial period. Well before the Revolution, there were Old Side and New Side Presbyterians, Old Light and New Light Congregationalists, not to mention Regular and Separate Baptists. The impulse to divide and separate continued on the American frontier as Cumberland Presbyterians, Disciples, Primitive Baptists, and other splinters organized

1. *The Search Light*, Dec. 29, 1922.
2. T. T. Martin, *The Inside of the Cup Turned Out* (Jackson, Tenn.: McCowat-Mercer Printing Co., 1932), p. 1.
3. Ibid., p. 2.

out of both theological and polity disputes—over salvation, ordination, missions, or revivalism. By the mid-nineteenth century, sectional, racial, and political issues had resulted in formal schisms between northern and southern Presbyterians, Methodists, and Baptists. In the early twentieth century, new controversies over science, evolution, biblical criticism, and other elements of "modernism" further factionalized American Protestants. Throughout this century, controversy spawned new denominations as liberals, conservatives, and fundamentalists disagreed over the nature of orthodoxy in a changing world. Consensus as to the meaning of orthodox Christianity was elusive even among conservatives. For example, after disputes between fundamentalists and liberals in the 1930s had led Princeton Seminary Professor J. Gresham Machen to leave the Presbyterian Church, U.S.A., and to found the Orthodox Presbyterian Church and Westminster Seminary, ultrafundamentalist Carl McIntire split with Machen and organized the Bible Presbyterian Church and Faith Seminary. Still later, Covenant College and Seminary were established as a result of schism in the ranks of McIntire's group. Few American denominations escape eventual fragmentation in some form.

Nor do denominations divide amicably. Theological objectivity and Christian charity wane as the defense of truth is pitted against the forces of darkness or ignorance. Lofty ideals and prophetic declarations often deteriorate into diatribes and character assassinations. Caricatures of the "enemy" abound. During the First Great Awakening of the 1740s, Presbyterian preacher Gilbert Tennent responded to criticism of the revivals by warning of the "danger of an unconverted ministry." He asked: "Is a dead Man fit to bring others to Life? . . . Isn't an unconverted Minister like a Man who would learn others to swim, before he has learn'd it himself, and so is drowned in the Act, and dies like a Fool?"[4] Tennent's contemporary, Charles Chauncy, the pastor of First Church, Boston, responded to such attacks by insisting that "A real, thorow Conversion from Sin to GOD in CHRIST is necessary; and to affirm it to be so is sound Doctrine; but to say that we can't be converted, unless we know the precise Time when this Change is wrought, is corrupt and false." He concluded that "Ministers should take heed to their doctrine, that it be real, not imaginary. . . . It should be Truth bottomed on the Word of GOD, and not a meer Notion, a Fancy that has Existence no where but in their own over-heated Brains."[5] Almost two centuries later evangelist

---

4. Gilbert Tennent, "The Danger of an Unconverted Ministry," in H. Shelton Smith et al., *American Christianity*, vol. 1 (New York: Scribner, 1960), pp. 325-26.

5. Charles Chauncy, "Errors of 'Enthusiasts,'" in Smith, *American Christianity*, vol. 1, pp. 402 and 403.

Billy Sunday described evolutionists as "loud-mouthed, foreign-lingo-slinging, quack-theory-preaching bolsheviki."[6] Liberal preacher Harry Emerson Fosdick answered that "now the Fundamentalists are giving us one of the worst exhibitions of bitter intolerance that the churches of this country have ever seen," and insisted that "cantankerousness is worse than heterodoxy."[7] As the twentieth century draws to a close, the polemic over the tension between orthodoxy and tolerance continues. Nowhere is this more evident than in The Controversy, as it is called, within the Southern Baptist Convention.

Begun as a result of powerful denominational fragmentation prior to the Civil War, the SBC flourished across the South and later throughout the nation, successfully avoiding a major schism for nearly a century and a half. During the turbulent 1960s and '70s, when many denominations lost ground in various statistical categories, Southern Baptist statistics showed continuing growth. Today, the SBC operates through an elaborate convention system that attempts to combine local church autonomy with denominational cooperation. Its foreign mission board fields the largest missionary task force in contemporary Protestantism. Its seminaries educate one of every five seminary students in the United States. Size and success, however, could not indefinitely protect the Southern Baptist Convention from the inevitable disputes that have always splintered denominations.

In 1979, a controversy emerged that undermined not only organizational but also personal relationships across the convention. In that year, a fundamentalist faction implemented certain political methods as a means of dominating the denominational structure. In response, a moderate faction took shape whose members were united less by a uniform theological position than by their opposition to the political maneuvers of the fundamentalists. The struggle between these two groups has led to the politicization and ultimate polarization of almost every segment of convention life. Fundamentalists describe the more liberal moderates as "snakes," "skunks," and "termites" at work within the Baptist house to destroy faith and undermine the veracity of the Word of God. Moderates view the fundamentalists as "totalitarians," "hit-men," and "super-apostles," determined to overturn denominational freedom, trust, and cooperation. Like no other previous debate in SBC history, a decade of intense controversy has left the denomination disoriented in its mission and uncertain about its future.

6. Willard Gatewood, *Controversy in the Twenties* (Nashville: Vanderbilt University Press, 1969), p. 342.
7. Harry Emerson Fosdick, "Shall the Fundamentalists Win?" in H. Shelton Smith et al., *American Christianity,* vol. 2 (New York: Scribner, 1960), p. 300.

On a Sunday night in June 1979, at the Summit in Houston, Texas, I sat with a group of seminary professors at the Pastors' Conference held prior to the annual meeting of the Southern Baptist Convention. We listened as a prominent Southern Baptist evangelist asked his audience, "Have you ever noticed how many of these instructors of higher learning look like they've been embalmed with the fluid of higher education? They . . . look like a God-forsaken corpse, pickled in intellectual skepticism. God forgive them."[8] On leaving the hall that night, we "instructors of higher learning" understood in starkly personal terms the sort of major upheaval that Southern Baptists were facing. But we failed to realize how much of our time and energy over the next ten years would be occupied by the ensuing struggle.

After ten years of monitoring The Controversy, several factors prompted me to write about it. First, the SBC provides a case study in the nature of church and culture in the American experience. Few American denominations have been so intricately related to a particular regional culture for so long. The SBC's debates over theology and politics or Scripture and authority cannot be understood apart from the cultural context of the denomination. To the extent this is a historical study, I make no attempt, for example, to explore the complex theological question of biblical inerrancy and its related dogmas except as an issue that informs the divisions in the SBC.

Second, the book explains the SBC to those outside the denomination. Southern Baptists are often something of a mystery to many Americans, both secular and religious. Northern liberals and evangelicals alike often have difficulty distinguishing Southern Baptist fundamentalists from nonfundamentalists within the overarching conservatism of the entire denomination. What passes for liberalism among Southern Baptists usually looks quite conservative compared to other religious liberalism. Similarly, observers of American evangelicalism often seem uncertain about the place of the SBC in that movement. Confusion about the denomination was evident, for example, in the attempts that were offered up to analyze the religion of Jimmy Carter, the only Southern Baptist to be elected president of the United States.

Third, this book is also intended for Southern Baptists themselves, many of whom seem unaware of the complex nature of their own convention's history and the diversity that characterized the denomination all along. Much of the history taught in SBC churches is hagiographical and allows little room for critical reflection. Even after ten years of

8. James Robison, sermon delivered at the Pastors' Conference of the Southern Baptist Convention, June 1979, audio tape recording.

upheaval, many Southern Baptists persist in believing that this is simply another of the "preachers' fights" that beset the denomination from time to time. They seem to think that it will eventually subside, and the SBC will continue to grow and prosper as it has in the past. Others insist that if the "enemies" on the other side, whether fundamentalist or liberal, can simply be disposed of, the convention will be saved and its spirituality secured. I hope that Southern Baptists who read this book will recognize that the roots of The Controversy were present in 1845, the year the SBC was founded. Our "intactness" endured longer than anyone had a right to expect.

Finally, there is a personal element to this book. This is an invigorating time to be a historian in the SBC. The Controversy offers an invaluable opportunity to observe and record denominational fragmentation from within. As an insider, however, I cannot claim complete objectivity in the face of the personal and communal trauma The Controversy has incurred. My historical analysis is informed by the individual and institutional turmoil within the denomination. Although my basic sentiments are discernibly "moderate," I am convinced that both warring factions—fundamentalists and moderates—must bear common, though different, responsibility for the current denominational state of affairs. If nothing else, perhaps a study of the last ten years of controversy will help the antagonists decide whether they want to spend another decade in such pursuits.

In writing this book I am indebted to many people. The project began at the suggestion of my friend Bill Thomason, whose advice was helpful throughout my research. I wrote the first draft of the manuscript while on a sabbatical leave at the Seinan Gakuin University, Fukuoka, Japan. My colleagues there, both Japanese and American, were an important source of friendship and encouragement. At the Southern Baptist Theological Seminary, Cindy Meadows and Fearn Pate supplied invaluable assistance in the preparation of the manuscript. My faculty colleagues at the Southern Baptist Theological Seminary have helped me reflect on The Controversy and its implications, past, present, and future. I am especially grateful to Dr. Larry McSwain, dean of the School of Theology at Southern Baptist Seminary, for taking time to read the final draft. Much editorial assistance came from Candyce Leonard, whose insights were as always both challenging and provocative.

Louisville, Kentucky   BILL J. LEONARD
Lent 1990

CHAPTER 1

Southern Baptists and Southern Culture: The Context of the SBC

GROWING UP SOUTHERN BAPTIST ONCE SEEMED RELATIVELY EASY. ELABO-rate denominational programs created a surprising uniformity among an otherwise diverse and highly individualistic constituency. In churches throughout the American South, Southern Baptist young people were taught how to behave in the church and in the world, on Sundays and throughout the week.

Sundays meant church, all-day church. Off you went to Sunday School armed with the three great symbols of Southern Baptist faith: a King James Version of the Bible, "genuine cowhide," zippered edition (white for girls, black for boys); a Sunday School quarterly outlining the prescribed Bible lesson; and an offering envelope containing the weekly tithe. The Sunday School envelope also offered an opportunity for detailing personal spirituality based on the denomination's "six point record system," which included points for attendance, being on time, having a prepared lesson, bringing a Bible, giving an offering, and attending preaching. The best Christians were those whose box scores totaled 100 percent each week. Sunday School classes were divided by age and sex. No "mixed" (co-ed) Bible classes were permitted. Lessons were taken from the International Sunday School Series used by numerous Protestant denominations, but written by and for Southern Baptists. On a given Sunday morning every Southern Baptist from Richmond, Virginia, to El Paso, Texas, studied the same lessons from the same literature. The International Series may have been to Southern Baptists what the Latin mass was to Roman Catholics. It provided a sense of continuity and security for a common community of faith. At home or while traveling, faithful Southern Baptists could study the same lesson in any congregation in the denomination.

After Sunday School came "morning worship." There, at least,

1

one discovered some diversity in homiletical styles and liturgical preferences. Big, old churches in Charleston, Augusta, or Nashville had ministers (the "Doctor") attired in morning coats, the pulpit garb of the South's gentlemen theologians. They preached ordered, erudite sermons after a robed choir sang the anthem. Other congregations had pastors (the "Reverend") who preached a little louder and a little longer, after the choir sang the "special music." Still other churches had preachers (the "Brother Pastor") belting out brimstone and warning of "the wrath that is to come"—all after the gospel quartet sang the "special." Whatever the format, each service concluded with an invitation to persons to believe in Jesus and be baptized, to move their membership from another church, "to rededicate" their lives, or "to surrender for full-time Christian service."

For the truly dedicated, Sunday morning was only the beginning. After a big Sunday dinner the faithful returned to church for assorted afternoon and evening activities. These often included visitation, committee meetings, choir practice, Training Union, and evening worship followed by a social gathering for "fellowship." Sunday ended as you finally fell into bed, exhausted after a Sabbath day's rest.

Growing up Southern Baptist meant no drinking, no smoking, and no "mixed" swimming. (Boys and girls did not swim or study the Bible together.) It meant Royal Ambassadors and Girls' Auxiliary (Baptist Boy Scouts and Girl Scouts), revivals in the fall and spring, and Vacation Bible School in the summer. Growing up Southern Baptist also meant you grew up southern. Thus you never sat next to a black person on a bus, in a restaurant, at school, or at church. You probably believed in segregation, states' rights, soul-winning, and going to a Southern Baptist church, one local expression of the greatest evangelistic endeavor since the time of the apostles. In 1948, Levi Elder Barton, an Alabama preacher, echoed the sentiments of multitudes when he declared that "the last hope, the fairest hope, the only hope for evangelizing this world on New Testament principles is the Southern Baptist people represented in that Convention. I mean no unkindness to anybody on earth, but if you call that bigotry then make the most of it."[1]

---

1. *Alabama Christian Advocate*, June 29, 1948, p. 2; and Kenneth K. Bailey, *Southern White Protestantism in the Twentieth Century* (New York: Harper & Row, 1964), pp. 153-54.

The Catholic Church of the South

That unity of Southern Baptist and southern culture led University of Chicago historian Martin E. Marty to describe southern Protestantism in general, and the SBC in particular, as one of the most intact religious subgroups in contemporary America. Intactness meant that the SBC retained a sense of continuity with its past and provided a powerful identity for its members in the present. Indeed, Marty suggested that southern Protestants, black Protestants, and Mormons were among the most "intact" religious subcultures on the American scene. Each of these traditions revealed "regularities of behavior and consistent norms for evaluation."[2] Intactness provided Southern Baptists with a denominational stability that many so-called mainline religious groups seemed unable to sustain. Marty also insisted that this distinct Southern Baptist identity was so closely linked to southern identity that it was possible to describe the convention as " 'the Catholic church of the South' so pervasive is its influence in so many dimensions of the culture."[3]

Under the huge umbrella of southernness and denominational organization there existed a variety of theological and practical approaches to the Christian gospel. Diverse expressions of theology, liturgy, piety, and ministry flourished within the bonds of cultural solidarity and denominational identity. Within this cultural and programmatic security there existed a spiritual unity based primarily on "the primacy of experience in religion."[4] Until recently, the diverse historical and theological traditions within America's largest Protestant denomination were held together by a powerful configuration of common cultural, organizational, and religious experiences.

No sooner had Marty's analysis been published in 1978, however, than the intactness that he described began to deteriorate. By 1979, the reality of cultural, denominational, and theological fragmentation within the SBC had become clear. The triumph of certain fundamentalist forces, intent upon imposing a particular ideological unity on the convention, gives evidence that the old cultural and denominational intactness no longer exists. The so-called fundamentalist "takeover" of the denomination is symptomatic of profound changes in southern cultural and Southern Baptist denominational self-consciousness.

In other words, it's not so easy to be a Southern Baptist anymore.

---

2. Martin E. Marty, "The Protestant Experience and Perspective," in *American Religious Values and the Future of America*, ed. Rodger van Allen (Philadelphia: Fortress, 1978), p. 40.

3. Ibid., p. 46.

4. Ibid., p. 47.

Gone is the King James Version as the standard text. While it continues to be a favorite in the pulpit, in the pew numerous other versions are used, including the RSV, ASV, New ASV, NIV, NEB, the *Good News Bible,* the *Living Bible,* and the *Jerry Falwell Faith Partner Bible.* Sunday School classes may now choose among a variety of study materials including the International Series, the Bible Book Series, and the Life and Work Curriculum—all produced by the Southern Baptist Sunday School Board. Some congregations eschew denominationally published materials altogether (too conservative for some, too liberal for others) in favor of literature produced by other Christian publishers. Southern Baptists in increasing numbers now designate their offerings toward agencies whose philosophy they embrace and away from those that they reject. Liturgical differences, long evident in the churches, have become even more divisive. Some preachers denounce "high church" practices—too much Bach and not enough "praise choruses"—as detrimental to true worship and genuine evangelism. Others bemoan the evidence of a "variety show" mentality in certain "low church" forms of worship. Many Southern Baptists now distinguish the church's witness through education and social action from its witness through personal evangelism and soul winning. Southern Baptist Democrats challenge Southern Baptist Republicans over the church's role in politics.

The Controversy in the SBC

Time and transition caught up with Southern Baptists in 1979. Since then the convention has divided into two opposing camps: fundamentalists who want to purge all vestiges of liberalism from the convention through control of boards of trustees, and moderates who oppose the fundamentalists' actions if not their theology. Each group claims to represent the genuine Baptist tradition. In 1979 a fundamentalist subgroup within the denomination began a successful effort to gain dominance of convention boards and agencies. Long present within the SBC, these fundamentalists sought to elect a series of convention presidents who would use the appointive powers of their office to secure majorities on all denominational boards of trustees, thereby promoting a fundamentalist agenda throughout Southern Baptist institutional life.

As a theological system and religious subgroup, fundamentalism is difficult to define with precision. Sociologist Nancy Ammerman writes that "fundamentalism, by definition, stands in opposition to the modern world. From the beginning, fundamentalists have identified themselves as those who opposed accommodation to pluralism, secularization, subjectivism, and—yes—even civility."[5] They came to oppose, primarily from a religious perspective, that phenomenon of Western culture they describe with such terms as modernity, modernization, or modernism. Characterized by a "capacity for dynamic change," modernism involves, among other things, the expansion of science, technology, and industrialism, "the erosion of the power and influence of religion, and the breakdown of primordial solidarities based on family and community."[6] For fundamentalists, such modernism undermines the unchanging truths revealed in Scripture, orthodox doctrine, and the historic creeds of the church.

As a movement fundamentalism is relatively recent in origin, having begun within nineteenth-century evangelicalism in response to the development of certain "modernist" trends evident in Western theology and culture. Historian George Marsden notes that "militant opposition to modernism" distinguished fundamentalism from such related movements as "evangelicalism, revivalism, pietism, the holiness movements, [and] millenarianism."[7] David Edwin Harrell suggests that fundamentalists, often taken for bigots in some quarters, were, from another perspective, "simply the keepers of the old order fighting for the survival of the Christian system against the powerful onslaught of authoritarian science and secularism."[8] Such a response produced a powerful militancy. Thus, Ammerman concludes, fundamentalists "are simply evangelicals who believe that nothing, not even civility, should get in the way of proclaiming the truth about the need for salvation."[9] In a sense, fundamentalism represents the more doctrinally militant wing of the larger evangelical community in America.

5. Nancy T. Ammerman, "Fundamentalists Proselytizing Jews: Incivility in Preparation for the Rapture," in *Pushing the Faith: Proselytism and Civility in a Pluralistic World,* ed. Martin E. Marty and Frederick E. Greenspahn (New York: Crossroad, 1988), p. 109.

6. Benton Johnson, "Modernity and Pluralism," in Marty and Greenspahn, *Pushing the Faith,* pp. 10-11.

7. George M. Marsden, *Fundamentalism and American Culture: The Shaping of Twentieth-Century Evangelicalism, 1870-1925* (New York: Oxford, 1980), p. 4. Such terms as modernism and modernity are also difficult to define, and many scholars hesitate to use them. Others, such as Ammerman and Marsden, continue to use them to describe various trends, of relatively recent origin, in science, religion, philosophy, and the culture in general which are characteristics of a spirit of "dynamic change." See Johnson, "Modernity and Pluralism," pp. 10-24; and Martin E. Marty, *Modern American Religion: vol. 1, The Irony of it All, 1893-1919* (Chicago: University of Chicago Press, 1986), pp. 1-14.

8. David Edwin Harrell, Jr., "The South: Seedbed of Sectarianism," in *Varieties of Southern Evangelicalism,* ed. David Edwin Harrell, Jr. (Macon: Mercer University Press, 1981), pp. 45-46.

9. Ammerman, "Fundamentalists Proselytizing Jews," p. 110.

Fundamentalism appeared on the American scene in the late nineteenth century in reaction to the efforts of various liberal factions in Protestant denominations to bring the claims of modern science and philosophy to bear on classical theology. With the publication of a series of pamphlets called *The Fundamentals* between 1910 and 1915, the movement was from the beginning characterized by its defense of such doctrines as the infallibility of Holy Scripture, the virgin birth of Christ, the bodily resurrection, and the sacrificial atonement. The so-called fundamentalist-modernist controversy of the early twentieth century created divisions in many major American denominations. While the Southern Baptist Convention experienced no serious divisions during this early period, it was involved in debates related particularly to the teaching of evolution in Baptist colleges. But throughout the century, Southern Baptists have argued frequently over various questions related to the influence of liberalism in the denomination.

Samuel Hill, Jr., places southern fundamentalists within four groups of evangelicals in the region. Evangelicals as a whole include the "Truth party," given to "correct belief"; the "Conversion party" committed to evangelism; the "Spirituality party," which promotes the experience of God's "intimate presence"; and the "Service party," which stresses "reconciliation" between people.[10] Hill identifies fundamentalists with the Truth party, concerned with establishing correct belief, exposing error, and maintaining an uncompromising allegiance to the unchanging truths of Christianity.[11] Contemporary southern fundamentalists tend to define themselves in terms of certain "points" characteristic of classic fundamentalism, including an inerrant Bible, Christ's virgin birth, substitutionary atonement and bodily resurrection, and his premillennial second coming, the belief that Adam and Eve were the first two human beings on earth, and the belief that Satan is a distinct, personal being. Yet fundamentalists, even in the South, are not a monolithic body. Hill writes that they differ,

> (1) in spirit, from harsh and judgmental, to aggressive and sarcastic, to self-contained and single-minded; (2) in relation to society, from negative and condemnatory, to transformative, to ecclesiastically sectarian; (3) on the status of theology from attention to doctrines, to doctrines and social morality, to texts and church organizational practices.[12]

---

10. Samuel S. Hill, Jr., "Fundamentalism and the South," in *Perspectives in Churchmanship*, ed. David M. Scholer (Macon: Mercer University Press, 1986), pp. 49-52.
   11. Ibid.
   12. Ibid., p. 51.

Southern Baptist fundamentalists reflect such diversity; many tend toward the conversionist or spirituality parties as well. Yet in 1979, a movement began which aimed at uniting all persons of fundamentalist persuasion in an effort to reshape the SBC into a uniformly fundamentalist denomination.

In this study, the term "fundamentalist" refers to those persons within the Southern Baptist Convention who accept a doctrine of biblical inerrancy as the only method for defining biblical authority and who seek to participate in a concerted movement to make that doctrine normative, particularly for those employed by convention-supported agencies and institutions. It is important to note, however, that other Southern Baptists may agree with fundamentalist doctrines but refuse to participate in an effort to impose such dogmas on the entire denomination. Thus the fundamentalist faction is opposed by a group that came to be called the moderates. This coalition is equally difficult to define. Moderates can be found in all four segments of Samuel Hill's definition of southern evangelicalism. They represent numerous doctrinal, regional, and political interests, many affirming the theological principles of the fundamentalists. They are unified to varying degrees in their opposition to the effort to reshape the SBC in an exclusively fundamentalist image. Some belong to discernibly moderate groups such as the Southern Baptist Alliance and Baptists Committed to the SBC. Others affirm the moderate approach on the state and national level. Many moderates consider themselves biblical inerrantists while others do not. Some have been influenced by such theological movements as neoorthodoxy and the social gospel while others reflect the heart religion of classic pietism. Their primary goal is to affirm what they view as traditional Baptist doctrine—biblical authority, missions, evangelism, soul competency, and religious freedom—while resisting fundamentalist dominance. Moderates are those who refuse to participate in an effort to reshape the denomination in an exclusively fundamentalist image.

Disturbed by what they believed to be a leftward drift of denominational institutions and emboldened by the growing impact of other religious right forces in the country, the fundamentalists began to turn the convention toward a particular doctrinal uniformity, grounded primarily in the dogma of biblical inerrancy. "Inerrancy" is the doctrine that the Bible is without error in all matters of faith, history, theology, biology, or any other issue that can be discussed in its light. While complete inerrancy belongs only to the original manuscripts of Scripture, contemporary Christians possess a Bible that is essentially inerrant in all its teachings. As James Hunter observes, the inerrancy hermeneutic (or method of interpreting Scripture) "is essentially literalistic, meaning that the Bible should be interpreted at face value whenever possible. This has not meant, as some have caricatured, that every single statement was to be understood in a literal sense."[13] Much of the last decade's debate has centered on the inerrancy issue, its relationship to historic Baptist doctrines, and the interpretation of those doctrines by and for convention employees.

Thus The Controversy has raged for over a decade. In 1980, Southern Baptist historian Walter B. Shurden delivered a series of lectures entitled "The Southern Baptist Synthesis: Is it Cracking?"[14] Ten years later it was clear that the synthesis had indeed cracked, and many analysts had begun to wonder if there had ever been much of a synthesis at all.

The Southern Baptist Convention constitutes an important case study in American denominationalism. Perhaps no major Protestant denomination retained so much of its nineteenth-century identity as long as the SBC. This book examines the present crisis—or, as it is popularly known, The Controversy—in the SBC in light of certain trends in southern culture and American denominationalism. It suggests that recent fundamentalist-moderate conflicts are symptoms of a broader and more complex fragmentation in the organizational and cultural context of the Southern Baptist Convention. In many respects the SBC has always lived on the edge of division over doctrine and practice. Indeed, the convention itself formed a denominational unity based less on rigid doctrinal synthesis than on denominational and regional identity. Such unity was grounded in a Grand Compromise in which ideologues on the right or the left were not allowed to control the center. Southern identity, denominational loyalty, and a sense of universal mission combined to create an institution built on compromise and motivated by the rhetoric of pietistic, populist triumphalism. Theology was defined narrowly enough to establish common Baptist identity but broadly enough to include a variety of historical interpretations relating to faith and practice. Efforts to narrow doctrine and practice—efforts that might exclude segments of the constituency from the great missionary endeavor—were avoided whenever possible. The Grand Compromise was thus protected by the same cultural and denominational myths that it promoted.

13. James Davison Hunter, *Evangelicalism: The Coming Generation* (Chicago: University of Chicago Press, 1987), p. 21; and James William McClendon, Jr., "Forged in the Crucible of Conflict," *Books and Religion*, Sept. 1986, pp. 3-7.
14. Walter B. Shurden, "The Southern Baptist Synthesis: Is it Cracking?" in the 1980-81 Carver Barnes Lectures, published by Southeastern Baptist Theological Seminary, 1981, pp. 5-6.

Like all compromises, however, it was always in danger of collapse. As cultural pluralism challenged the remaining myth of southernness and religious pluralism presented new alternatives to denominational loyalty, the convention inevitably faced an identity crisis. Theological diversity, if not contradiction, long present in the convention simply became more pronounced in the new context. The current theological debates must therefore be understood in the light of cultural and denominational dysfunction. Questions of doctrine cannot be separated from related issues of social and organizational instability. In short, the very things that held the SBC together had the potential to break it apart.

This book explores the fragmentation of the Southern Baptist Convention from several perspectives. First, it examines the role of the SBC within its particular cultural environment—in this case the American South. Second, the book focuses on the nature of Southern Baptist denominationalism and the development of the Grand Compromise upon which the close-knit unity of the convention was built. Third, other chapters explore the nature of doctrine within the convention and the theological tenets around which Southern Baptists unite. Was there ever a genuine doctrinal consensus? How did doctrinal uniformity relate to theological and ecclesiastical diversity? Fourth, this study investigates the nature of popular piety in Southern Baptist life and its impact on the theology of conversion, on spirituality, and on worship and preaching. Finally, the book evaluates the nature of the present controversy in SBC life in terms of cultural and denominational transitions. It traces the powerful rise of fundamentalism as well as the demise of that Grand Compromise on which the convention was established and reflects on possibilities for the future.

Church and Culture in the American South

The relationship between church and culture is an important topic for scholars of American and southern religion. Many writers begin with Clifford Geertz's idea that culture "denotes an historically transmitted pattern of meanings embodied in symbols, a system of inherited conceptions expressed in symbolic forms by means of which . . . [persons] communicate, perpetuate, and develop their knowledge about and attitudes toward life."[15] Through culture a particular group establishes

15. Clifford Geertz, *The Interpretation of Cultures* (New York: Basic Books, 1973), p. 89.

norms for behavior, promotes values, interprets events, and identifies other significant aspects of common life. M. J. Herskovits writes that if "a society is composed of people, the way they behave is their culture."[16] Frederick Buechner uses a phrase that might represent a more pastoral description of culture as "the world into which you are born and the world that is born in you."[17] No religious group can ignore its cultural context.

Geertz's belief that cultural patterns are transmitted through myths and their accompanying symbols is an important concept for understanding the relationship between southern culture and the Southern Baptist Convention. It was by means of common myths and symbols that diverse and devastated segments of the post–Civil War South were reunited. Symbols provided outward and visible signs of the inward and spiritual reality evident in certain myths. The issue, of course, is not whether the details of the myths were entirely factual, or whether southerners, individually or collectively, knew all the "facts" related to the narratives. The question was whether the myths became an effective, and in that sense a "true," way of defining collective existence. As Mark Shorer suggested, "A myth is a large, controlling image that gives philosophical meaning to the facts of ordinary life; that is, which has organizing value for experience."[18] Through its myths a society gives meaning to the actual empirical events of its history. Such myths thus provide cultural identity and are perpetuated by the culture they help define.

The American South has been one region where myths and symbols have provided a major source of cultural unity and security. Paul Gaston writes, "what does distinguish the South, at least from other parts of the United States, is the degree to which myths have been spawned and the extent to which they have asserted their hegemony over the Southern mind."[19]

16. Marty, "The Protestant Experience and Perspective," p. 33, citing Philip Bagby, *Culture and History: Prolegomena to the Comparative Study of Civilizations* (Berkeley: University of California Press, 1963), pp. 84, 104-5.

17. Frederick Buechner, *The Sacred Journey* (San Francisco: Harper & Row, 1982), p. 9.

18. Mark Shorer, "The Necessity for Myth," in *Myth and Mythmakers*, ed. Henry A. Murray (Boston: Beacon, 1960), p. 355, cited in Patrick Gerster and Nicholas Cord, *Myth and Southern History: The Old South* (Chicago: Rand McNally, 1974), p. 2.

19. Paul M. Gaston, *The New South Creed: A Study in Southern Mythmaking* (New York: Knopf, 1970), p. 8, cited in Gerster and Cord, *Myth and Southern History*, p. xv.

Southern Culture, Southern Religion

The significance of myth in defining the nature of southern culture is illustrated in Charles R. Wilson's work *Baptized in Blood: The Religion of the Lost Cause, 1865-1920*. Wilson shows how southern churches utilized the Lost Cause—the idealization of the southern heritage even in defeat—to rebuild the South's spiritual and moral identity following the war. In an effort to help a vanquished people overcome their despair, southern churchmen and women provided a theological explanation for secular events. Wilson writes that southern ministers "saw little difference between their religious and cultural values, and they promoted the link by constructing Lost Cause ritualistic forms that celebrated their regional, mythological and theological beliefs."[20] For Wilson's purposes, the actual events of defeat were less important than the way certain events—Stonewall Jackson's death, Lee's persona, the surrender—became symbols of and for southern society. As southern religionists willingly defended the myth of southernness prior to the Civil War, so they set themselves to remythologizing southern culture following the surrender at Appomattox. The dream of nationhood was replaced with "the dream of a cohesive Southern people with a separate cultural identity." Religion, Wilson insists, "was at the heart of this dream."[21] He believes that the religion of the Lost Cause provided southerners with a renewed sense of chosenness and the possibility of spiritual victory in the aftermath of political defeat. In a sense, the southern churches themselves were "baptized in blood," and, if they would be faithful to their calling, they would rise again to greater spiritual heights.[22]

Such a myth was evident in the preaching of Southern Baptist ministers who, like the Puritan preachers before them, continually called their flock to remain true to its mission lest God remove his blessing. These jeremiads warned that the loss of evangelical zeal, the compromise of doctrinal orthodoxy, or lack of cooperation could lead God to reject Southern Baptist efforts. Like the New England Puritans, the southern preachers insisted that their region was chosen by God. Unlike the Puritans, however, the southerners had to convince a defeated people that they were still chosen and that their terrible ordeal was part of a divine plan through which faithfulness, truth, and perseverance would ultimately prevail.[23]

20. Charles R. Wilson, *Baptized in Blood: The Religion of the Lost Cause, 1865-1920* (Athens, Ga.: University of Georgia Press, 1980), p. 11.
21. Ibid., p. 1.
22. Ibid., p. 8.
23. Ibid., pp. 78-79.

Baptized in Blood is only one of several recent studies that examine the powerful relationship between southern religion and culture. In discussing the antebellum South, historian Donald Mathews notes that "religion and the American South are fused in our historical imagination in an indelible, but amorphous way."[24] Mathews observes that evangelical religion enabled both blacks and whites to understand their place in southern culture. Each appropriated a religious experience that provided its adherents with "a sense of personal esteem and liberty." Mathews insisted that even before the Civil War, southern religion was closely identified with "social solidarity." Thus, church attendance was at once a "religious act" and "a civic responsibility."[25] Religious life and rituals helped southern people understand who they were and how they fit into the divine plan for their region and the world.

In his well-known 1942 social analysis *Millhands and Preachers*, Liston Pope contended that southern churches were among the most powerful social forces in perpetuating a spirit of regional isolation and "idealizing antebellum civilization."[26] Samuel Hill, Jr., another prominent analyst of southern culture and religion, suggests that the "religion of the Southern people and their culture have been linked by the tightest bonds. That culture, particularly in its moral aspects, could not have survived without a legitimating impetus provided by religion. . . . For the South to stand its people had to be religious and its churches the purest anywhere."[27]

In many respects the intimate relationship between religion and culture in the South endured throughout most of the twentieth century. Writing in 1968 Thomas Clark noted that "no institution in the modern South so clearly reflects conditions of regional life as the church. Though deep change is at once noticeable, there is still an underlying fact of historical continuity."[28] He claimed that "Old South issues" retained a powerful hold on the modern church in the region and noted that neither "the economic revolution" created by the Great Depression nor the upheavals caused by two world wars caused any major changes in "the fundamental structure of the southern church."[29] Southern Protestant-

24. Donald G. Mathews, *Religion in the Old South* (Chicago: University of Chicago Press, 1977), p. xiii.
25. Ibid., p. 249; and Samuel S. Hill, Jr., *The South and the North in American Religion* (Athens, Ga.: University of Georgia Press, 1980), p. 7.
26. Liston Pope, *Millhands and Preachers* (New Haven: Yale University Press), p. 34.
27. Samuel S. Hill, Jr., *Religion and the Solid South* (Nashville: Abingdon, 1972), p. 36; and Wilson, *Baptized in Blood*, p. 7.
28. Thomas Clark, *The Emerging South* (New York: Oxford, 1968), p. 248.
29. Ibid.

ism remained a bulwark against change and transition—modernity—in the South. In many respects the Southern Baptists were the leaders in the "rugged domination" of Protestantism in the region. Clark concluded: "Not a single southern issue, political or religious, has arisen in the last half century which has not been influenced to some degree by Baptist attitudes."[30] In the aftermath of defeat and the humiliation of Reconstruction, southern religionists set themselves to the task of remythologizing their place in the divine plan and restoring faith in the ultimate victory of their spiritual, if not their political, cause.[31] Myths and symbols, old and new, provided a source of southern unity and security.

What were the myths that have helped to form southern self-identity? They were many: the genteel society—educated, erudite, and thoughtful; the relationship between the sexes, that is, chivalrous gentlemen and graceful ladies; the sense of neighborliness; and the nurturing of children to civic responsibility. Racial myths persisted from the days of slavery in segregationist Jim Crow laws. Perhaps the Great Southern Myth was this: the people who lost the war retained the vision. Even in defeat, the southern people were more righteous, more decent, more moral, and more God-fearing than their Yankee counterparts ever could be. Through some mysterious process of purification God was working out his purposes with the southern people.

What then was The Great Southern Baptist Myth? The denomination of the defeated, itself born of schism and racism, had become God's "last" and "only hope" for evangelizing the world according to New Testament principles. Its numerical, financial, and spiritual growth, as well as its evangelistic zeal, was evidence of God's blessing on its ministry, its mission, and its method. Schism would mean the death of the myth, so schism must be avoided at all cost. Nothing could be allowed to deter the South's most southern denomination from its calling to redeem itself and win the ultimate battle against evil. This passion for triumph, for spiritual and numerical success among Southern Baptists, cannot be understood apart from the surrender at Appomattox.

The denomination likewise was unified in its response to the southern ethical and social status quo. Many scholars have examined the social agenda of the SBC within the context of southern culture. John Eighmy concluded that during the first sixty years of its history the convention "assumed the role of a cultural establishment by sanctifying

30. Ibid., p. 268.
31. Wilson, *Baptized in Blood*, p. 1.

a secular order devoted to states' rights, white supremacy, *laissez faire* economics, and property rights."[32] Eighmy believed that southern churches were in cultural captivity since they required a consensus of distinct values that validated their existence as a separate body from Northern Baptists.[33] He concluded that while supporters of the social gospel were present in the SBC, they were by no means a dominant theological force. Rather, a majority of Southern Baptists focused their attention on individualistic issues of personal conversion and morality, not on the corporate sins of southern society. In the epilogue to Eighmy's work, Samuel Hill observed that Baptist evangelical individualism served as a way of preserving and perpetuating certain aspects of southern culture. He called this "a primary means of preserving the region's cultural unity." Hill further suggested that the southern churches served, "usually unwittingly, as agents of [social] reinforcement. This has been the case because both Christianity and southernness have been effective frameworks of meaning—cultural symbols for communicating, perpetuating, and developing knowledge and attitudes."[34] Eighmy's study also shows, however, that the SBC was influenced to some extent by its own social gospel advocates and that questions over the corporate and personal implications of evangelism were represented in segments of the denomination.[35] These diverse approaches became more pronounced as the convention became more pluralistic.

Other scholars agree with Eighmy that southernness was a significant factor in determining Baptist responses to social issues. Rufus Spain observed that Southern Baptists were limited in their social awareness in part because of their "intensely 'Southern' outlook." Spain concluded that "Northern-born social Christianity had first to overcome Southern sectionalism before it could find acceptance among Southern Baptists."[36] Even in matters of personal morality, about which Southern Baptists were outspoken, they continued to reflect the existing mores of southern culture. Spain claimed that Southern Baptists were important to southern life, but not because they shaped the environment according to Baptist standards. Rather, "their importance as a social force was in supporting and perpetuating the standard of the society at large."[37]

32. John Lee Eighmy, *Churches in Cultural Captivity* (Knoxville: University of Tennessee Press, 1976), p. x.

33. Ibid., pp. 75, 94; and Wilson, *Baptized in Blood*, p. 10.

34. Ibid., p. 202.

35. Ibid., pp. x-xi.

36. Rufus B. Spain, *At Ease in Zion: Social History of Southern Baptists, 1865-1900* (Nashville: Vanderbilt University Press, 1967), p. 211.

37. Ibid., p. 214.

Sometimes it seemed that southern values and Southern Baptist values were one and the same.

Southern Baptist identification with southern society developed alongside another important source of identity, the denomination. This denominational consciousness provided an increasing sense of unity and uniqueness for churches affiliated with the SBC. It served to distinguish Southern Baptists from their northern counterparts and from other more independent Baptists in the South. Indeed, the first one hundred years of the convention's history give evidence of the steady growth of a powerful denominationalism. The seeds of denominationalism were present from the beginning. Southerners rejected the northern Baptist "society" approach to denominational endeavors for a more centralized order in which agencies were linked by an overarching convention system. Each body retained an independent board of trustees, but appointments to those boards were made at the yearly meeting of the convention.

From its schismatic beginning in 1845 the Southern Baptist Convention evolved into something resembling the Established Church of the South. Certainly it was not the only denomination to perpetuate the religion of the Lost Cause, to remythologize the South's divine mission after its terrible defeat, or to perpetuate the social and racial attitudes of the culture. Over time, however, not only did the SBC become the largest of the southern denominations but also its close identification with the culture lasted longer than that of mainline southern churches. In assuming the role of establishment, the SBC also lost something of the dissenting tradition long characteristic of the broader Baptist heritage. Generally speaking, Southern Baptists have not reflected the dissenting position of other smaller Baptist groups in America and Europe in matters of politics, economics, and social issues. Traditional Baptist devotion to the separation of church and state has often been blurred by issues involving segregation, civil rights, and recent support for certain agendas of the new religious-political right.

The Fragmentation of Southern Culture

Sociologists, historians, and politicians have long since proclaimed the demise of the solid South. There is, however, considerable debate as to the nature of this cultural fragmentation. While most scholars agree that the South has experienced considerable cultural transition, particularly since the end of World War II, they cannot agree on the character and chronology of the process. Nonetheless, it seems clear that during the last two decades, the South has experienced "the disappearance of regional distinctiveness; the growing resemblance of the region to the rest of the country; [and] the merging of the South into the American mainstream."[38] In 1960, C. Vann Woodward wrote "the time is coming, if it is not already arrived, when the Southerner will begin to ask himself whether there is really any longer much point in calling himself a Southerner."[39] Woodward described the South in terms of a cultural revolution that would affect all of the major institutions in the region. As regional distinctions disappeared, a cultural vacuum was created. Certain typically southern "faults" such as sharecropper agriculture, one-party politics, and Jim Crow laws were being replaced with less distinctive faults common to other regions of the country.[40] Likewise, typically southern values were confronting the values of a more pluralistic nation. Thus, Woodward wrote, "Bereft of . . . myths, . . . peculiar institutions, even . . . familiar regional vices," southerners faced the loss of their very identity.[41]

Also in 1960, Samuel Hill noted that while the forces of the "Southern regional faith and culture" had influenced each other, a variety of new cultural disruptions were driving a "formidable wedge" between the two. Hill concluded that "the future may well seem ominous to a conservative and culturally pampered institution as it confronts a new social order and climate of opinion."[42] Clearly the cultural upheavals within the region have had a significant impact within the Southern Baptist Convention. Indeed, one of the powerful appeals of fundamentalism has been its promise to protect the convention from the upheavals of modernity and cultural transition.

In an article entitled "The Ever-Vanishing South" published in 1982, historian Charles Roland took issue with those who asserted the South's cultural demise too quickly. He acknowledged that major changes have occurred but insisted that southerners would not give up their distinctiveness without a fight. Roland wrote that "many ancient emotions, loyalties, and traits of unmistakably southern origin" continued to have a powerful impact on the region.[43] He had a point. By the

38. Charles Roland, "The Ever-Vanishing South," *The Journal of Southern History* 48 (Feb. 1982), p. 3.

39. C. Vann Woodward, *The Burden of Southern History* (Baton Rouge: Louisiana State University Press, 1960), p. 3.

40. Ibid., p. 5.

41. Ibid., p. 15.

42. Samuel S. Hill, Jr., *Southern Churches in Crisis* (Boston: Beacon, 1966), p. xiii.

43. Roland, "The Ever-Vanishing South," p. 6.

end of the 1980s, the booming economy of the southern Sun Belt had moderated considerably, particularly in the oil-producing and farming industries. Politically, the South seems to have returned to a one-party system, this time in the Republican camp, at least in presidential elections. Racism remains extensive, though perhaps more subtle. In the face of cultural disillusionment, traditionalism in religion is again being promoted, particularly in the theology of fundamentalism and the politics of the new religious right.

Sociologist Nancy Ammerman, using studies from the Center for Religious Research at Emory University's Candler School of Theology, concluded that there is indeed a "New South," characterized by radical changes fostered by demography, education, and cultural pluralism. In light of those transitions she suggested that the conflict in the SBC "cannot be separated from the vast cultural changes that have revolutionalized the region that is its home."[44] Fundamentalism reasserted itself in southern religion in general and the SBC in particular in reaction to the loss of the old cultural securities. At the same time, the inability of the convention itself to resist the onslaught of fundamentalist. extremism—as it did in the past with other movements—is due in part to the loss of the same cultural stability. In other words, the cultural pluralism and transition that turned many people to fundamentalism also rendered the old Southern Baptist coalition powerless to respond to a fundamentalist takeover of the denomination itself.

The Unity of Southernness

From the beginning, the unity of the SBC was built on cultural loyalty and security. Initially the denomination was founded around a geographic unity. From its establishment in 1845 until well into the twentieth century, to be a Southern Baptist generally meant that one was a resident of the American South. The constituency of the convention lived almost exclusively along the southeastern seaboard, in the Deep South and in the Southwest as far as Texas. Even before the formation of the Confederate States of America, the SBC had defined itself geographically. Its unity was more than geographic, however.

The convention was formed as a result of sectional and cultural differences, North and South, that anticipated and paralleled the broader

---

44. Nancy Ammerman, "The New South and the New Baptists," *The Christian Century*, May 14, 1986, p. 486.

divisions in the American nation. In a sense, the SBC united around certain southern attitudes—political, religious, economic, and social—but also helped articulate those ideas as the Confederacy itself took shape. As C. C. Goen has shown, the divisions of the three major Protestant denominations—Methodist, Baptist, and Presbyterian—prepared the way for national schism, giving the nation itself "permission" to divide.[45] Like their southern counterparts in the Congress, Southern Baptist leaders insisted that their regional and personal rights had been violated by the abolitionist dominated "federal" bureaucracy of the mission societies. When the Baptist Foreign Mission Society refused to appoint a known slaveholder, James Reeve, to missionary service, the southerners knew that it was time to "secede." They declared that the mission board had exercised undue ecclesiastical authority and had given a political issue priority over a spiritual calling, thereby "FORBIDDING US to speak UNTO THE GENTILES," as South Carolinian William B. Johnson wrote.[46] Slaveholding was an extraneous issue being used to thwart the divine call given to southern mission volunteers.

Contemporary Southern Baptists, moderate and fundamentalist alike, are fond of saying that the SBC was formed as a missionary denomination. They note that the convention was established in May 1845, "for the purpose of carrying into effect the benevolent intention of our constituents, by organizing a plan for eliciting, combining and directing the energies of the whole denomination in one sacred effort, for the propagation of the Gospel."[47] But a missionary commitment was not something new with the new denomination. Baptist churches in the South had been united with Baptist churches in the North for missionary activity since the formation of the Triennial Convention in 1814. The original unity of the SBC was based less on a new concern for missionary outreach than on a common rejection of earlier ecclesiastical alignments. To remain in union with the Triennial Convention meant that Baptists in the South could no longer be appropriately southern. This they would not do. Their unity around certain "sectional" issues—particularly slavery—was the basis for their break with the North and their decision to form a new denomination. The SBC was therefore southern before it was missionary. William B. Johnson, the first president of the SBC, wrote in an "Address to the Public" in 1845 that the mission board had wrongfully sanctioned "anti-slavery opinions" and required missionary

---

45. C. C. Goen, *Broken Churches, Broken Nation* (Macon, Ga.: Mercer University Press, 1985).

46. Robert Baker, *A Baptist Source Book* (Nashville: Broadman, 1966), p. 120.

47. Ibid., p. 116.

appointees to oppose slavery. He concluded that "these brethren, thus acted upon a sentiment they have failed to prove—that slavery is, in all circumstances, sinful."[48] Denied the right to hold their views on slavery and fulfill their missionary imperative, the southerners began a new movement that was at once united around evangelical zeal and southern cultural mores.

With the formation of the Confederacy, the SBC united in its support of the new nation. A committee on the State of the Country, elected by the convention, made its report on May 13, 1861, supporting the formation of the Confederacy. The second of ten resolutions approved by the convention declared: "That we most cordially approve of the formation of the Government of the Confederate States of America, and admire and applaud the noble course of that Government up to this present time."[49] By 1863, Southern Baptists had intensified their concern for the new nation and its place in the divine plan. In that year resolutions denounced the U.S. government for "the war which has been forced upon us." The convention also expressed its "opposition to a reunion with the United States on any terms whatever." It declared that "we gratefully acknowledge the hand of God in the preservation of our government against the power and rage of our enemies, and in the signal victories with which he has crowned our arms."[50] Early Southern Baptist unity was closely related to the unity of the Confederacy and its glorious cause. When the war was over, therefore, Southern Baptists shared in the unity of defeat. That defeat not only drew them together but kept them from pursuing immediate and long-term reunion with the separated brothers and sisters of the North. A postwar resolution declared: "Resolved, 1st. That the Southern Baptist Convention is a permanent institution. . . . The necessity of sustaining it is more imperative now than at any former time."[51] As Charles Wilson and others have shown, Southern Baptists were among those religious groups which united around the mythology of the Lost Cause in an effort to provide a spiritual response to a political defeat. The way in which Southern Baptist leaders sought to explain the defeat of the South's righteous cause provides insight into their continuing response to divisive theological and cultural issues. The formula seems to be: When in doubt, spiritualize. That tendency remains a significant element of SBC life.

Rufus Spain suggested that postwar Southern Baptists could not

---

48. Ibid., p. 120.
49. W. W. Barnes, *The Southern Baptist Convention, 1845-1953* (Nashville: Broadman, 1954), p. 44, citing *Proceedings of the Southern Baptist Convention*, 1861, pp. 63-64.
50. Ibid., p. 45, citing *Proceedings of the SBC*, 1863, pp. 54-55.
51. Ibid., p. 68, citing *Proceedings of the SBC*, 1866, p. 25.

bring themselves to acknowledge the error of their cause. Defeat had come not because the vision was faulty but because the people were sinful. God had permitted their defeat because his people had not been faithful enough. Spain wrote that such an approach "evidently satisfied Baptists, for expressions of skepticism regarding the cause disappeared, at least from state Baptist newspapers, by 1866."[52] He concluded that "attributing defeat to God's will enabled Baptists to save face and obviated the necessity of sacrificing cherished beliefs."[53] Questions of repentance over the sinfulness of the Cause were obscured and ignored, for to admit any culpability would have negated the sacrifice of so many who died in the war. It would also have meant acknowledging that the Southern Baptists had been wrong from the beginning, that their culture, nation, and denomination should never have been formed. That kind of confession was impossible. Instead, they fell back upon divine sovereignty and their own spiritual weakness. A Georgia Baptist editor concluded that "it is clear that God has taken our case out of our own hands and substituted *his* judgment in the guidance of our affairs for our own. . . . If God has placed us where we are, we ought to be content with our condition."[54] Such a spiritual interpretation was the only possible way to preserve both the security of the faith and the validity of the Lost Cause.

The surrender at Appomattox left another theological problem for Baptists and other southern religionists involving biblical hermeneutics and the slavery issue. With the Emancipation Proclamation and the northern victory, Southern Baptists confronted a major dilemma. How could they retain their belief in biblical authority when their proslavery hermeneutic proved politically untenable? If the Bible was wrong in its apparent support of human slavery, could it still remain trustworthy for redemption? Thus the question of slavery became the first of many "slippery slopes" to challenge Southern Baptist biblical literalism and hermeneutical method. Both the opponents and the defenders of slavery had built their cases on the authority of Holy Scripture. Richard Furman of South Carolina, one of the South's most articulate defenders of the Bible and slavery, wrote in 1845 that the New Testament detailed the Christian treatment of slaves, not their emancipation. To suggest that slavery was a sin was "to abandon the Bible or make it teach an expediency."[55] The South had created a hermeneutic that used biblical interpretation as a source of social and religious solidarity.

---

52. Spain, *At Ease in Zion,* p. 18.
53. Ibid.
54. Ibid., citing *Christian Index,* Jan. 13, 1866, p. 10.
55. Richard Furman and Francis Wayland, *Domestic Slavery Considered as a Scriptural Institution* (New York: Lewis Colby, 1845), p. 9.

Recent studies have shown that many religious leaders in the antebellum South opposed slavery in principle and longed for a time when the Peculiar Institution would be ended. But with the rise of abolitionism, the demand for immediate manumission, and the denunciation of slave holding as unchristian, the southern religious establishment rose to the defense of the social and political status quo. At that point they made a fateful decision to link biblical authority with the practice of human slavery. As Randy J. Sparks comments, southern evangelicals discovered that they could "follow one of two paths: either continue their opposition to the institution and defend the rights of slaves or restructure their beliefs to accommodate slavery and slaveholders. The first path . . . could destroy the church in the South."[56] Rufus Spain shows that many Southern Baptists simply could not accept the idea that their biblical interpretation of slavery had been incorrect. He cites a Virginia editor who insisted that God would not have permitted such great suffering merely "that an inferior race might be released from nominal bondage and endowed with a freedom which, to them, is but another name for licentiousness, and which must end in complete extermination."[57] Still others suggested that God delivered the slaves, not because God opposed slavery but because southerners neglected their calling to evangelize the blacks properly. That mandate to win blacks to the gospel remained intact even after the war.[58]

Following the war, many white Baptists viewed the problems of emancipation and free blacks as proof that their original views on slavery were correct. Blacks, they believed, could not adapt themselves properly to freedom and the privileges of civilized society. Thus most Southern Baptists, well into the twentieth century, accepted a biblical hermeneutic that sanctioned segregation as readily and uncritically as they had accepted divine approbation of slavery. The southern cultural status quo not only informed the denomination's attitudes toward segregation, but it also used its own biblical literalism to give divine support to the practice. Such an approach informed missionary strategy throughout the first half of the twentieth century.

J. Franklin Love, for example, the executive secretary of the Foreign Mission Board from 1915 to 1928, was convinced that Southern

56. Randy J. Sparks, "Religion in Amite County, Mississippi, 1800-1861," in John B. Boles, *Masters and Slaves in the House of the Lord: Race and Religion in the American South, 1740-1870* (Lexington: University Press of Kentucky, 1988), p. 68.

57. Spain, *At Ease in Zion*, pp. 18-19, citing *Religious Herald*, Feb. 22, 1866, p. 1.

58. Ibid., p. 19.

Baptists should first convert Anglo-Saxons to Christianity so that they might win the darker races. He wrote: "Let us not forget that to the white man God gave the instinct and talent to disseminate His ideals among other people and that he did not, to the same degree, give this instinct and talent to the yellow, brown or black races. The white race only has the genius to introduce Christianity into all lands and among all people."[59] Naturally, Love based his ideas on the Bible. In his recent study of the Foreign Mission Board, Robert Nash suggests that "Love's theory of Anglo-Saxon supremacy was rooted in the idea that God had called Paul to go over into Europe rather than to continue his ministry in Asia."[60] Love believed that God's plan "was first to evangelize the white Gentile world . . . to move toward the coming Anglo-Saxon civilization, and so get his hands on the mightiest national life of the world."[61]

In 1956 W. A. Criswell, the pastor of First Baptist Church, Dallas, told the South Carolina legislature that "he not only strongly favored racial segregation, but that it would be best for religious groups to 'stick with their own kind.'"[62] He suggested that few blacks desired to integrate white churches, and observed of those who did, "Let them integrate. Let them sit up there in their dirty shirts and make all their fine speeches. But they are all a bunch of infidels, dying from the neck up."[63] Those who opposed segregation were infidels—unbelievers who denied Bible teaching on the separation of the races. By 1968, Criswell had moderated his views for the sake of evangelism, and in 1970 he noted, "I came to the profound conclusion that to separate by coercion the body of Christ on the basis of skin pigmentation was unthinkable, unchristian and unacceptable to God."[64]

The Southern Baptist responses to questions of slavery, segregation, and race illustrate some significant issues in Southern Baptist biblical literalism and the influence of southern culture. Criswell and others did not confess that their earlier views on segregation and the

---

59. 1890 SBC *Proceedings*, pp. 14-15.

60. Robert N. Nash, Jr., "The Influence of American Myth on Southern Baptist Foreign Mission, 1845-1945" (unpublished Ph.D. Thesis, Southern Baptist Theological Seminary, 1989), p. 170.

61. J. Franklin Love, *The Appeal of the Baptist Program for Europe* (Richmond: Foreign Mission Board of the Southern Baptist Convention, 1920), p. 7.

62. W. A. Criswell, "Like John Brown's Soul, He Goes Marching On," *Baptist Bible Tribune*, July 5, 1968; and "Seminary Spokesman Takes Issue with Dr. W. A. Criswell, Dallas, Texas," *Western Recorder*, Mar. 8, 1956, p. 16.

63. Ibid.

64. C. Allyn Russell, "W. A. Criswell: A Case Study in Fundamentalism," *Review and Expositor* 81 (Winter 1984), p. 122.

races were wrong; they simply modified them for the sake of a higher imperative, the evangelization of all persons. The literalist hermeneutic was preserved while previously ironclad biblical teachings were adapted in response to changing cultural and political situations. Fundamentalists thus adapted their views with changing times and culture in much the same way others did, but in such a way that the literalist hermeneutic survived intact. Those who challenged such a hermeneutic in such issues as peace-war, wealth-poverty, or male-female roles in the church were the new "infidels" who, like abolitionists and civil rights leaders, were making Holy Scripture an "expediency." Cultural captivity perpetuated hermeneutical captivity which allowed large segments of the SBC to avoid the hard questions regarding their use of the Bible. That effort to link biblical authority and a social status quo and the attempt to adapt to cultural changes in such a way as to preserve biblical literalism provide important insights into the "Battle for the Bible" that descended on the SBC in 1979.

Throughout much of its history Southern Baptist biblicism helped reinforce the southern cultural status quo while elements of southern culture helped reinforce Southern Baptist biblicism and social solidarity. The old denominational coalition of the SBC developed within the reasonably protective environment of southern culture. Thus, Nancy Ammerman concludes that "only when conservative beliefs lost their cultural dominance was it necessary for people to organize and identify themselves specifically as holders of those beliefs."[65] As the South changed, the culture became more pluralistic and one valuable source of denominational stability was no longer intact. The so-called moderates in the SBC therefore adopted various approaches to this cultural transition that were particularly disturbing to fundamentalists within the SBC. Some moderates sought to change with the culture, urging the denomination to adapt to new economic, social, racial, and theological realities. They longed for a more positive and immediate Southern Baptist response to modernity. Others who would ultimately gravitate toward the moderate camp recognized that the culture was changing but believed that the old denominational coalition and machinery would adapt to the present and the future as readily as it had in the past. They continued to behave as if the old cultural and denominational forces were still intact, declaring—at times against all evidence to the contrary—that The Controversy of the 1980s was no different from previous controversies and insisting that the denomination would ultimately move back toward the center. Fundamentalists recognized the growing cultural pluralism in

---

65. Nancy Ammerman, "The New South and the New Baptists," p. 487.

the South and reacted against it. They warned that the liberalism of the New South would ultimately destroy the spiritual and doctrinal solidarity of the SBC and its churches. They attributed the declines of other American denominations—particularly Methodists and Presbyterians—as directly related to their compromise with modernity. As Ammerman observes, SBC fundamentalists "are reasserting a less pluralistic reality in conscious opposition to a world in which old beliefs are no longer assumed to be true."[66] The culture might change but the faith would be preserved.

Fundamentalists also recognized that the old denominational coalition which had long frustrated their attempts to control the convention was breaking down. Through the use of their considerable rhetorical skill and certain methods of modern media, they redefined Southern Baptist dogma in such a way as to challenge the old theological and missionary *via media* of the denomination. Without the old protections of culture and denominational solidarity, the denominational pragmatists were unable to keep a more narrow definition of dogma and identity from dominating the convention and ultimately from controlling its boards and agencies. Thus the transitions in southern culture contributed to the downfall of the old denominational coalition and the rise of a right wing movement that promised to purge the SBC of the destructive elements of liberalism, pluralism, and the compromise of truth for the sake of unity. While that movement gained widespread control of the convention, however, its actions merely hastened the inevitable fragmentation of the denomination itself.

66. Ibid.

CHAPTER 2

Denominationalism: The Shape of the SBC

THE SOUTHERN BAPTIST CONVENTION WAS ESTABLISHED DURING THE "FORmative years" of American denominationalism.[1] While certain doctrinal and organizational alignments were evident throughout the colonial period, the impetus to gather in denominations flourished among the Protestant churches of nineteenth-century America. During the period from 1787 to 1850 the development of denominationalizing tendencies was particularly evident among such evangelical groups as Methodists, Baptists, Presbyterians, and Congregationalists. Millenial expectations, a concern for revivalism, and the missionary imperative together with the spirit of democratic optimism helped to move local congregations and benevolent societies to unite in a common evangelical endeavor. As Elwyn A. Smith observed, the modern denomination represents "the gathering of local and regional efforts into comprehensive organizational unity specifically joined with an early tradition of American Christianity."[2] This organizational effort was so successful that generations of religious Americans understood their Christianity in terms of membership in a specific denomination. In the religiously pluralistic context of American society, the denomination became a means for effecting certain evangelical activities.

As a modern organizational "theory and pattern" the denomination represents "the most basic administrative change in the church in fourteen hundred years."[3] If, as Sidney Mead suggests, denomina-

---

1. Sidney E. Mead, "Denominationalism: The Shape of Protestantism in America," in *Denominationalism,* ed. Russell Richey (Nashville: Abingdon, 1977), p. 74.

2. Elwyn A. Smith, "The Forming of a Modern American Denomination," in Richey, *Denominationalism,* p. 113.

3. Martin E. Marty, *Righteous Empire* (New York: Dial Press, 1970), pp. 67-68; and Richey, *Denominationalism,* p. 14.

tionalism in general represents "the shape of Protestantism in America," then denominational identity reflects the shape of the Southern Baptist Convention in particular.[4] Within the protective confines of southern culture, Southern Baptists developed a powerful denominational self-consciousness around which their autonomous congregations and diverse theological traditions were united. This organizational self-consciousness provided an increasing sense of programmatic loyalty and solidarity for churches in the SBC. The success of fundamentalists in bringing their theological and political agenda to bear on Southern Baptist life is a direct result of the decline of the old denominational coalition. No study of The Controversy in contemporary convention politics can ignore the development and subsequent fragmentation of Southern Baptist denominationalism.

The Denomination: Selected Interpretations

In 1977 historian Russell Richey compiled a valuable collection of essays that examined the nature of American denominationalism. The compendium provided numerous interpretations regarding the impact of the denominational phenomenon on American churches. They range from Winthrop Hudson's belief that the denomination was originally an ecumenical device for promoting unity among the fragmented Protestant communions to H. Richard Niebuhr's insistence that it represented "the moral failure of Christianity."[5] Most agreed, however, that the denomination was a new way of understanding the nature of the Christian church. It reflected an ecclesiastical category distinct from traditional church-sect typologies. The denomination was neither church nor sect but a new method of organizing and identifying multiple religious groups in a society where disestablishment and religious liberty prevailed. The constitutionally mandated freedom of religion ultimately put an end to an officially established church in America. Religious majorities and dissenting sects were forced to work out their own identity in relationship to and competition with each other. The denomination, therefore, became an effective means of organizing the churches in a nation where there was no

4. Mead, "Denominationalism: The Shape of Protestantism in America," in Richey, *Denominationalism,* pp. 70-105.

5. Richey, *Denominationalism,* p. 11.

state-sanctioned religion.[6] It was an alternative to Troeltsch's single church religious establishment.

Nor was the American denomination primarily a sect. Sectarian dissent against state-supported religion was no longer necessary in the American context of religious freedom. In fact, historian Timothy Smith suggested that in its earliest stages, denominationalism was "the very opposite of sectarianism; for it admits no claim to the exclusive possession of truth."[7] Religious liberty had created peculiar problems for certain evangelical sects. They were compelled to balance the exclusive nature of their theological claims with the inclusive right of all religious groups to proclaim their views. This was no easy task since many displayed a "'sectarian' tendency" in their claims to be the closest to the doctrine and practice of the New Testament church.[8] Nineteenth-century denominations often sounded very sectarian in their efforts to establish the distinctiveness of their doctrines and attract the attention of potential converts. Denunciation of other Christian traditions was necessary and widespread. Indeed, the public debate became an important forum in which evangelical churches declared their own views while challenging the theology and practice of their competitors. Nineteenth-century Methodists, Baptists, Presbyterians, Disciples, and others sought to prove that they were the true church and that their competitors were mistaken, if not heretical. Denominationalism set the boundaries for such confrontations, however. It channeled sectarian zeal into organized action. It also helped to "civilize" groups toward greater "social inclusiveness" and wider acceptance by the culture at large.[9]

In his analysis of the phenomenon, Sidney Mead concluded that

> the denomination, unlike the traditional forms of the church, is not primarily confessional, [and] it is certainly not territorial. Rather it is purposive. . . . A church as a church has no legal existence in the United States. . . . Neither is the denomination a sect in a traditional sense. . . . It is, rather, a voluntary association of like-hearted and like-minded individuals, who are united on the basis of common beliefs for the purpose

6. Winthrop Hudson, "Denominationalism as a Basis for Ecumenicity: A Seventeenth-Century Concept," in Richey, *Denominationalism*, pp. 21-42.

7. Timothy L. Smith, "Religious Denominations as Ethnic Communities: A Regional Case Study," in Richey, *Denominationalism*, p. 48.

8. Mead, "Denominationalism: The Shape of Protestantism in America," in Richey, *Denominationalism*, p. 15.

9. Russell Richey, "The Social Sources of Denominationalism: Methodism," in Richey, *Denominationalism*, p. 136.

of accomplishing tangible and defined objectives. One of the primary objectives is the propagation of its point of view.[10]

Mead's description seems particularly applicable to those groups that reflect a decidedly evangelical approach to Christian faith. It is less appropriate for the more ethnically distinctive, liturgically oriented churches.

The denominations he described demonstrate a variety of common characteristics. These qualities were evident from the beginning of the SBC and continue to inform its popular self-perception. They include: (1) the presence of certain sectarian, antihistorical tendencies and a claim to direct New Testament lineage; (2) a view of the church as a voluntary association of individuals, an approach which "tends to push tangible, practical considerations to the fore by placing primary emphasis on the free, uncoerced consent of the individual";[11] (3) a strong concern for the missionary enterprise and the worldwide propagation of the gospel; (4) revivalism as a primary means of doing evangelism; (5) a strong pietistic approach to faith with a concomitant antirationalistic bias; and (6) a tendency toward competition with other denominations as a means of gaining "volunteers and distinguishing true religion from false."[12] While Mead's approach has its limitations and does not apply to all American religious groups, his six characteristics are most helpful for understanding the ideas and actions that shaped the denominational consciousness of Southern Baptists. Not only did the SBC unite around the characteristics Mead described, but the convention also sought to preserve and perpetuate those nineteenth-century elements as long as possible, thus guaranteeing orthodoxy and identity. Indeed, few other American denominations retained their nineteenth-century identity, and thus resisted modernity, as long as the Southern Baptist Convention. In many ways, the SBC remains one of America's most enduring nineteenth-century denominations.

It could not last forever. As modernity insinuated itself into the culture and the convention, fragmentation was bound to occur. In response, fundamentalists promised to preserve the denomination's faithfulness to its nineteenth-century evangelical and cultural heritage. Moderates sought to use nineteenth-century denominational machinery to preserve the old structures and loyalties in the face of changing times.

10. Ibid., p. 167, citing Sidney Mead, "Denominationalism: The Shape of Protestantism in America."
11. Mead, "Denominationalism: The Shape of Protestantism in America," in Richey, *Denominationalism*, p. 81.
12. Ibid., pp. 75-105.

Ultimately, both groups were doomed to failure as both merely fueled the inevitable fragmentation.

The idea that the denomination is primarily "organizational" rather than "confessional" is also important for understanding the Grand Compromise on which the SBC was built. The denomination became a means for uniting the people called Baptists "in one sacred effort, the propagation of the Gospel."[13] The convention was a means to accomplish an evangelical end. Baptists were particularly concerned that the denomination never supersede the local congregation as the basic source of ecclesiastical authority. Nonetheless, convention programs served to unite diverse congregations across the South in a joint endeavor involving evangelism and missions. Churches that tenaciously guarded their autonomy were willing to join in denominational cooperation in order to accomplish broader evangelistic and missionary tasks than their individual resources could sustain. The denomination created a certain catholicity of action among various Baptist churches in the South.

Like other evangelical groups, Southern Baptist denominationalism reflected three "constitutive elements." These included "a purposive system of executive and promotional agencies; . . . the association of this structure with a particular American religious tradition; and a conservative, sometimes legalistic, determination to maintain a distinctive identity in the face of change."[14] This conservative instinct to maintain the status quo often caused great frustration for those who wanted to effect more rapid change. It also served to protect the denomination from capricious or faddish movements, thereby avoiding the possibility of schism. Mead notes that a denomination often maintains "a kind of massive and stubborn stability, inertia, and a momentum of its own." Likewise, denominationalists learned how to utilize the system to maintain the cooperative coalition needed to achieve the desired ends. This fact leads Mead to conclude "that whatever else top denominational leaders *may be*, they *must* be denominational politicians."[15] Those who wanted to make the organization effective had to learn how to work within it.

This tendency of denominations to maintain the theological and cultural status quo strongly influenced H. Richard Niebuhr's idea that

---

13. Robert Baker, *A Baptist Source Book* (Nashville: Broadman, 1966), p. 116.

14. Elwyn A. Smith, "The Forming of a Modern American Denomination," in Richey, *Denominationalism*, pp. 134-35.

15. Mead, "Denominationalism: The Shape of Protestantism in America," in Richey, *Denominationalism*, p. 82.

denominationalism represented the death of dynamic, prophetic Christianity. For Niebuhr, each denomination ultimately becomes an end in itself, more concerned with self-preservation than with the proclamation of the kingdom of God.[16] Denominationalism, Niebuhr believed, institutionalized the life out of the spiritual, conversionist awakenings of the eighteenth and nineteenth centuries. In this way denominations turned the kingdom of God into "a human possession, not a permanent revolution."[17] Denominational churches became more concerned with inviting sinners to join their organization than with introducing them to faith in God. As Niebuhr concluded, "it must justify and praise itself, its gospel and its faith, instead of living in the forgiveness of sin, doing its work, and making its confession."[18] Niebuhr acknowledged that some corporate institutionalism was inevitable as the church sought to organize itself. Nonetheless, denominationalism represented "the accommodation of Christianity to the caste system of human society."[19] He warned that it led churches "to sublimate their loyalties to standards and institutions only remotely relevant if not contrary to the Christian ideal" and tempted them to make "their own self-preservation and extension the primary object of their endeavor."[20] The inertia Niebuhr describes accounts for the frustrations of many SBC fundamentalists and liberals alike in their efforts to effect change in the institutions and agencies of the convention.

Denominationalists, of course, disagreed. They insisted that the bureaucratic machinery of the denomination was merely a tool for realizing the church's primary calling: the evangelization of the world. They were simply laboring together with God in the work of bringing in the kingdom. For the convention builders, the denomination was an instrument by which evangelicals would Christianize America and preach the gospel to all nations.[21] Russell Richey suggests that the denominationalism which matured in the early decades of the nineteenth century was "purposive" in nature. It represented "the joint testimony of distinct peoples and traditions that the Christianization of American society was to be their individual and common endeavor."[22]

---

16. Richey, "The Social Sources of Denominationalism: Methodism," in Richey, *Denominationalism,* p. 170.

17. H. Richard Niebuhr, "Institutionalization and Secularization of the Kingdom," in Richey, *Denominationalism,* pp. 242-43.

18. Ibid., p. 240

19. H. Richard Niebuhr, *The Social Sources of Denominationalism* (New York: World, 1957), p. 6.

20. Ibid., p. 21.

21. Richey, "The Social Sources of Denominationalism: Methodism," in Richey, *Denominationalism,* p. 169.

22. Ibid., p. 178.

If denominations later became ends in themselves, that did not obscure their original purpose and vision.

The Southern Baptist Convention was formed under that kind of mandate. Clearly, the early leaders felt a divine imperative to Christianize society—particularly southern society—and to take the gospel to the ends of the earth. Denominational programs and policies were almost always articulated in terms of the evangelical mission. The denomination was the instrument by which Southern Baptist people would fulfill the Great Commission (Matthew 28:19-20). Denominationalists called on Southern Baptists to look beyond their considerably diverse liturgical, educational, historical, even theological differences to the united tasks of evangelization and Christianization. In the process, they created a particular programmatic and organizational identity which, with southern culture, bound the constituency together. There were always those—Calvinists, Landmarkists, Social Gospelers, evangelists, and fundamentalists—who insisted that the cost of denominational loyalty was too great a price to pay, that in preserving its institutions, programs, and public unity, it sacrificed dogma, orthodoxy, or prophetic witness. Southern Baptist denominationalism prevailed, however, enabling the convention to avoid a major schism longer than anyone might have expected. It was a Grand Compromise, constructed by individuals who sought to bring some unity of purpose to a sometimes unruly constituency wary of any threat to local church autonomy and individual freedom. A century of denomination builders did their work well. Traditional loyalties could not last, however. When the old coalition faltered and modernity caught up with southern culture and Southern Baptists, the wolves were already at the door.

The SBC: Theological and Regional Traditions

Perhaps the wolves were always at the door. In many ways, cooperation and stability were always elusive for the SBC. For one thing, an individualistic ecclesiology undermined cooperation. The local congregation stood at the center of all ecclesiastical authority. Local church autonomy was to be maintained above all. Southern Baptists also reflect a fierce individualism in their concern for conscience and personal freedom. Neither church nor state, hierarchy nor creed were to interfere with personal liberty. A strong emphasis on subjective religious experience helped create suspicion of objective religious authority and organizations. Many members held strong anti-institutional and antidenominational sentiments, which contributed to a widespread mistrust of bureaucracy shared by Southern Baptists on both the right and the left. Yet in spite of these attitudes, Southern Baptist history reveals the evolution of a powerful denominational consciousness. That loyalty remains so strong that many Southern Baptists seem willing to accept almost any proposals and changes made by the current fundamentalist leadership as long as they can retain the name Southern Baptist. That such a strong organizational identity should be inculcated in a people suspicious of hierarchies and bureaucratic alignments is a tribute to the work of the early denomination builders.

Analysts of Southern Baptist denominationalism have made much of the diverse theological and regional "traditions" which coalesced to create the SBC. Walter B. Shurden of Mercer University was one of the first to explore the nature of what he called the Southern Baptist "synthesis." Shurden charted "four distinct traditions" that existed among Baptists in the South and that became part of the denominational makeup after 1845. They reflect surprising theological and regional diversity.

The Charleston Tradition

Shurden called the first strain the Charleston Tradition, after the Baptists who established First Baptist Church, Charleston, South Carolina, in the later seventeenth century. Dedicated Calvinists, they are sometimes called Regular Baptists. Shurden suggests that this tradition was characterized by "order"—theological, ecclesiastical, and liturgical. Its theology was expressed in the Philadelphia Confession of Faith, adopted in 1742, and grounded in Reformed theology. The Regular Baptists sought to balance local church autonomy with associational connectionalism.[23]

The Charleston Tradition reflects a concern for ordered worship in the simple yet dignified Calvinist mode. These Baptists emphasized the importance of baptism and the Lord's Supper along with a concern for personal piety and ethics. Committed to education, they founded numerous institutions including Furman University, Wake Forest University, the University of Richmond, and later the Southern Baptist Theological Seminary, the denomination's first seminary.[24] Many of the

---

23. Walter B. Shurden, "The Southern Baptist Synthesis: Is it Cracking?" in the 1980-81 Carver Barnes Lectures, published by Southeastern Baptist Theological Seminary, 1981, p. 5.

24. Ibid., p. 6.

preachers in this tradition could be numbered among what Brooks Holifield calls the "gentlemen theologians" of the South.[25] Unashamedly evangelistic, they tended to be educated individuals concerned for church order within the context of Reformed theology.[26] During the nineteenth and early-twentieth centuries representatives of the Charleston Tradition occupied prominent Baptist pulpits in Richmond, Augusta, Atlanta, and other urban areas of the South.

The Sandy Creek Tradition

Shurden labeled a second source of Southern Baptist identity the Sandy Creek Tradition of the Separate Baptists. These Baptists came into the South filled with religious fervor fostered by the First Great Awakening and a mandate to spread Christianity across the American frontier. A group of Separate Baptists under the leadership of Shubal Stearns and Daniel Marshall formed the Sandy Creek Baptist Church, Sandy Creek, North Carolina. That congregation became the mother church of over forty churches in the region.

The Separate Baptists were characterized by revivalistic conversionism, "individualism, congregationalism, biblicism, and egalitarianism."[27] Their worship tended toward spontaneity, enthusiasm, and emotional outburst, and they often experienced dramatic conversion and expressed it with shouts, tears, groans, and spirited singing. They looked to ministers whose preaching demonstrated spiritual enthusiasm in calling sinners to conversion. Many feared that too much education inhibited the religion of the Spirit. Highly individualistic, they were suspicious of alignments which might threaten congregational autonomy and the liberty of the individual soul. Their biblical loyalty and literalism made the Separate Baptists anticreedal. They would allow no "man-made" collections of dogma to become substitutes for the authority of Holy Scripture.[28]

Separate Baptists were an unruly lot who carried their revivalistic fervor west into Kentucky, Tennessee, Arkansas, Louisiana, and Texas. Theologically, they were heirs of Reformed doctrine, yet their penchant for mass evangelism and immediate conversion pushed the Separate

---

25. E. Brooks Holifield, *The Gentlemen Theologians: American Theology in Southern Culture, 1795-1860* (Durham, N.C.: Duke University Press, 1978).

26. Shurden, "The Southern Baptist Synthesis: Is it Cracking?" p. 6.

27. Ibid.

28. Ibid.

Baptists closer to Arminian theology regarding general atonement and free will than most Baptist historians have been willing to acknowledge. Shurden cites Virginia Baptist John Leland's view that, "It is a matter of fact that the preaching that has been most blessed of God, and most profitable to men, is the doctrine of Sovereign grace in the salvation of souls, mixed with a little of what is called Arminianism."[29] Such theological admixtures are a major factor in the contemporary controversy in the SBC.

The Georgia Tradition

Shurden called the third source of Southern Baptist identity the Georgia Tradition, evident in two particular locations, Augusta and Atlanta. The convention that was formed in Augusta coalesced, Shurden believed, around southern sectionalism related primarily to the question of slavery and "cooperative denominationalism," a more centralized form of denominational organization. The genius behind this denominational configuration was William B. Johnson of South Carolina, the convention's first president.

This denominational solidarity was reinforced in 1882 under the leadership of I. T. Tichenor, secretary of the Home Mission Board in Atlanta. Tichenor, Shurden said, led Southern Baptists to break with the Northern Baptist Home Mission Society and to concentrate missionary work through a centralized board rather than individual state conventions. While the Georgia Tradition fostered extensive denominational cooperation it also perpetuated sectional attitudes relating to southern provincialism and racial biases.[30]

The Landmark Tradition

The fourth tradition that Shurden charted was the Landmark Tradition, which gained prominence in the 1850s, creating controversy and threatening the unity of the convention.[31] Born in Tennessee and Kentucky, Landmarkism, as promoted by its early leaders J. R. Graves, J. M. Pendleton, and A. C. Dayton, was a form of Southern Baptist primitivism. Its proponents claimed that Baptists were the true church because

29. Ibid., pp. 6-7.
30. Ibid.
31. Ibid.

they alone could trace their lineage through an unbroken succession to John the Baptist immersing Jesus in the Jordan River. Landmarkism represented the sectarian side of the SBC. Taking their name from Proverbs 22:28, "Remove not the ancient landmark, which thy fathers have set," these Baptists sought to purify the convention of all who would not conform to their dogmatic definitions regarding the nature of the church, baptism, the Lord's Supper, and salvation. Their ecclesiology helped provide the often traditionless, ahistorical Baptists with an identity suitable for refuting the claims of Methodists, Presbyterians, Disciples, and other groups. While those denominations might claim John Wesley or John Calvin as founders, Baptists could point to direct descent from Jesus himself. They had maintained the true church order in its pristine purity all the way from New Testament times. Thus Baptists alone possessed the true ordinances. Those who had received baptism, even by immersion, outside the Baptist house were compelled to be baptized again. "Alien immersion"—non-Baptist immersion—was unacceptable in Landmark churches. The Lord's Supper could be received only by members of the specific congregation in which it was administered. This was the doctrine of "close communion."

For the Landmarkists, local churches alone constituted the true church of Christ. They suggested that a line of Baptist churches existed throughout Christian history, preserving the true New Testament doctrines. In a sense, Landmarkism was a kind of history "in the neighborhood of make-believe," constructed as a means of verifying Baptist doctrine, defining Baptist ecclesiology, and maintaining Baptist identity in competition with other religious groups. Landmarkists took great liberties with historical materials in their effort to establish their primitive credentials. The efforts of Landmarkists to impose their theology on the entire convention led the SBC to the brink of schism on several occasions.

The Evangelical Denominational Tradition

Since its publication in 1981, Shurden's thesis has become a helpful tool for understanding the diverse regional, theological, and liturgical traditions that were incorporated into the SBC. Other scholars have continued to expand and refine the thesis by noting other traditions not covered in the original study. In a recent doctoral dissertation at the Southern Baptist Theological Seminary, John Loftis explored the varying traditions in terms of ministerial roles or types. Loftis describes a fifth tradition that he calls the "Evangelical Denominational Tradition" in

SBC life.[32] He viewed this segment of the convention as growing out of the American Southwest—particularly Texas—with its roots in denominational pragmatism and conservative theology. This tradition placed great emphasis on a Southern Baptist way of believing, acting, worshiping, and evangelizing. Its adherents were convention loyalists, willing to use whatever worked to grow churches and expand the missionary mandate.[33]

The Texas Baptist Tradition

Historian Leon McBeth recently traced the development of what he termed the "Texas Baptist Tradition" in the SBC.[34] Expanding on Shurden and Loftis, McBeth insisted that the Texas Tradition began in the early twentieth century and that B. H. Carroll (1843-1914), founder of Southwestern Baptist Seminary in Fort Worth, was its chief architect. Southwestern Seminary was its major denominational institution, and the *Texas Baptist Standard* its primary publication.

McBeth distinguished between the southern and southwestern regions and the cultural impact that those two geographical areas had on the SBC itself. While the Southwest certainly had ties to the Confederacy, it was shaped by other cultural and political forces as well. He noted that the early Texas settlers claimed a vast expanse of territory that they would conquer "like a collective sponge." Texas Baptists absorbed this "militant spirit of conquest," McBeth said.[35] He suggested that the Texas Baptist Tradition is characterized by a particular style of "Baptist imperialism." Its supporters never doubted that "they would build in the Southwest one of the greatest Baptist empires in the world."[36] Denominational unity and cooperation were linked to the spirit of regional conquest. Theology was conservative and practical, most beneficial as it aided the church in fulfilling its evangelistic task.

The Texas or Southwestern Tradition represents a twentieth-century reassertion of the earlier denominational commitment to the Christianization of society. God had placed Southern Baptists in a fron-

---

32. John Franklin Loftis, "Factors in Southern Baptist Identity as Reflected by Ministerial Role Models, 1750-1925" (unpublished Ph.D. dissertation, Southern Baptist Theological Seminary, 1987), pp. 232-50.
    33. Ibid.
    34. Leon McBeth, Denominational Heritage Week Lectures, The Southern Baptist Theological Seminary, May 1988, audio tape recording.
    35. Ibid.
    36. Ibid.

tier culture for the purpose of winning souls and building the kingdom of God in a new wilderness. The Southwest, with all its economic, political, and spiritual potential, would be another "city upon a hill" which would renew America's mission and its place in the divine plan. The society would be conquered for Christ. It is no coincidence that many of the largest churches in the SBC are now west of the Mississippi River. The Texas Baptist Tradition is characterized by an unabashed triumphalism intent on winning the region to Christianity.

A Southern Baptist Synthesis?

The existence of these varied theological and regional traditions in SBC life illustrates that there was great diversity in the convention from the very beginning. In surveying this diversity, Shurden concluded that "the synthesis of the convention was missionary, not doctrinal, in nature."[37] Given his approach to the issue, Shurden's thesis was an appropriate method for understanding the SBC's unity in diversity. Yet there is another way of approaching the question of synthesis. Most Southern Baptists have perceived themselves, rightly or wrongly, as doctrinally united and theologically homogeneous. In the minds of most Southern Baptists, the convention's "synthesis" was both missionary *and* doctrinal. In popular perception, the denomination was united around the great theological truths of the Baptist-biblical tradition. How was it possible for so diverse a constituency composed of so many traditions to perceive themselves as doctrinally unified? One explanation is found in an often overlooked article written in 1874 by James P. Boyce, faculty member and first president of the Southern Baptist Theological Seminary.

Boyce wrote in response to an editorial published in *The Baptist* (Tennessee) which objected to the fact that certain ideas promoted at the seminary contradicted doctrinal positions advocated by "four or five state [Baptist] conventions."[38] The writer, a Landmarkist, insisted that Southern Baptists should not be asked to support professors whose doctrines were contrary to those preached in Baptist churches. He concluded that the seminary was hopelessly adrift from its theological moorings, "too far removed from the people to ever recover from its embarrassment."[39]

Boyce responded by reminding readers that every seminary pro-

37. Shurden, "The Southern Baptist Synthesis: Is it Cracking?" p. 8.
38. Elder M. P. Lowery, *The Baptist*, Feb. 28, 1874.
39. Ibid.

fessor was required to sign a doctrinal statement, or Abstract of Principles, approved in 1859. He noted that neither the Philadelphia (1742) nor New Hampshire Baptist Confessions of Faith (1833) were used exclusively in preparing the Abstract since various factions of the convention objected to articles within each of those early Baptist documents. As the convention sought to develop a doctrinal statement for its seminary, it had followed three basic principles. First, it was to provide a clear expression of the "fundamental doctrines of grace." That is, it would incorporate the great evangelical doctrines of the Christian faith. Second, the Abstract should delineate those basic principles that were "universally prevalent" among the people called Baptists. The seminary was identifiably Baptist in its distinctive doctrines. Third, Boyce concluded, "upon no point, upon which the denomination is divided, should the Convention, and through it the Seminary, take a position."[40] Boyce, a Calvinist, recognized that there were differences among nineteenth-century Southern Baptists that should not be allowed to undermine denominational unity.

The success of those principles is evident in the Abstract itself. The document affirms the inspiration of Scripture, but no specific theory of inspiration is advocated. Christ's work as mediator is acknowledged, but no single view of the atonement is explicit in the statement. The return of Christ is asserted, but no specific millennial theory is advanced. Baptist concepts of salvation, believer's church, and the ordinances are maintained. Where differences of opinion prevailed among nineteenth-century Baptists in matters such as ecclesiology and Landmarkism, no specific position was stated.[41]

As it was with the seminary, so it was with the denomination as a whole. Clearly, Southern Baptists understood themselves in terms of both a missionary *and* doctrinal identity. Yet the doctrines were articulated in such a way as to make room for congregations that represented a variety of diverse theological traditions. Each could believe that its way was the Baptist way. There was less a synthesis than a Grand Compromise based in an unspoken agreement that the convention would resist all attempts to define basic doctrines in ways that excluded one tradition or another, thereby destroying denominational unity and undermining the missionary imperative. Doctrinal positions were articulated in terms general enough to unite as many Southern Baptists as

40. James P. Boyce, "The Two Objections to the Seminary," part 5, *Western Recorder,* June 20, 1874, p. 2.

41. "The Abstract of Principles," in *Catalog, 1987-89,* Southern Baptist Theological Seminary, pp. 2-3.

possible in fulfilling the missionary task. Boyce himself refused to make questions of double predestination, alien immersion, or close communion a test of fellowship at the seminary. He did, however, accept the resignation of Professor Crawford Toy, concluding that Toy's views on Scripture were outside the bounds of the Abstract. How Boyce would respond to contemporary doctrinal debates in the SBC is at best speculative.[42] His vision of the way in which his nineteenth-century seminary would respond to convention divisions does inform the denominationalizing process.

Modifications in theology continued in Southern Baptist denominational life. When the convention finally did approve an official doctrinal statement—the Baptist Faith and Message (1925)—it chose to follow the more moderate New Hampshire Confession over the more explicitly Calvinist Philadelphia Confession. This approach to dogma represents one of the major strengths of the SBC in its efforts to avoid schism. It permitted those who affirmed certain "universally prevalent" Baptist beliefs to unite in missionary action. It allowed room for a variety of interpretations and traditions among churches and individuals who considered themselves Baptist. These diverse approaches helped expand Southern Baptist ministries and numbers. It also forced church leaders to look to denominational programs as the source of uniformity and solidarity rather than elaborate doctrinal conformity among Southern Baptist people and churches.

The Grand Compromise was also the denomination's weakness. It meant that the SBC always lived on the edge of controversy and potential schism as representatives of one particular theological viewpoint sought to impose their interpretation on the entire body. This explains why the history of the denomination is characterized by continual controversy and political struggle. Denominationalism served not only to provide a sense of unity and identity, but also to become a means of dealing with efforts to narrow doctrine and divide the convention. Denominationalists learned how to allow dissident groups enough power or doctrinal specificity to keep them within the convention, but to withhold enough power to prevent their impinging on the beliefs and practices of other traditions in the SBC. Ideologues were not permitted to distract the convention from its larger programmatic agenda. This way of proceeding kept the SBC theologically conservative and historically Baptist while allowing for surprising diversity in the churches.

42. William A. Mueller, *A History of Southern Baptist Theological Seminary* (Nashville: Broadman, 1959), pp. 135-42.

The SBC: A Historical Overview

Southern Baptist history illustrates the continuing struggle for denominational consensus among a constituency influenced by various ecclesiastical traditions and theological viewpoints, each, with some legitimacy, claiming to represent historic Baptist principles. It provides a fascinating case study in the evolution of an American denomination. A brief survey of the development of the SBC illustrates the growth of denominational identity.

First, the denomination itself was formed around a convention system, a relatively new type of organizational structure for Baptists in America. Earlier cooperative efforts took the form of loose-knit societies, each autonomous and funded through membership subscriptions from individual supporters. Through the early Triennial Convention, founded in 1814, Baptists in America first established missionary work. In this way they united in missionary and benevolent activity without threatening congregational autonomy or individual freedom. Denominational structure and identity were minimal.

Baptists in the South took a different approach, organizing boards and agencies around a more centralized convention system that would coordinate all denominational endeavors. Membership in the new convention was composed, not of individuals, but of those churches that agreed to unite in corporate action. Regional associations of churches and state Baptist conventions also developed alliances. Initially, denominational efforts were limited in scope. As historian W. W. Barnes wrote: "During the formative years, as it was finding its direction, the influence of the society method and the possible fear of centralized, more comprehensive organization held the Convention to a program of missions only."[43] Funding for denominational missionary endeavors was still based on the society method. Each agency subscribed its own budget through direct appeal to the churches. Each church could "designate" the specific work for which its funds were to be used.

Southern Baptist historians suggest various reasons for the gradually increasing tendency toward centralization. W. W. Barnes noted the popularity of the Philadelphia Confession of Faith with its concern for the unity of the invisible church as one important factor. Another factor was the Separate Baptist appreciation for Presbyterian church government, and another was the centralizing tendency of En-

---

43. W. W. Barnes, *The Southern Baptist Convention, 1845-1953* (Nashville: Broadman, 1954), p. 34.

glish General Baptists also present in the South.[44] Robert Baker insisted that the formation of Baptist state conventions encouraged centralization. Likewise, the early denominational leaders, particularly William B. Johnson and Richard Furman, were advocates of centralization. Baker concluded that "the continued use of the society plan of financial representation totally isolated the centralized convention from any interference whatsoever with the autonomy of the churches."[45]

William B. Johnson of South Carolina was the chief architect of such a plan. He wrote: "In its successful operation, the whole Denomination will be united in one body for the purpose of well-doing, with perfect liberty secured to each contributor of specifying the object or objects, to which his amount shall be applied, as he please, whilst he or his Delegation may share in the deliberations and control of all the objects, promoted by the Convention."[46] Whether they realized it or not, however, Johnson and the other denomination builders changed the way Baptists organized themselves, laying the foundation for the modern, multi-agency SBC. As Southern Baptists came to accept denominational identity more fully they also developed a program for collective funding of all agencies. Again, that program of denominational cooperative finance was to prove both the convention's greatest strength and, ultimately, its weak link.

In spite of the decision to form a unified convention, various forces opposing denominational organization were present from the beginning. Alexander Campbell's opposition to denominational alignments attracted many Baptist sympathizers. Campbell (1788-1866) attacked those who organized missionary and benevolent societies as establishing unscriptural agencies not evident in the true New Testament church. Others, such as hyper-Calvinist Daniel Parker, denounced missionary activity entirely. Parker (1781-1844) insisted that each individual entered the world with the seed of salvation or the seed of damnation. Their eternal destiny was decreed at birth so missionary activity was both futile and unbiblical.[47] Many Baptists in the South accepted Parker's doctrine of "two seeds in the spirit" or gospel primitivism, thus rejecting all missionary alliances. Moreover throughout the convention's history there remained an abiding suspicion of the denomination manifested within the SBC itself. Landmarkism was the source

---

44. Ibid., p. 118.
45. Robert A. Baker, *The Southern Baptist Convention and Its People, 1607-1972* (Nashville: Broadman, 1974), p. 174.
46. Ibid., p. 165.
47. Ibid., p. 151.

of much internal mistrust. Landmarkists condemned any ecclesiastical organization that threatened the autonomy and authority of the local congregation. No board or agency was to have authority over the local church. Landmarkist challenges to Southern Baptist denominationalism occur well into the twentieth century.

In the twentieth century, fundamentalism also promoted various forms of antidenominationalism. One of the most powerful attacks on the convention structure was led by the infamous Texas preacher J. Frank Norris, longtime pastor of First Baptist Church, Fort Worth. Norris was a constant critic of SBC denominationalists and their bureaucratic efforts to control local churches and protect liberals. By the 1930s Norris led his congregation out of the SBC, but that did not stop him from continuing to denounce the denomination and its leaders. The Independent Fundamentalist Baptist movement which Norris and others developed became a major challenge to denominationalism among Baptists in the South. Jerry Falwell is perhaps the best-known pastor in the Independent Baptist Fundamentalist tradition in contemporary America. Independent Baptists have long been some of the SBC's most persistent critics. The fundamentalist dominance of the convention, however, has produced improved relations with various elements of the Independent Baptist movement. The presence of antidenominational sentiments both within and without the SBC indicates that many Southern Baptists have long maintained an ambivalent relationship with their own convention. Critics could generally find a sympathetic response to their antidenominational rhetoric among the autonomous churches and independent-minded constituency.

These attitudes reveal that the denominationalists in the convention had their work cut out for them. Yet, in spite of continued controversy and a long series of challenges to denominational development, the Southern Baptist Convention became one of the most organized, efficient, and numerically successful ecclesiastical bodies in North America. More important, convention leaders inculcated a profound sense of denominational loyalty and identity among the people in the churches. As we have seen, the denomination became a means of uniting those of various regional, theological and liturgical traditions and holding at bay those who sought to impose narrower doctrinal or ecclesiastical norms on the entire body. In spite of its success, however, SBC unity was tenuous, relying on the intricate relationship of culture and denominational loyalty to prevail against continuing assaults from a diverse and restless constituency. As pluralism invaded both church and culture, the possibility of maintaining the fragile balance became increasingly problematic.

CHAPTER 3

Southern Baptist Denominationalism: The Sources of Unity

WHAT WERE THE SOURCES OF SOUTHERN BAPTIST DENOMINATIONAL UNITY? How did a denomination so committed to personal individualism and local autonomy avoid major schism for so long? The answers to these questions are complex, sometimes contradictory. Southern Baptist unity developed slowly and was never completely secure; it was the result of many forces that evolved during the first hundred years of the convention's history. As we have seen, southern culture provided an important source of unity from without. Southern Baptists were united by common social values and traditions as well as struggles related to the Civil War, Reconstruction, and other elements of their cultural situation. There were also various sources of unity that came from within the convention and shaped Southern Baptist self-understanding and sense of cooperation.

Denominationalists Promote Unity

First, Southern Baptist identity was fostered by generations of leaders who were committed to denominational unity and organizational success. In the beginning, the advocates of denominational unity were aided in their task by the vulnerability of the churches in the post–Civil War era. Not only were most Baptist churches located in rural areas but also they were devastated by the ravages of war and the massive spiritual and physical needs that confronted the entire region. There were no "super churches" able to go it alone with elaborate programs and extensive financial resources. The churches needed each other if they were to provide an evangelistic and pastoral response to their region and the world. The early leaders learned important lessons from the war, the slavery controversy, and the schism with Baptists in the North. If they were to establish an effective denominational organization and grow as a successful institution, they must avoid schism at all cost. It is not insignificant that the people who constructed the Grand Compromise and avoided a major schism for over a century were heirs of the great schism that divided American Baptists in 1845.

From the devastation of the Civil War and Reconstruction the SBC grew to become America's largest Protestant denomination. In 1988, the convention reported a total membership of 14,618,567 members in 37,116 churches. The convention system incorporated a variety of autonomous units, each related through cooperative relationships. Local churches are autonomous entities, based in congregational polity, which means that each congregation is responsible for its own budget, ministries, and theological emphasis. Associations are larger denominational units, still autonomous, that incorporate Southern Baptist churches in relative proximity for the purposes of fellowship and combined local ministries. State conventions, also autonomous, receive contributions from local churches to the Cooperative Program of denominational finances. States retain a portion for their regional ministries—establishing new churches and supporting state Baptist universities and colleges—and send a portion to the Southern Baptist Convention, the denomination's national organization. Administered through an Executive Committee, the national SBC controls agencies that include the Home and Foreign Mission boards, six theological seminaries, the Annuity Board, the Brotherhood Commission, the Historical Commission, the Radio and Television Commission, the Education Commission, the Stewardship Commission, the Christian Life Commission, and the Sunday School Board. Local churches relate to associations, state conventions, and the national SBC individually through "messengers" sent to annual meetings. Churches are entitled to send messengers to the national meeting based on congregational size—one messenger for each affiliated congregation and one additional messenger for each 250 members or each $250 paid to the convention, to a maximum of ten.

In establishing this system the early denominationalists worked in various ways. Above all, they sought to maintain a spirit of compromise while inculcating a strong denominational identity among a people suspicious of hierarchical alliances. Denominationalists affirmed a conservative theological consensus, while avoiding those narrow definitions that would prove divisive, thereby focusing attention on practical Christian action. This approach to leadership is evident in generation after generation of prominent Southern Baptists, particularly during periods of controversy. The following individuals are only a few examples of a consistent pattern of denominational leadership.

R. B. C. Howell

R. B. C. Howell (1801-1868), a prominent pastor and the second president of the SBC, opposed an attempt to impose Landmarkist doctrines on the entire convention. As editor of *The Baptist* (Tennessee), Howell worked to unite Tennessee Baptists into a state convention and to promote broader denominational harmony. One writer observes: "For thirteen years Howell used *The Baptist* as an instrument for information, promoting harmony, healing schismatic frictions, furthering benevolent objectives, and pursuing hopes for education and unification."[1] In 1848, the editorship of *The Baptist* passed to Landmark leader J. R. Graves who utilized the paper to broadcast his own antidenominational sentiments. Graves not only attacked denominational mission boards but also urged the SBC to unite around Landmark doctrines of the church, baptism, communion, and ordination. He insisted that all SBC churches should practice close communion and require the rebaptism of all who had not received immersion in a Baptist church. These doctrines would thus become normative for all Southern Baptist churches, thereby considerably narrowing doctrinal parameters.

As the pastor of First Baptist Church, Nashville, Howell led that congregation to take disciplinary action against Graves, a member of his congregation, for defaming the church in his speeches and writings. Graves carried the matter to the 1859 meeting of the SBC in Richmond, Virginia, hoping to thwart Howell's election to a sixth term as convention president. He warned that Howell's election would destroy support for the convention and create an immediate schism. Howell's response was that of a classic denominationalist. Although elected by a comfortable majority, Howell promptly resigned in order that any hint of schism might be avoided.[2] His election marked the defeat of Graves's attempt to impose Landmark definitions on the SBC. His resignation as president allowed Landmark supporters to remain within the convention. Doctrinal obscurantism was rejected, schism was avoided, and denominational unity preserved.

Howell was convinced of the destructive nature of the Landmark movement. He wrote in 1859:

> There are elements at work that threaten the disruption of the relation of the Convention and the Foreign [Mission] Board to the body of the Southern Baptists. There are schemes of consolidation and centralization

1. Linwood T. Horne, "Leadership in Times of Crisis: A Study in the Life of R. B. C. Howell," *Baptist History and Heritage* 20 (Jan. 1985), p. 39.
2. Ibid., p. 42.

now urged by certain brethren who exercise a controlling influence in the
... Convention which, if they succeed in consummating, will as certainly
destroy the present union of Southern Baptists in Foreign Missions as the
Convention meets in May next. And there is a determination on the part
of some, moved more by partisan than missionary zeal, to make the next
Biennial Convention an ecclesiastical Court and to force its decision into
antagonism with Churches and Associations.[3]

Southern Baptist historian Albert McClellan comments that "concerning
the denomination, Howell appears to have had two assumptions:
(1) Cooperative missions is the reason for the existence of the Southern
Baptist Convention, and (2) the Convention is not a rigid legislative
body."[4] W. W. Barnes concluded that while 1859 represented the last
effort on the part of Landmarkists to destroy the convention it was not
the end of their attempt to change convention structure, eliminate "the
financial basis of co-operative work," and shape the convention "into an
ecclesiastical body composed of churches."[5] Where Landmarkists failed,
fundamentalists succeeded, due in part to the demise of the Grand
Compromise which R. B. C. Howell and others set in motion.

James Bruton Gambrell

James Bruton Gambrell (1841-1921) was another leader who contributed
to the development of denominational identity in the SBC. Once a scout
in Lee's army, Gambrell had an illustrious career as an editor, a Baptist
college president, a seminary professor, and executive secretary of the
Baptist General Convention of Texas. A committed denominationalist,
Gambrell was a strong supporter of the voluntary principle in religion.
He insisted "that all true religion is voluntary, and that all true service is
responsive to the claims of Jesus Christ upon the individual heart and
conscience." Churches were "voluntary organizations," with each congregation "a complete unit in itself."[6] Baptist efforts to unite for missionary action were based on the uncoerced cooperation of each congregation. In their common activity on behalf of the gospel, churches stood
"on equal footing."[7]

---

3. *Tennessee Baptist,* Feb. 5, 1859, p. 2, as cited in Albert McClellan, "The Leadership
Heritage of Southern Baptists," *Baptist History and Heritage* 20 (Jan. 1985), p. 9.

4. McClellan, "The Leadership Heritage of Southern Baptists," pp. 9-10.

5. W. W. Barnes, *The Southern Baptist Convention, 1845-1953* (Nashville: Broadman,
1954), p. 113.

6. J. B. Gambrell, *The Years in Texas* (Dallas: Baptist Standard, 1970), pp. 45-46.

7. Ibid., p. 49.

For Gambrell, the primary basis for denominational cooperation was missionary activity. Those local congregations that refused to minister beyond themselves were sinful and selfish. Baptist churches, therefore, should unite in establishing mission boards and missionary activities, at home and abroad.[8] Like R. B. C. Howell, Gambrell was disturbed by attempts to undermine missionary cooperation. He wrote that a few "gospel missioners" (Landmarkists) should not be permitted to destroy the unified work of the mission boards. He asked: "Have brethren who do not believe in the cooperative system of missions the right to membership in cooperative bodies and in general to use the meetings, the papers, the boards and the machinery of cooperation to hinder and destroy cooperation? Certainly not."[9]

Gambrell was also concerned about what he saw as an equally ominous threat to denominational identity: participation with other denominations in the cause of Christian union. During the late-nineteenth and early-twentieth centuries many Southern Baptists responded positively to ecumenical cooperation with other groups, particularly those of similar evangelical and missionary sentiments. Evangelical endeavors such as the Student Volunteer Movement and the Laymen's Missionary Movement attracted the attention of many Southern Baptist leaders. Gambrell led in the effort to discourage Southern Baptist participation in ecumenical affairs. He urged the convention to avoid any organizational alignment that might dilute Southern Baptist principles. Gambrell advocated the development of a genuine Southern Baptist identity, untainted by contact with other non-Baptist groups. Southern Baptists were encouraged to read denominationally produced literature, utilize denominationally developed programs, and think of themselves as a unique New Testament people. Baptist patriarch E. Y. Mullins wrote of Gambrell's views and his contribution to denominational identity:

> He did not believe in entering into evangelistic and missionary combinations with other denominations because it would hamper us in bearing full witness to the truth of the New Testament as we understand it. . . . In a sentence, the outstanding service which he rendered to his generation of Baptists was in unifying the various elements among Southern Baptists, on the one hand, and on the other in restraining them from unwise combinations with alien forces.[10]

8. Ibid., pp. 178-80, 223ff., and 307ff.
9. Ibid., p. 130.
10. E. C. Routh, *The Life Story of Dr. J. B. Gambrell* (Oklahoma City: Baptist Book Store, 1929), pp. 93-94.

Gambrell's intent was to promote Southern Baptist doctrine and practice while protecting the denomination from those influences, however helpful, that would undermine Baptist identity.

In 1913, the Baptist General Convention of Texas approved a statement on Christian union drafted by Gambrell and George W. Truett, the well-known pastor of First Baptist Church, Dallas. It described the Baptist position on the doctrines of personal faith, baptismal immersion, believer's church, and congregational polity—each based on a particular understanding of biblical teachings. It also declared that no "organic union" of the churches could be achieved apart from these scriptural doctrines. Any attempts at union on any other terms were "impossible with Baptists."[11] The document concluded that "our most cherished beliefs, our deep sense of duty will not permit us to enter into any federation, council, or what not that would, in any way, obscure the position set out above, or hinder us in the full and fill preaching of the whole counsel of God to all the people of the world."[12]

Gambrell's approach provides important insight into the development of Southern Baptist denominational unity. First, not only were denominationalists concerned about avoiding internal division, they were also careful to avoid external alignments that would compromise Baptist doctrine or dilute denominational consciousness. Gambrell's insistence that Southern Baptists avoid associations that would sacrifice specific Baptist doctrine again indicates that theology was important to SBC self-understanding, unity, and cooperation. Second, Gambrell's actions demonstrate the way in which convention leaders sought to shape a denominational identity for churches and individuals within the SBC. Southern Baptists were to follow their own unified program of missionary and denominational outreach. Only in that way could the doctrines and convictions of the Baptists be preserved. Such "Baptist blinders" would protect the identity and the mission of the denomination. They also provided a valuable sense of identity for a diverse constituency. In 1921, George W. McDaniel, the pastor of First Baptist Church, Richmond, Virginia, acknowledged that Gambrell's "firm judgment and avowed convictions kept Southern Baptists from expensive entangling alliances which others entered to their embarrassment and regret."[13] Only by developing their own programs and policies could the uniqueness of the Southern Baptists be assured.

11. J. B. Gambrell, *Christian Union, in Parable and Precept* (New York: Revell, 1917), p. 179.

12. Ibid., p. 181.

13. George W. McDaniel, *A Memorial Wreath* (Dallas: Baptist Standard, 1921), p. 71.

Edgar Young Mullins

In many respects, Edgar Young Mullins (1860-1928) personifies the Grand Compromise that characterized the SBC throughout most of the twentieth century. As few other Southern Baptist leaders, Mullins represented the nature of denominational compromise and identity in the convention. In his role as preacher, professor, and theologian he helped shape Southern Baptist public, if not popular, theology. As president of the Southern Baptist Theological Seminary, the Southern Baptist Convention, and the Baptist World Alliance, he was at once a denominational leader and a world Baptist statesman. As Walter Shurden comments, "Denominational politics was something he loved and the art of politics something in which he excelled."[14] Mullins did not win all his battles in the convention, but successes in denominational controversies probably helped Southern Baptists avoid major compromise in the turbulent period of the 1920s.

Even Mullins's election as president of the Southern Baptist Theological Seminary in 1899 reflects the nature of Southern Baptist denominational compromise. Mullins, then pastor of First Baptist Church, Newton Centre, Massachusetts, was chosen to replace William Whitsitt, seminary president and professor of church history. Whitsitt's 1896 historical study *A Question in Baptist History* demonstrated that English Baptists had not practiced baptismal immersion until 1641. That controversial conclusion was a direct contradiction of the Landmark claim that historic Baptist churches had maintained immersion in unbroken succession since the time of John the Baptist. So intense was the controversy that Whitsitt was forced to resign. (His views are almost universally accepted now by Baptist historians.) Mullins was a credible candidate to succeed Whitsitt not only because of his stature as a preacher and theologian but also because, although a southerner, he had been outside the Whitsitt controversy while in distant New England. At the same time, it seems clear that Mullins was indeed sympathetic to Whitsitt's scholarly investigations and generally accepted his conclusions.[15] Again, the Grand Compromise remained intact.

From his position as president and professor of theology at the Southern Baptist Seminary, he shaped the development of Southern Baptist public theology in significant ways. His book *The Axioms of*

---

14. Walter B. Shurden, "The Pastor as Denominational Theologian in Southern Baptist History," *Baptist History and Heritage* 15 (July 1980), p. 20.

15. W. Morgan Patterson, "The Southern Baptist Theologian as Controversialist: A Contrast," *Baptist History and Heritage* 15 (July 1980), p. 10.

Religion provided "a fresh statement of Baptist views to 'enable the world to understand us better.'"[16] Mullins's work as a theologian reflects his gifts as a denominationalist. Clearly, he was no theological liberal. Much of his work was produced in response to modernism and its threat to evangelical Christianity. He defended such classic Christian doctrines as biblical inspiration and authority, the virgin birth of Christ, the bodily resurrection, the reality of the supernatural in religion, and the significance of religious experience for every individual.[17] At the same time, he insisted that new scientific discoveries were no threat to the biblical revelation. He noted that the theory of evolution was gaining in popularity among scientists but warned that it should not be taught as if it were "a definite or established truth of science."[18] Faith and reason were not contrary to each other.

The response of Mullins's critics gives further evidence of his use of the Grand Compromise that bound the convention together. One of Mullins's friends and sometime critics was J. Gresham Machen, a Princeton professor and fundamentalist leader. Machen opposed Mullins's suggestion that religion was not controlled by scientific and philosophical principles but by its own unique "personal relation," confirmed by "the immediate experience of God."[19] Subjective religious experience, according to Mullins, was the foundation of faith. Machen responded that religion could not be compartmentalized. Like science and philosophy, it depended on facts. George Marsden comments that, "Machen regarded Mullins's position as a dangerous concession in principle to the chief tendency in modern thought—away from direct knowledge of facts to subjective experience."[20] This difference reflects at least one point of departure between the conservative Mullins and the fundamentalist Machen. Fundamentalists frequently attack Mullins's understanding of religious experience as too closely tied to the views of the German philosopher Friedrich Schleiermacher. Baptist inerrantists Tom Nettles and Russ Bush praise Mullins's defense of biblical orthodoxy in the face of modernism, but agree with Bernard Ramm that he did not provide "an adequate doctrine of authority."[21] Ramm further suggested that Mullins lived and wrote "under the charm of pragmatism and pursued

16. Ibid., p. 11.
17. Ibid., p. 13.
18. Ibid., citing SBC *Annual, 1923*, pp. 19-20.
19. George M. Marsden, *Fundamentalism and American Culture: The Shaping of Twentieth-Century Evangelicalism, 1870-1925* (New York: Oxford, 1980), p. 216.
20. Ibid.
21. L. Russ Bush and Tom J. Nettles, *Baptists and the Bible* (Chicago: Moody, 1980), p. 298.

its faulty logic."[22] For inerrantists, Mullins's appeal to religious experience was his greatest theological weakness. Other Southern Baptists view it as one of Mullins's greatest strengths.[23] Still other scholars see Mullins's efforts at compromise as indicative of another kind of weakness. Norman Furniss, an early analyst of the fundamentalist-modernist controversy in America, suggested that Mullins "never clarified his convictions sufficiently" to exercise significant influence over the controversy. He cites another historian who concluded that "Dr. Mullins wobbled around a good deal, and on the whole gave encouragement to the anti-evolutionists."[24] Furniss regarded Mullins's compromise as equivocation.

E. Y. Mullins was no one-dimensional individual as ideologues often seek to portray him. His theology was constructed in a denomination founded on a precarious compromise. For Mullins, freedom was at the heart of the Baptist legacy. He wrote that "the doctrine of the soul's competency in religion under God is the historical significance of the Baptists."[25] He concluded: "If there is any one thing which stands out above all others in crystal clearness in the New Testament it is Christ's doctrine of the soul's capacity, right and privilege to approach God directly and transact with him in religion."[26] His ability to exercise leadership within that context is a monument to his understanding of the political, theological and ecclesiastical realities present in the SBC.

Herschel H. Hobbs

Herschel H. Hobbs, longtime pastor of First Baptist Church, Oklahoma City, echoes Mullins's approach to Southern Baptist controversy and the art of denominational compromise. Walter Shurden calls Hobbs " 'the E. Y. Mullins' of the 1960s and 1970s."[27] He notes that Mullins had a profound impact on Hobbs; both served as president of the SBC during turbulent times, and both were guiding forces behind the construction

22. Ibid., citing Bernard Ramm, "Baptists and Sources of Authority," p. 10.

23. James Leo Garrett, James Tull, and E. Glenn Hinson, *Are Southern Baptists "Evangelicals"?* (Macon: Mercer University Press, 1983), pp. 136-38.

24. Patterson, "The Southern Baptist Theologian as Controversialist," p. 14, citing Norman F. Furniss, *The Fundamentalist Controversy, 1918-1931* (Hamden, Conn.: Archon Books, 1963), p. 120.

25. E. Y. Mullins, *The Axioms of Religion* (Philadelphia: American Baptist Publication Society, 1908), p. 56.

26. Ibid., p. 63.

27. Shurden, "The Pastor as Denominational Theologian in Southern Baptist History," p. 21.

of Southern Baptist confessions of faith, Mullins in 1925 and Hobbs in 1963. Like Mullins, Hobbs mastered the art of denominational compromise, affirming conservative theology while refusing to define that theology so narrowly as to exclude large segments of the constituency or precipitate schism.

This process of denominational compromise is illustrated in Hobbs's own account of the work of the committee charged with revising the 1925 Baptist Faith and Message, a committee that he chaired. He reports that one committee member proposed to define the doctrine of the Lord's Supper in terms of the Landmark idea of close communion, in which only members of each local congregation were permitted to participate in communion at their specific church. Hobbs recalls that another committee member responded that while he accepted such an interpretation, as would most Baptists in his state, "we must remember that we are not preparing a statement of faith for any one state but for all Southern Baptists. It must be broad enough for all of them to live comfortably with."[28] That approach to theological and practical issues illustrates something of the Grand Compromise on which the convention was built. It was crucial to Hobbs's own attitude toward SBC unity.

His work as a denominational leader reflects his successful attempts to maintain the convention's conservative *via media*. With conservative rhetoric and denominational solidarity, Hobbs helped preserve unity in the face of numerous twentieth-century conflicts. Hobbs's method of compromise failed, however, at the convention's 1980 annual meeting in St. Louis, Missouri. The failure illustrated that a new day had dawned in the SBC. This was the second year of the fundamentalist plan to take control of convention leadership, and tensions between factions showed no signs of easing as the week neared its end. At that point, Hobbs exercised a tactic that many denominationalists had used when all other efforts at reconciliation failed. As a senior statesman and past convention president, Hobbs asked for a point of personal privilege and an opportunity to call the convention messengers beyond their differences to a renewed commitment to a common denominational task— evangelism and missions—and away from "creeping creedalism."[29] Before he could complete his remarks, Herschel Hobbs was drowned out by a chorus of boos from the audience. Watching from the press room, Marse Grant, the editor of the *Biblical Recorder*, observed in disbelief:

28. Herschel Hobbs, "Southern Baptists and Confessionalism," *Review and Expositor* 76 (Winter 1979), p. 60.

29. Terry Mattingly, "Old Baptists, New Baptists: A Reporter Looks at the Battle to Control the SBC," *Southwestern Journal of Theology* 28 (Summer 1986), p. 6.

"They're booing Herschel Hobbs. Am I at the Southern Baptist Convention? They're booing Herschel Hobbs. What is happening to us?"[30]

What was happening was a collapse of the old methods of denominational compromise. In an interview with reporter Terry Mattingly, Hobbs himself recalled: "Of course, no one likes to be booed. I still can't express how I felt except that it was a real feeling of sadness that things should come to that. . . . I had never, ever, seen us leave a convention, no matter how bitter the fighting had been, without some kind of reconciliation at the end, some kind of love feast. Now, it seems like I can't even remember what the old days were like."[31] Hobbs and other older leaders slowly realized that this controversy was somehow different from earlier ones. Traditional remedies for healing wounds and uniting a divided constituency no longer worked.

Hobbs's 1980 experience was compounded at the SBC meetings throughout the decade of the eighties. Denominationalists fruitlessly attempted to utilize old methods of compromise for restoring unity and slowing the fundamentalist takeover. Privately, if not publicly, traditional denominationalists were forced to admit that things had changed. Most still could not believe that the system that had worked so well in their day would not somehow save the convention from fragmentation or schism. What denominationalists failed to realize, however, was that denominational loyalty itself had begun to disappear long before The Controversy erupted. Fundamentalists recognized that the shape of denominational unity had changed and acted on that reality while many moderates continued to hope that old loyalties and methods would again prevail.

Organizational Unity

Throughout most of the twentieth century denominational unity prevailed, however, holding in balance the almost irreconcilable forces of local autonomy, theological conservatism, and doctrinal imprecision. Convention leaders imbued their constituency with a sense of organizational unity that withstood many a controversy. They established a convention system by which evangelical, educational, and benevolent activities became increasingly centralized. They created agencies and programs around which Southern Baptists invested intensive loyalty

30. Ibid.
31. Ibid., pp. 6-7.

and energy. The SBC thus evolved into a highly centralized corporation supported by a loose confederation of autonomous congregations and theologically diverse subgroups. Robert Baker concludes that "sensitiveness relative to centralization in the Convention began to disappear rapidly during the 1920's."[32]

In 1917, an Executive Committee was established to coordinate all denominational programs and to administer policies as the "defacto year-round corporate voice of the Convention."[33] The Home and Foreign Mission Boards, the state Baptist colleges and denominational seminaries, the Woman's Missionary Union, and the Sunday School Board helped create what Walter Shurden calls a "Southern Baptist Spirit" of denominational identity and action.[34] These agencies developed uniform programs that shaped the life of local congregations large and small. Denominational programs contributed to the formation of a Southern Baptist calendar of the Christian year that all churches affiliated with the convention were encouraged to observe. Since most Southern Baptist congregations eschewed the traditional liturgical calendar of the larger Christian community, these denominational holy days served an important and unifying purpose. For example, Christmas was characterized less by traditional Advent observances than by an emphasis on foreign missions. The Christmas season included emphasis on a special missionary offering named in honor of Lottie Moon, a nineteenth-century SBC missionary to China, the epitome of missionary dedication and self-sacrifice. The Easter season was devoted to promoting the Annie Armstrong Home Missions Offering, a program that in many SBC churches received greater attention than traditional Lenten observances. Other special denominational Sundays now include Race Relations Sunday, Cooperative Program Day, World Peace Sunday, and Sanctity of Life Day. Churches were Southern Baptist not only because they affirmed certain basic doctrines but also because they acted like Southern Baptists were supposed to act, through conformity to convention programs and practices. After 1925, this denominational unity was further solidified by financial cooperation through support for the Cooperative Program, a unified financial plan.

32. Robert A. Baker, *The Southern Baptist Convention and Its People, 1607-1972* (Nashville: Broadman, 1974), pp. 400-401.

33. Ibid., p. 401.

34. Walter B. Shurden, "The Southern Baptist 'Synthesis': Is It Cracking?" in the 1980-81 Carver-Barnes Lectures, published by Southeastern Baptist Theological Seminary, 1981.

The Cooperative Program

The Cooperative Program represents an important denominationalizing force in Southern Baptist life. First, its adoption put an end to the last vestiges of the society method in the increasingly centralized convention organization. No longer would each agency be compelled to send representatives, hat in hand, to individual churches. Through one collective program Baptists could fund all the agencies related to the convention. This not only streamlined the collection of funds but also solidified the centralization of the convention system begun in 1845.

Second, the Cooperative Program made collective funding the primary means of supporting denominational agencies. It created a system of allocation whereby each agency received specific amounts from the total undesignated receipts subscribed by the churches. Mission boards retained special seasonal offerings but they also received major funding directly from the Cooperative Program.

Third, the Cooperative Program solidified the relationship between state Baptist conventions and the national denomination. Even today, Cooperative Program monies go first to the state Baptist conventions which retain a portion of those receipts for their own budgets. States then decide how much to allocate to the national convention. The success of denominationalizing trends is evident in the ability of the national convention to convince the states to share an increasing portion of their Cooperative Program budgets with the convention as a whole. Robert Baker comments that "this fusion between the state programs and the Convention's activities brought a new denominational unity to Southern Baptists."[35]

That arrangement is now being called into question. In 1988, E. Glenn Hinson, professor of church history at the Southern Baptist Seminary, Louisville, suggested that state conventions, many of which remain under the control of convention moderates, might reevaluate their allocations to the national convention. Instead of sending their monies to the fundamentalist controlled Executive Committee of the SBC, the state conventions might designate directly which agencies should receive specific sums of money, thereby circumventing the Executive Committee altogether. At their 1988 state convention, Virginia Baptists developed a proposal to reevaluate their funding of the national convention if the SBC presidents refused to accept the counsel of a special committee regarding appointments to convention boards and agencies. This proposal could become a new means of

35. Baker, *The Southern Baptist Convention*, p. 404.

funding and a new approach to The Controversy on the part of moderates.

Finally, support for the Cooperative Program became a means of identifying "cooperating" Southern Baptist churches. By 1931, messengers from local churches to the annual SBC convention were recognized as those whose churches were in cooperation with the work of the denomination and which had been "during the fiscal year preceding ... a bona fide contributor to the work of the convention."[36]

From the beginning, securing support for the Cooperative Program was not easy. J. E. Dillard, chairman of the Commission on the Cooperative Program from 1925 to 1946, wrote, "Our problem is to get our people, *all of them,* promoting our program."[37] Thus stewardship promotion became an integral part of denominational solidarity. It united national, state, and local agencies and churches in a common task. On every level of convention life, the denomination provided churches and individuals with uniform, practical programs for promoting stewardship and soliciting financial commitments from constituents. Again, the denominationalists did their work well. Support for the Cooperative Program became a primary means of financing denominational projects while at the same time it enabled congregations to identify with the purposes of the denomination.

By the 1970s, however, the Cooperative Program was showing signs of decline if not disintegration. Increasing demands from boards and agencies strained its resources to the breaking point. Many denominational institutions began pursuing their own independent funding programs, which many feared would siphon off funds otherwise intended for the Cooperative Program. Local churches, many facing their own budget problems, were reevaluating their participation in the Cooperative Program.

Then came The Controversy. Many fundamentalist churches had long hesitated to contribute large amounts of their overall budgets to the Cooperative Program, insisting that they could not in good conscience support those programs or institutions which they believed to be heretical—particularly certain seminaries. They chose to keep their money at home, using it for special mission projects or for their own direct ministries. In 1988, Robert Edwards documented this trend in a study of the giving patterns of certain well-known fundamentalist and moderate congregations. His findings are published here, not as a means of judging denominational loyalty, but as an illustration of

36. Ibid., p. 405.
37. J. E. Dillard, *Promoting Our Program* (Nashville: Executive Committee, nd), p. 4.

trends in support for the Cooperative Program. The following list illustrates the practice of Cooperative Program giving among fundamentalists. The six churches listed below represent some of the flagship churches of the fundamentalist movement in the SBC. The figures show the amount of Cooperative Program giving as a percent of the total church budget. They represent some of the flagship churches of the fundamentalist movement.

Church	Percent of Total Budget to CP
First Baptist, Euless, Texas	8.0%
First Baptist, Dallas, Texas	4.8%
First Baptist, Atlanta, Georgia	2.6%
Bellevue Baptist, Memphis, Tennessee	4.3%
First Baptist, Jacksonville, Florida	2.7%
Second Baptist, Houston, Texas	2.7%

In 1987, the six churches collected combined gifts totaling $60,002,858. They gave a combined total of $2,327,976 to the Cooperative Program for a combined percentage of 3.9 percent—at a time when the average SBC congregation gave around 9 percent of its total annual income to the Cooperative Program. Clearly, leading fundamentalist churches have given reduced percentages of their income to the Cooperative Program. Whether they will substantially increase that amount now that they are in control remains to be seen.

At the same time, many moderate churches, once the backbone of Cooperative Program support, are reevaluating their response to denominational funding. This survey of giving patterns from certain moderate congregations also illustrates a pattern.

Church	Percent of Total Budget to CP
First Baptist, Amarillo, Texas	16.1%
First Baptist, Decatur, Georgia	5.2%
Kirkwood Baptist, St. Louis, Missouri	19.7%
Northminster Baptist, Jackson, Mississippi	11.2%
Park Cities Baptist, Dallas. Texas	7.2%
North Phoenix Baptist, Phoenix, Arizona	14.8%

In 1987, these churches received a combined total of $22,563,335 in receipts. They gave a combined total of $3,153,624 to the Cooperative Program for a total combined percentage of 14 percent. Whether they will continue to contribute at a similar level to a fundamentalist-controlled SBC is an important question for the financial future of the SBC. If churches such as these decrease their Cooperative Program allocations and fundamentalist churches do not considerably increase their financial support of the Cooperative Program, the SBC will soon be in serious financial difficulty. The fragmentation over finances is a clear indication of the changing denominational consciousness in the SBC.[38]

Denominational Unity in the SBC

The fact remains that Southern Baptists developed and retained a powerful denominational consciousness throughout most of the twentieth century. That denominationalism was shaped by numerous factors. First, in the aftermath of the Civil War, southernness provided an important cultural identity and security for a denomination born of schism and racism. Second, though composed of groups representing a variety of theological traditions, Southern Baptists articulated a theology of basic Baptist beliefs around which a doctrinal consensus could be constructed. They defined those doctrines broadly enough, however, to allow for a surprising diversity in belief and practice among local congregations. Third, they developed a common program for proclaiming, funding, and accomplishing certain evangelical, missionary, and educational tasks. Fourth, they accepted a common piety based on personal religious experience, devotional study of the Bible, and a Christian life guided by Baptist understanding of the faith. In short, denominational stability and uniformity created a sense of Southern Baptistness that held in balance theological, liturgical, and regional diversity. By mid-twentieth century, Southern Baptist identity was increasingly programmatic. Committed denominationalists sought to maintain unity, encourage compromise, and keep the corporation spiritually alert, financially solvent, and statistically successful.

Samuel Hill, Jr., notes that by the 1950s and 1960s, three types of convention leaders helped preserve denominational unity. "Organization men" kept programs updated and ongoing, assuring churches that all denominational programs were optional while insisting the conformity to such programs would enhance denominational success. Others stressed the convention's "spiritual" unity in its attempts to send missionaries abroad and train disciples at home. And certain "charismatic personages" utilized their powerful personalities and rhetorical

---

38. Robert R. Edwards, "Un-Cooperative Program," unpublished paper, Southern Baptist Theological Seminary, July 1988.

skills to turn the convention from "potentially divisive issues" to unified cooperation.[39]

Denominationalists sought to maintain the conservative middle while keeping the convention from moving too far to the right or left in ideology or practice. As James Sullivan, a longtime denominational executive, observed:

> The most basic principle of administration for any [SBC] agency or institution, therefore, is that it must operate at the center of its constituency. A true leader is one with skill who will never identify himself with either extreme group (the 10 percent on the left or right on any issue). Insofar as he is able, he will operate near the center of the silent middle, and with listening ears in both directions, more valid answers can be found and positions held.[40]

Responding to Sullivan's comments, sociologists Larry McSwain and Tom Wilkerson conclude: "In the three decades following World War II, the denominational leadership functioned basically with this perspective and was able to maintain an essentially harmonious approach to the issues of convention life."[41] The principle that underlay that approach, however, had been present in the SBC from the days of R. B. C. Howell, James P. Boyce, J. B. Gambrell, and E. Y. Mullins.

This principle was evident throughout denominational life. It was simply the way denominational administrators learned how to function in the turbulent world of SBC politics. It meant that while persons on the right or left of the theological spectrum were often appointed to convention boards and agencies, every effort was made to keep ideologues from controlling convention procedures. They could participate but not dominate, since denominationalists like Sullivan feared that moving the convention too far right or left would destroy the fragile compromise on which unity was built. When forced to take a stand on particular issues the denomination was encouraged to move toward the conservative middle. James Sullivan was among those denominational administrators who believed that right wing efforts at controlling the convention moved in seven-year cycles before swinging back toward the center. He and others were very surprised when The Controversy extended to ten years with no sign of abating.

The claim by contemporary SBC fundamentalists that they had

39. Samuel Hill, Jr., "Epilogue," in John Lee Eighmy, *Churches in Cultural Captivity* (Knoxville: University of Tennessee Press, 1972), p. 206.

40. Larry L. McSwain and Tom Wilkerson, "Negotiating Religious Values: Dilemmas of the SBC 'Peace Committee' in Resolving Denominational Conflict," typescript, nd.

41. Ibid.

previously had no voice in convention policy is debatable. Conservative and fundamentalist advocates had always participated in convention leadership and served on boards of trustees. W. A. Criswell, the pastor of First Baptist Church, Dallas, and a leader of the fundamentalist faction, is a case in point. Criswell served as president of the convention for two terms, from 1960 to 1962. His second term was opposed by a group of Southern Baptist educators who were distressed by Criswell's literalist approach to Scripture. Criswell's reelection was supported by Duke K. McCall, at the time president of the Southern Baptist Theological Seminary, whose theological views were perceived as liberal by many SBC fundamentalists. McCall supported Criswell's right to be president of the convention both because of and in spite of his views on the Bible. Criswell was a committed Southern Baptist and had every right to be convention president. Criswell was reelected to a second term during the very years which fundamentalists later claimed to be a period when they were shut out of convention leadership.

Fundamentalists were never refused participation in the life of the SBC. They were kept from controlling the convention, however, lest their drive for narrower doctrinal definitions and ideological purity alienate other segments of the convention, thereby threatening denominational unity. The old formula went something like this: Let the fundamentalists into the denominational system; then they will see how well it works and that it is basically conservative in its administration. They will also discover that "bureaucrats" who run convention agencies are sincere, pious people who can be trusted to follow a basically conservative course. Ultimately, the great inertia of denominational machinery will wear them down before they can make any significant ideological changes away from the conservative middle. To alleviate the threat of schism, it might be necessary to force the resignation of a seminary professor or other convention employees who become the center of a controversy. But others who might hold similar controversial views would be allowed to remain, thereby preserving unity and avoiding wholesale purges. Schism was to be avoided at all costs for the sake of the mission enterprise, the stability of the denomination, and the continuation of the basic Southern Baptist program.

Somehow this approach worked, particularly in the turbulent twentieth century when other Protestant denominations were being torn asunder. At the same time, the obsession to keep within the convention as diverse factions as possible meant that there was always the threat of takeover or schism from one ideological segment or another and that every convention action—particularly regarding theology and politics—had the potential for controversy or division. In its effort to retain every theological faction, the SBC sowed the seeds of the fragmentation it so obsessively sought to avoid.

Following World War II, forces were at work in both the culture and the denomination that would significantly effect the denominational apparatus for dealing with controversy and divisiveness. Pluralism in both church and society led to changes in denominational life. Denominational programs became more pluralistic in an effort to appeal to an increasingly diverse constituency. In general, uniform adherence to SBC programs was less regimented as churches exercised broader options that reached beyond applying Southern Baptist organization to local concerns and ideological positions. By the 1970s and 1980s, denominational statistics became increasingly static, with some evidence of decline. Certain fundamentalist mega-churches, displeased with the "liberalism" they found in denominational programs and agencies, developed their own materials and ministries outside the convention. Certain moderate congregations, disturbed by the rightward direction of convention literature, also began to look elsewhere for Bible study materials and other educational programs for their churches. By 1989, the Southern Baptist Alliance, an organization of moderates, began to publish alternative literature for use in Southern Baptist congregations. By this time Southern Baptists were no longer accepting denominational programs as readily as before. As the position of the conservative middle became more difficult to articulate, denominational literature and programs could not appeal to one segment of the convention without alienating another.

The traditional denominational approach to controversy and compromise was frustrating to those Southern Baptists, right and left, who felt that the convention bureaucracy seemed less concerned for the truth or for prophetic witness than for the preservation of the status quo in the name of unity. During the civil rights movement of the 1960s, for example, those Southern Baptists who were sympathetic toward the cause of blacks and other minorities frequently criticized the denomination's failure to respond prophetically to the struggle against racism. They warned that the denomination was equivocating on racial justice as it had on the slavery issue a century before. In order to protect its assets, programs, and corporate status, the SBC was giving minimal response to the crises that were dividing the nation. At the same time, many conservatives within the convention feared that the denomination had gone too far in not condemning the civil disobedience that accompanied civil rights demonstrations. Some wanted to cut off funds to the denomination's Christian Life Commission because its support for the civil rights movement identified the denomination too closely with political and theological liberalism.

By the 1970s and 1980s fundamentalists in the SBC were pressing their longtime complaints that the convention, through its boards and bureaucrats, was compromising theological truth—namely the doctrine of biblical inerrancy—for the sake of denominational solidarity. Paul Pressler, a Houston appeals court judge, became an outspoken leader of a movement to wrest control of the denomination from the control of bureaucrats and restore it to the real conservatives in conformity to the will of the SBC majority.[42] The stage was set for a major confrontation.

The pluralism of American life tends to weaken denominational life from the outside. As the South lost more and more characteristics of its traditional identity, as nonsoutherners moved in and as Southern Baptists moved outside the region, pluralism threatened traditional denominational coalitions. Since the 1950s Southern Baptists have taken their faith to so-called "pioneer" areas beyond the South. Often these efforts were begun by transplanted southerners who wanted a little piece of Alabama or Texas to provide security in the backside of the American desert—Chicago, New York, or Boston. As these churches evangelized the "natives," however, persons became Southern Baptist who had never been south of the George Washington bridge. Many denominationalists lamented the fact that these northerners did not understand the need to do things the way they were done in the Baptist Zion of the South. Southernness in outlook and program again confronted pluralism. Southern Baptist youth in increasing numbers disregarded the warnings of their elders and married persons "outside the faith" (that meant Methodists, not Muslims). This significant sociological and biological phenomenon brought people into the denomination who had not been raised Southern Baptist, or even southern. Many were not pleased when rebaptism was required of them before they could join a Southern Baptist church. Others questioned the rationale behind organizational practices that most of the faithful had always accepted as both Baptist and biblical. Pluralism again created a crisis in Baptist denominational identity.

In the face of these challenges, denominational executives and administrators seemed unable to rally the troops around common goals and programs. They could no longer summon the rhetoric necessary to turn the denomination away from controversy and divisiveness. This may be due to the fact that denominational bureaucrats, while terribly efficient in their administrative ability to make programs work, lost their ability to articulate a collective vision for the convention. In 1971, H. C. Brown, a professor of homiletics at Southwestern Baptist Theological Seminary, noted that "Professors, administrators and other denomi-

---

42. Paul Pressler, interview with Gary North, "Firestorm Tapes," audio cassette.

national leaders generally have allowed their pulpit skills to atrophy while attending to other responsibilities, but a number of them are strong preachers."[43] Walter Shurden suggested that this decline in preaching skills among denominational workers helped explain "the rise of the pastor as denominational theologian" in the SBC.[44] Preaching remained the primary means for galvanizing opinion and shaping the agenda for Southern Baptist people.

Denominational administrators and employees have become something of a third column—neither clergy nor lay—within the convention. Many are ordained and have served as ministers in local churches. Yet they are not seen as belonging to the clergy since they do not function within the context of the congregation. Denominational staff members report that family and friends often think they left the ministry when they began to work for the convention. In 1971, theologian Clyde Fant observed that "while denominational workers are not entirely shut out of participating in the denominational process in general, they largely are. . . . This is a mistake that needs immediate remedy."[45] In the 1980s the distance between convention staff and constituents had increased. By then, denominational employees showed limited ability to shape the direction of the denomination.

A growing number of articulate fundamentalist pulpiteers also denounced any denominational unity that obscured theological orthodoxy. The compromise necessary to maintain denominational unity was denounced as an equivocation from orthodox truth. Fundamentalists insisted that their ideological and theological positions were nonnegotiable and not subject to the old compromises on which the denomination had been built. This meant that the old methods of denominational compromise no longer applied. The basis of earlier denominational unity had been obliterated in the name of orthodoxy. At the same time, the increasing absence of denominational solidarity meant that the power base of denominationalists had eroded significantly.

As early as 1963, historian Samuel Hill anticipated such a moment in SBC life. Hill observed that the "trend toward greater centralization of power in the convention" might backfire on denominationalists and prove their undoing. He noted that while convention programs had become more centralized, primary authority remained with local con-

43. Shurden, "The Pastor as Denominational Theologian in Southern Baptist History," p. 22.
44. Ibid.
45. Ibid., citing Clyde Fant, "I Returned to the Pastorate," *The Baptist Program*, Jan. 1980, p. 8.

gregations. He wrote: "This means that any grass-roots movement, or
for that matter any single local church, can shape or upset the life of the
entire convention."[46] Hill concluded that, "the convention's polity being
as it is, wresting of control by the ultra-conservatives from the moderates
is not impossible."[47] Given such a precarious balance of power it was
almost inevitable.

Southern Baptist denominational unity has always been precarious, based on a fragile compromise of diverse local groups. As the
protective environment of southern culture and the programmatic unity
of denominational organization became more pluralistic, the time was
ripe for a takeover by those long disturbed by what they saw as the
ambiguity of Southern Baptist theology. Theological disputes, while
significant, are merely symptoms of a broader cultural and denominational identity crisis. The old denominational coalition could not last
forever. Fundamentalism merely hastened its demise. For years Southern Baptists managed to have it all denominationally, statistically, and
theologically. From the ashes of Civil War and Reconstruction they built
the largest Protestant denomination in the United States. Though continually plagued by controversies, they were able to avoid a major
schism or the loss of a large segment of their constituency. In the cultural
cloister of the South and the protective environment of denominational
loyalty an amazingly diverse liturgical, hermeneutical, even doctrinal
tradition existed.

And as the old protections of culture and denomination have
collapsed Southern Baptists still want to have it all. Moderates continue
to believe that the old denominational coalition will prevail, that the
pendulum will swing to the conservative center, and schism will be
avoided. Many continue to act as if they can regain their rightful place
and restore the Grand Compromise by winning the next presidential
election. Fundamentalists, on the other hand, believe that they can
maintain the old denominational triumphalism and success, that they
can control the Southern Baptist coalition after having destroyed it
completely. They still insist that they have made a simple "course correction" that will preserve the denomination's heritage. In fact, nothing
could be further from the truth.

46. Samuel Hill, Jr., "The Southern Baptists: Need for Reformation, Redirection,"
The Christian Century, Jan. 9, 1963, p. 40. Hill used the term "moderate" earlier than anyone
else.

47. Ibid.

CHAPTER 4

Southern Baptist Theology:
The Shape of Dogma

IN A BOOK PUBLISHED IN 1983, BAPTIST PROFESSORS JAMES E. TULL, E. GLENN Hinson, and James Leo Garrett responded to the question *Are Southern Baptists "Evangelicals"?* Their answers—yes (Garrett), no (Hinson), maybe (Tull)—provide an insightful summary of the history of theology in the SBC. Given his particular approach to the source materials, each scholar makes a convincing case, a fact that illustrates the eclectic nature of Southern Baptist theology.[1] That such a question would be asked is evidence that Southern Baptist theology does not admit of easy definition. This theological "elasticity" is one of the denomination's greatest strengths and one of its most significant weaknesses.

From the beginning Southern Baptists understood themselves as bound by certain doctrines that were at once distinctly Christian and discernibly Baptist. Yet within that general doctrinal framework there existed surprising theological diversity, sometimes even contradiction. The denomination's religious language often combined dogma, piety, and rhetoric in such a way as to make theological precision extremely difficult to maintain. This allowed the convention to incorporate multiple regional and doctrinal traditions—Calvinist, modified Calvinist, Arminian, modified Arminian, fundamentalist, Landmarkist, social gospel, even liberal—without major schism. Establishing a consensus on "what all Southern Baptists believe" was a formidable task, particularly the more precise such definitions became. This theological diversity was often a matter of some public pride for the individualistic Baptists.

---

1. James Leo Garrett, Jr., E. Glenn Hinson, James E. Tull, *Are Southern Baptists "Evangelicals"?* (Macon: Mercer University Press, 1983).

Journalists and preachers alike often joked that to put four Southern Baptists in a room meant at least five opinions on a given subject. All would agree, however, on the need to win souls and send out missionaries in some form or another.

Such diversity also meant that the entire convention was always at the mercy of those restless subgroups—Landmarkists, fundamentalists, inerrantists, premillennialists, or others—that claimed a divine mandate to impose their specific doctrinal definitions on the entire convention. In a 1988 news conference shortly after his narrow election as SBC president, fundamentalist leader Jerry Vines warned that neo-orthodox "liberals" in the convention "use our vocabulary, but not our dictionary."[2] In Vines's view, both sides in The Controversy might use similar terms but only fundamentalists possessed the genuinely Baptist definitions. Not surprisingly, moderate Southern Baptists said the same thing about fundamentalists, particularly regarding such classic Baptist doctrines as soul liberty and the priesthood of all believers. The moderates maintained that fundamentalists used Baptist vocabulary but with non-Baptist interpretations.[3]

From the beginning of their takeover movement, the fundamentalists have insisted that the problems in the denomination were primarily, if not exclusively, theological. They declared that liberalism, neoorthodoxy, the social gospel, and other leftwing ideologies were turning the convention away from its Baptist roots and undermining the beliefs of the majority of true Southern Baptists. In the early years of the debate, moderates insisted that the struggle was essentially political, the effort of a fundamentalist-oriented political faction to dominate convention life and distract the denomination from its unified goals of missions and evangelism. But as fundamentalists promoted various doctrinal positions regarding the nature of Holy Scripture, the role of women in the church, religious liberty, and the priesthood of all believers, the moderates were forced to respond to the denominational upheavals in theological terms. Many moderates now warn that fundamentalists are changing not only the way the convention works but also the way Southern Baptists believe. Theology is at the heart of The Controversy in the SBC.

Theology was a primary factor in most of the controversies that bedeviled Southern Baptists throughout their history. Given the fragile

2. Rodney Clapp, "America's Southern Baptists: Where They Are Going," *Christianity Today*, Nov. 4, 1988, p. 27.

3. Grady Cothen, "Southern Baptists Face Great Confusion on Why They Exist," *SBC Today* (Jan. 1989), p. 6; and Dan Martin, "Lolley Says SBC May Be 'Mortally Wounded,'" *Baptist Standard*, Sept. 14, 1988, p. 4.

coalition around which the SBC was formed, however, theological debate was inseparable from denominational influence and control. No Southern Baptist controversy is ever completely theological or political. Ideology and politics were present from the first. As noted earlier, the SBC itself embraced a wide range of theological traditions within its denominational organization. Most early Southern Baptist churches maintained a strong appreciation for Reformed theology, but Regular Baptist Calvinism was modified significantly by Separate Baptist revivalism. Indeed, revivalism in the SBC, as in many evangelical denominations, served to "Arminianize" the churches toward greater emphasis on free will, individual choice, and salvation for "whosoever will" believe. Those Southern Baptists who mourn the decline of Reformed theology in SBC life might well blame evangelists, revivals, and statisticians, not neoorthodox liberals, for the Arminian orientation of popular theology.

Arminianism, though publicly renounced in classrooms and pulpits throughout the convention—particularly its doctrine of falling from grace—has had far greater popular impact on SBC evangelism than most analysts admit. Those who describe Southern Baptists as modified Calvinists could just as easily classify them as modified Arminians so strong is the emphasis on free will and general atonement. If the old acronym TULIP (Total depravity, Unconditional election, Limited atonement, Irresistible grace, Perseverance of the saints) serves to define the five points of Calvinism, then many Southern Baptists are one-point Calvinists and four-point Arminians. Although retaining perseverance of the saints and thus rejecting the possibility that one might fall from grace, Baptists otherwise generally reflect an Arminian understanding of election, atonement, and free will.

In a similar way, Landmarkism, though unsuccessful in imposing its successionist ecclesiology on the entire denomination, remained a powerful influence in the SBC. But so did varying degrees of social and theological liberalism that were also evident in support for such issues as the social gospel, the civil rights movement, peace movements, Christian feminism, and biblical criticism.[4] (Nevertheless, Southern Baptist "liberals" often seem conservative when compared to liberals outside the denomination). In spite of their apparent cultural and theological homogeneity, Southern Baptists demonstrate surprising diversity of thought and practice.

4. John Lee Eighmy, *Churches in Cultural Captivity* (Knoxville: University of Tennessee Press, 1976), pp. 57-80, 124-30, 147-50; and David Whitlock, "Southern Baptists and Southern Culture: Three Visions of a Christian America" (unpublished Ph.D. dissertation, Southern Baptist Theological Seminary, 1988). Whitlock documents the fundamentalist, conservative, and liberal theological diversity in the SBC.

Southern Baptist Confessions of Faith

Since 1845, the Southern Baptist Convention has approved only three documents that delineate specific theological positions affirmed by the denomination and its churches. The first doctrinal statement was the "Abstract of Principles" approved in 1858, not for the entire convention, but as a guide for faculty members at the Southern Baptist Theological Seminary. The other two statements are contained in the Baptist Faith and Message, the denomination's official confession of faith, ratified in 1925 and revised in 1963. These documents place Southern Baptists solidly within the Baptist tradition. They are grounded in two earlier Baptist documents, The Philadelphia Confession of 1742, and the New Hampshire Confession of 1833. The confessions outline doctrinal positions on Holy Scripture, the Trinity, the church, ordinances, salvation, baptism, judgment, and Christian ethics. The confessions are specific enough to identify the SBC as a theologically conservative, distinctly Baptist denomination while they are general enough to allow for a variety of diverse interpretations among the autonomous congregations that make up the convention. No doubt the early convention builders took some unspoken theological consensus for granted. They also hesitated to define dogma too narrowly lest they alienate large segments of the constituency, thereby increasing the possibility of fragmentation or schism.

The Abstract of Principles

The Abstract of Principles of the Southern Baptist Theological Seminary illustrates the point. Faculty members are required to teach "in accordance with, and not contrary to" the document.[5] The Abstract contains twenty articles that reflect basic Christian and Baptist beliefs, strongly shaped by Reformed theology. With surprising consistency, however, the articles avoid specific definitions on many potentially divisive issues.

Article I asserts that the Scriptures "are given by inspiration of God, and are the only sufficient, certain and authoritative rule of all saving knowledge, faith and obedience." It affirms the authority of Scripture but offers no specific theory of biblical inspiration.[6] Article VII, "The Mediator," acknowledges Christ's role as "mediator between God and man" but does not delineate a particular theory of atonement:

5. *Catalog*, 1987-1989, Southern Baptist Theological Seminary, p. 2.
6. Ibid.

ransom, substitution, federal, or example.[7] Article XIV on the Church declares that Christ is "Head of the Church" but gives no theory of ecclesiology—although nineteenth-century Landmarkists would have desired a more specific definition.[8] Article XVI on the Lord's Supper declares that "it is in no sense a sacrifice," but "is designed to commemorate" Christ's death. Yet the article does not require acquiescence to either an open or close communion policy. Likewise, the final article (XX) on "The Judgment" acknowledges that God will ultimately "judge the world by Jesus Christ," but no theory of eschatology—premillennial, postmillennial, or amillennial—is set forth.[9]

Does this lack of specificity suggest that nineteenth-century Southern Baptists took it for granted that they held the same specific interpretations of these general dogmas? Hardly. The Abstract illustrates James P. Boyce's idea that "upon no point, upon which the denomination is divided, should the Convention, and through it the Seminary, take a position."[10]

In today's fundamentalist-charged atmosphere, however, confessional documents are interpreted not only by what they say but also by what they do not say. A mere affirmation of the authority of Holy Scripture may no longer be sufficient apart from an inerrantist theory of biblical inspiration, and an expressed belief in Christ's atoning work requires in addition an acceptance of the substitutionary theory alone.

The Baptist Faith and Message

The denomination's official confession, The Baptist Faith and Message, was a response to specific theological controversies in the convention. The 1925 confession was a reaction to the fundamentalist-modernist debate that dominated American Protestantism in the 1920s. The 1963 revision came about as a result of a controversy involving seminary professor Ralph Elliott's book on Genesis and the use of higher criticism in biblical studies. Though born of controversy, the Faith and Message documents also indicate the effort of Southern Baptists to define doctrine in terms general enough to incorporate diverse segments of the convention.

Article One states that Holy Scripture is "without mixture of error for its matter," a phrase taken directly from the New Hampshire Confes-

7. Ibid.
8. Ibid.
9. Ibid., p. 3.
10. James P. Boyce, "Two Objections to the Seminary," part 5, *Western Recorder,* June 20, 1874, p. 2.

sion. The interpretation of that phrase lies at the heart of the debate over biblical inerrancy. Fundamentalists believe that the statement requires adherence to the doctrine of inerrancy. They view it as an affirmation that Scripture is without error in all "matters" whether doctrine or history, theology or science. Non-inerrantists, however, suggest that the phrase speaks to the trustworthiness and absolute authoritative nature of the Bible in "matters" of faith—the essential issue that Scripture addresses. In addition, adherents of each camp often disagree among themselves on the specific meaning of inerrancy or authority. A number of studies have explored that debate and its implications.[11] It is evident that both sides in the debate adhere to a high view of Scripture as authoritative guide for the church and the individual. But the important issue here involves the way in which contemporary Southern Baptists seek to interpret what seems a less specific statement than many currently desire.

The Faith and Message statement also illustrates the influence of modified Calvinism-Arminianism on the SBC. Between the approval of the Abstract of Principles in 1858 and the Baptist Faith and Message in 1925, considerable modification in Reformed theology occurred. In fact, the articles on "election" in the Abstract and the Baptist Faith and Message display considerable divergence, if not downright contradiction. Concerning the doctrine of election, the Abstract states: "Election is God's eternal choice of some persons unto everlasting life—not because of foreseen merit in them, but of His mere mercy in Christ—in consequence of which choice they are called, justified and glorified."[12] The words "God's eternal choice of some persons" clearly indicate the influence of the Reformed doctrine of single predestination. The Baptist Faith and Message, on the other hand, taken almost verbatim from the earlier New Hampshire Confession, states that "election is the gracious purpose of God, according to which He regenerates, sanctifies, and glorifies sinners. It is consistent with the free agency in man, and comprehends all the means in connection with the end. It is a glorious display of God's sovereign goodness. . . ."[13]

The idea of "free agency" in human beings is less evident in the

11. Robeson B. James, ed., *The Unfettered Word* (Waco: Word, 1987); L. Russ Bush and Tom J. Nettles, *Baptists and the Bible* (Chicago: Moody, 1980); Duane A. Garrett and Richard R. Melick, Jr., eds., *Authority and Interpretation* (Grand Rapids: Baker, 1987); Gordon James, *Inerrancy and the Southern Baptist Convention* (Dallas: Southern Heritage Press, 1986); and Joe Edward Barnhart, *The Southern Baptist Holy War* (Austin: Texas Monthly Press, 1986).

12. *Catalog, 1987-1989*, p. 12.

13. "Baptist Faith and Message," in Bill J. Leonard, *Baptist Ideals: Distinctives of our Faith* (Nashville: The Sunday School Board of the Southern Baptist Convention, 1988), p. 53.

more Calvinist Abstract. While prevailing popular interpretation no doubt understands election within the context of the general atonement, the convention has long included many persons who held varying opinions—Calvinist, modified Calvinist, modified Arminian—regarding the doctrine.

The use of these confessions also demonstrates the determination of denominational leaders to avoid schism over doctrine whenever possible. When theological disputes threatened denominational unity, the convention acted, usually leaning toward the right. Yet this rightward tilt alleviated enough pressure to allow the denomination to drift back toward the "conservative middle" without a wholesale purge or debilitating schism.

Controversy in the SBC

In their analysis of denominational conflict, sociologists Larry McSwain and Tom Wilkerson describe three major controversies that threatened SBC unity during the twentieth century. They suggest that "each of these was a conflict of values where the issues were essentially theological."[14] They conclude that in each of the controversies, the "bureaucratic approach failed" and a fundamentalist theological perspective "prevailed" by majority vote of the convention.[15] In other words, rightwing ideologues prevailed over conservative centrists.

The Evolution Controversy

The evolution controversy of the 1920s was a major threat to SBC unity. In 1925, denominationalists like E. Y. Mullins succeeded in securing convention approval for a moderate statement aimed at maintaining a balance between faith and science. The initial version of the Baptist Faith and Message was approved that year as a statement of theological consensus. The statement angered fundamentalists who wanted no compromise with evolution. The threat of schism loomed large. Led by president George W. McDaniel, the 1926 meeting of the convention approved a strong antievolution position. The messengers also passed a

14. Larry L. McSwain and Tom Wilkerson, "Negotiating Religious Values: Dilemmas of the SBC 'Peace Committee' in Resolving Denominational Conflict," typescript, nd.
15. Ibid.

resolution requiring all denominational employees to subscribe to the antievolution statement. But while the fundamentalist forces won, it is doubtful many convention employees signed the statement as required, and no employee was removed for failing to affirm the resolution. Denominationalists lost the public debate, but their policy of inclusion and tolerance prevailed in the long run.[16]

The Elliott Controversy

Another significant conflict of values occurred in the SBC in 1963. This controversy concerned the publication of a study of Genesis written by Ralph Elliott, a professor at Midwestern Baptist Theological Seminary, in Kansas City, Missouri. Elliott's use of the historical-critical method of biblical interpretation created a major controversy that led to the revision of the Baptist Faith and Message, Elliott's subsequent removal from his teaching position, and the refusal by Broadman Press to reissue the book. Again, the fundamentalists won in the public arena, yet the historical-critical method continued to be utilized in many Southern Baptist seminaries and universities. Denominationalism lost in public but prevailed in private. This phenomenon in SBC politics continued to frustrate and infuriate fundamentalists.[17]

The Broadman Commentary Controversy

The same was true in a later, related theological dispute over the publication of volume one in the denomination's Broadman Bible Commentary series. The original edition, published in 1969 and written by British Baptist G. Henton Davies, also used the historical-critical approach to Old Testament studies. In a heated dispute, the convention voted to recall the volume and have it rewritten, this time by Clyde T. Francisco, professor of Old Testament interpretation at Southern Baptist Seminary. Although Francisco was a man of widely recognized conservative credentials, he was also influenced by the historical-critical method. Again the convention leaned rightward but avoided a major purge or a significant departure from the denominationally committed, conservative middle that allowed for varying hermeneutical methods to exist in SBC life.

The result of this two-sided approach to controversy, Walter

16. Ibid.
17. Ibid.

Shurden observes, is that Southern Baptists "usually end up 'non-settling' the issue by saying both things at the same time."[18] The reason for this, Shurden concludes, is generally that "denominational unity is more important to Southern Baptists than theological arguments about the Bible."[19] Denominationalists recognized that once the SBC began to scrutinize doctrine too closely, and demand a greater degree of uniformity, the whole fragile enterprise could come tumbling down.

Baptist Distinctives: Sources of Theological Consensus

This is not to say that Southern Baptists have had no theological consensus whatsoever. It has never been possible to be an "orthodox" Southern Baptist without affirming certain foundational beliefs. What were those basic doctrines that formed the theological center of Baptist belief? In his *A History of the Baptists*, Robert Torbet delineated certain "distinctives" that characterize Baptist doctrine. They include:

1. "The sacred Scriptures the sole norm for faith and practice." The Bible is the authoritative guide for faith and order in the church and in the life of the individual.
2. "The New Testament church composed of baptized believers." Each individual is called to personal faith in Christ as a prerequisite to baptism and church membership. Baptism and the Lord's Supper are "ordinances" of the church.
3. "The priesthood of the believer and the autonomy of the local congregation." All Christians have direct access to God through Jesus Christ. Each local church governs itself under the authority of Christ. Laity and clergy cooperate together.
4. "The principle of religious liberty and the separation of church and state." Each person is responsible to God for religious choices and commitments. The state cannot compel faith from any individual.[20]

Clearly, these distinctives are not exclusively Baptist, since they characterize the belief and practice of various other groups within the

18. Walter B. Shurden, "The Problem of Authority in the SBC," *Review and Expositor* 75 (Spring 1978), p. 225.
19. Ibid.
20. Robert Torbet, *History of the Baptists* (Philadelphia: Judson, 1950), pp. 16-32.

Free Church tradition. Nor do they provide a convenient checklist for identifying and defining a "true" Baptist church. Each represents one facet in the entire Baptist mosaic. "Distinctives" are combined in singularly Baptist modes.

At best, these basic doctrines are held together in a kind of creative tension. Biblical authority is inseparable from soul competency. Confessionalism is balanced by anticreedalism. The authority of the clergy is balanced by the authority of the congregation. The guidance of the democratic majority is tempered by the conscience of the dissenting minority. Balancing such powerful ideas is a difficult task for any religious group, particularly in local congregations where controversy, fragmentation, and schism readily occur. Local autonomy, however, allowed individual churches to emphasize certain Baptist distinctives according to the will of a majority of the church members. Those who did not identify with one Southern Baptist congregation could find another with which they did agree. Thus a Southern Baptist church that promoted biblical inerrancy and fundamentalist dogma and rejected women's ordination and ecumenical relationships might coexist in the same community with a Southern Baptist church that espoused an opposite philosophy. The denomination, therefore, represented a *via media* by which churches stressing diverse expressions of the basic Baptist distinctives were bound together in common Christian endeavor.

But as differences became more pronounced and more entrenched, the classic unity-in-diversity soon began to unravel. Fundamentalists claimed that their vision of the Baptist heritage represented that of a majority of Southern Baptists. They demanded that this position be reflected in all denominationally funded institutions if not in all SBC churches. In their zeal to impose a fundamentalist dogma on the entire convention fundamentalists sowed the seeds of denominational fragmentation, thereby dealing a mortal blow to the Grand Compromise on which Southern Baptist cooperation was built.

The Quest for Balance

Historian William R. Estep observes that

> One of the factors contributing to the fragmentation of the Baptist witness into splinter groups has been the attempt on the part of some to force a degree of conformity upon others without safeguarding the individual conscience from the tyranny of the majority. In the absence of any binding

authority (creed, bishop, councils) to hold Baptists together, a certain degree of diversity within biblical parameters is as necessary as it is inevitable. . . . When held in proper balance, these principles make possible a rich diversity within a dynamic unity.[21]

When that balance is no longer maintained, however, defining a "true" Baptist becomes extremely difficult. The fact that the SBC was able to maintain that fragile balance for so long without a major schism is a testimony to the success of denominational compromise. Certain sets of distinctives were held in tandem in an attempt to form a balanced approach to faith and practice.

Biblical Authority and Soul Competency

For Southern Baptists, biblical authority and soul competency are closely related. While affirming the authority of Scripture, Baptists also recognize the competency of the soul in discerning religious matters. The outer witness of Scripture was confirmed by the inner witness of the Holy Spirit in the heart of the believer. For Southern Baptists, fundamentalist and moderate alike, the Bible is the sole rule of faith and practice for the individual and the church. Many refer to themselves as "people of the Book," or "Bible-believing Christians." The Bible is viewed as the guide for doctrinal belief, ethical behavior, and personal salvation. E. Y. Mullins asked, "What is the distinctive message of the Baptists to the world?" His answer: "The authority of the Scriptures lies at the basis of our plea. We do not believe any form of Christianity which breaks with the Scripture as the revealed and authoritative word of God can long serve the interests of God's kingdom on earth in a thoroughgoing way."[22] Yet Mullins also insisted that, "The biblical significance of the Baptists is the right of private interpretation and obedience to the Scriptures." He continued, "But as comprehending all the above particulars, as a great and aggressive force in Christian history as distinguished from all others and standing entirely alone, the doctrine of the soul's competency in religion under God is the distinctive historical significance of the Baptists."[23] Thus the authority of Scripture was closely related to the concept of soul compe-

---

21. William R. Estep, "Baptists and Authority: The Bible, Confessions and Conscience in the Development of Baptist Identity," *Review and Expositor* 84 (Fall 1987), p. 599.

22. E. Y. Mullins, *The Axioms of Religion* (Philadelphia: Griffith and Rowland, 1908), p. 26.

23. Hinson, in *Are Southern Baptists "Evangelicals"?*, citing Mullins, *The Axioms of Religion*, pp. 73-74.

tency, that inner authority through which persons recognized and responded to biblical truth. Christians were responsible to seek out the truth of Scripture for themselves. They were not to receive it unquestioningly from a church hierarchy or ministerial tribunal. Such freedom involved significant personal responsibility. It was not a rabid individualism but a "freedom for interdependence" and community in the church.[24]

Southern Baptists sought to unite the objective authority of the Bible with the subjective experience of the individual, and they often wrote as if each was *the* most important single doctrine of their history. Mullins's appeals to both Scripture and conscience, for example, have led many to identify him with their particular side in the present denominational controversy: Dr. Mullins the inerrantist, and Dr. Mullins the prophet of soul liberty. Russ Bush and Tom Nettles argue that Mullins's theology reflects an inerrantist view of Scripture. They insist that Mullins repudiated the idea that "those holding to an authoritative Bible are in fact bibliolaters."[25] E. Glenn Hinson, however, suggests that while Mullins affirmed the authority of Scripture, he "was no biblicist." Rather, "he drove in a beeline to the Baptist principle of voluntarism or soul competency as the essence of biblical religion."[26] Mullins himself apparently saw no contradiction in holding both doctrines simultaneously. He helped shape a denomination in which respective proponents could find common ground. Reconciliation over these Baptist distinctives now seems increasingly impossible. Rather than struggling for balance or allowing groups that emphasize the doctrines in different ways to coexist within the denominational house, each faction is forced to choose one doctrine over the other.

Reluctantly Confessional, Selectively Creedal

"Baptists are not a creedal people," Southern Baptist patriarch Herschel Hobbs once wrote.[27] A cursory look at Baptist history might lead one to respond, "Well, sort of." During the twentieth century, Southern Baptists have moved steadily, albeit reluctantly, toward creedalism, all the time insisting that it was not really happening. They often attempt to clarify their growing use of doctrinal statements with the phrase, "confessional,

---

24. Ibid., p. 137.
25. Bush and Nettles, *Baptists and the Bible*, p. 291.
26. Hinson, *Are Southern Baptists "Evangelicals"?*, p. 137.
27. Herschel Hobbs, "Southern Baptists and Confessionalism: A Comparison of the Origins and Contents of the 1925 and 1963 Confessions," *Review and Expositor* 76 (Winter 1979), p. 55. As noted throughout this book, the use of confessions is a major issue in The Controversy.

not creedal." In one sense, this is an appropriate qualification. In another, the distinction is essentially academic. Confessions of faith, originally used by denominationalists to preserve unity and avoid schism, have become a source of division as competing groups debate the definition of specific dogmas. When cultural and denominational ties were intact, intricate doctrinal definitions were less essential. As those sources of stability collapsed, many Southern Baptists turned to dogma to reinforce their diminishing identity. Confessions offered security; they also became tools for wielding power and provided a means for resolving conflicts. The more corporate the relationship, the more necessary the creed.

From their beginnings in the seventeenth century, Baptist groups have not hesitated to use confessions of faith to delineate basic doctrines, provide a source of unity, and establish a basis for membership. English Baptists, both General (Arminian) and Particular (Calvinist), made extensive use of confessions. William Estep suggests that these documents were confessional but not creedal. Creeds, he suggests, were

> authoritative and often viewed as final, unalterable, and binding statements of faith. . . . For Baptists, confessions of faith have never constituted ultimate authority. All major confessions from 1610 to 1963 were considered abstracts of biblical truth as the group formulating the confession perceived it. These confessions have often been uneven and incomplete expressions of the Christian faith. Thus the nature of a particular confession was largely shaped by the purpose for which it was conceived at the time.[28]

Confessions had a derivative authority drawn from Scripture and the community of faith. William Lumpkin, an authority on Baptist confessionalism, notes that most seventeenth-century Protestant groups in Europe and Britain identified themselves through the publication of confessions of faith. Baptist confessions were distinctive in four specific areas. First, their ecclesiology emphasized local communities of believers. Second, they defined the ordinances of baptism and the Lord's Supper in identifiably Baptist ways. Third, they gave strong emphasis to evangelism and missions. Fourth, they stressed freedom of conscience and the separation of church and state. He writes, "There was little fear of the confessions' dominating the groups owning them and even less of their usurping the place of the scriptures."[29] Confessions were never placed above or even alongside biblical authority.

28. Estep, "Baptists and Authority," pp. 600-601.
29. William L. Lumpkin, "The Nature and Authority of Baptist Confessions of Faith," *Review and Expositor* 76 (Winter 1979), p. 24.

Among Southern Baptists, however, a strong anticreedal, even anticonfessional, sentiment flourished from the beginning. The organizers of the SBC declared in 1845 that, "We have constructed for our basis no new creed; acting in this matter upon a Baptist aversion to all creeds but the Bible."[30] This aversion to creedalism was due to several factors. Separate Baptists, strong in the South, opposed confessions as detrimental to personal religious experience. They feared that mental assent to dogma would undermine both radical conversion and biblical authority. The Campbellite movement of the mid-nineteenth century was militantly anticonfessional, rejecting creeds as "authoritative symbols" that threatened biblical faith. Nineteenth-century Baptists, in a competitive struggle with Disciples, did not want to be cast as creedalists.[31]

When the fundamentalist-modernist controversy finally forced the SBC to produce its first official confession of faith in 1925, the document was introduced with an elaborate disclaimer qualifying the way in which such a confession was to be used. Southern Baptists are the only Baptist denomination to include such a qualification as a guide for interpreting confessions. These statements concluded:

> (1) [That confessions] constitute a consensus of opinion of some Baptist body, large or small, for the general instruction and guidance of our own people and others concerning those articles of the Christian faith which are most surely held among us. They are not intended to add anything to the simple conditions of salvation revealed in the New Testament. . . .
>
> (2) That we do not regard them as complete statements of our faith, having any quality of finality or infallibility. As in the past so in the future Baptists should themselves be free to revise their statements as may seem to them wise and expedient at any time.
>
> (3) That any group of Baptists, large or small, have the inherent right to draw up for themselves and publish to the world a confession of their faith whenever they may think it advisable to do so.
>
> (4) That the sole authority for faith and practice among Baptists is the Scriptures of the Old and New Testaments. Confessions are only guides in interpretation, having no authority over the conscience.
>
> (5) That they are statements of religious convictions, drawn from the Scriptures, and are not to be used to hamper freedom of thought or investigation in other realms of life.[32]

---

30. SBC *Annual*, 1845, p. 19; and Walter B. Shurden, "Southern Baptist Responses to their Confessional Statements," *Review and Expositor* 76 (Winter 1979), p. 69.

31. Lumpkin, "The Nature and Authority of Baptist Confessions of Faith," p. 25.

32. Ibid., p. 26.

These disclaimers support the prevailing idea that Southern Baptists were always confessional but not creedal. Yet they also illustrate once again the Southern Baptist genius for compromise. The 1925 Baptist Faith and Message, including its introductory disclaimer, satisfied those who wished to define basic Southern Baptist dogma while also placating those who were wary of creedal entanglements. Again, Southern Baptists sought to have it both ways, to be creedal and noncreedal at the same time, temporarily forestalling a decision on the use and meaning of confessions. They approved a basic and rather general statement of Baptist beliefs, but added an escape clause. Those who differed with the statements on the basis of conscience could still remain Southern Baptists. Perhaps it was less that denominationalists feared creeds than that they wanted to retain unity among those both for and against the use of confessions in Baptist life.

Once a confession was written down and officially approved, however, the scene was set for its more arbitrary use in defining the doctrinal parameters of the SBC. The line between a confession and a creed is thin indeed. In retrospect, it seems Southern Baptists were naive in their effort to distinguish between confessionalism and creedalism. Since 1979, the distinction has become particularly academic.

William Lumpkin concludes that "the fear of creeds is, largely, an irrational fear," that all religious traditions subscribe to creeds—a consensus of belief—written or not.[33] Lumpkin himself uses the terms creed and confession interchangeably to refer to documents that "state facts," but do not necessarily provide interpretation of facts.[34] These confessions-creeds, he believes, were "recommendations" extended to churches and individuals, but "never as decrees."[35]

In the current denominational controversy, many fundamentalist leaders would agree with Lumpkin that creeds are inevitably theological guides for every religious group. They disagree as to the application of such statements to the constituency. In their view, confessional statements should provide precise definitions of dogma, and employees of the SBC must agree with these definitions. Since 1979, they have gone to great lengths to ensure that the statement on Holy Scripture included in the Baptist Faith and Message—"without mixture of error for its matter"— be interpreted in light of the doctrine of biblical inerrancy. Others have sought to establish their own list of nonnegotiables as the basis for Southern Baptist theological unity. Still others have attempted to clarify

33. Ibid.
34. Ibid.
35. Ibid., pp. 26-27.

the meaning of the Baptist Faith and Message by using other creedal documents such as the Chicago Statement of Inerrancy, a document with no official relationship to the SBC but one that is being promoted by some as a guide for faculties at denominational seminaries.

The events at The Southern Baptist Theological Seminary in Louisville, Kentucky, illustrate the way in which selective creedalism is spreading throughout the denomination. Since 1859, faculty members have been required to sign the Abstract of Principles as a prerequisite for teaching at the school. As noted earlier, faculty are required to teach "in accordance with, and not contrary to" the articles of the Abstract. With the success of the fundamentalist movement, however, new documents have been unofficially added to the list of confessional guides. New faculty members are asked to concur with the statements of the Baptist Faith and Message, although they are not asked to sign the document. In 1988, the faculty of the school unanimously approved "A Resolution of Recommitment and Renewal" by which they renewed commitment to "our cherished Baptist heritage" and the school's Abstract of Principles. They also renewed commitment to the "seminary president's intention to work toward reconciliation of the conflict in the convention," pledging faithful cooperation in the "action plan for reconciliation."[36] New faculty members report that part of their trustee interview prior to their hiring involved a discussion of the Chicago Statement. The increase in confessional "qualifiers" illustrates the changing nature of creedalism in the SBC.

These developments support Walter Shurden's contention that Southern Baptist creedalism has increased steadily throughout the twentieth century as both "strict-confessionalists" (fundamentalists) and "mainstream denominationalists" (moderates) have "unwittingly (or perhaps 'wittingly'!) given prominence to the Confession by indirectly using it as a call for denominational unity."[37] In Shurden's view, confessionalism and centralization combined to make Southern Baptists a creedal denomination. He cites a prophetic observation made by historian William W. Barnes regarding the 1925 confession. Barnes wrote:

> The reception that that creed has received, or perhaps one should say, has not received, seems to suggest that Southern Baptists are not yet ready for doctrinal centralization, but the first step has been taken. It may be another century, but if and when the doctrinal question again arises, succeeding generations can point to 1925 and say that the Southern

36. "A Resolution of Recommitment and Renewal," Southern Baptist Theological Seminary.

37. Shurden, "Southern Baptist Responses to their Confessional Statements," p. 82.

Baptist Convention, having once adopted a creed, can do so again. Perhaps by that time other centralizing forces will have been developed and the convention may have the means and the method of compelling congregations to take notice of the creed adopted.[38]

Barnes recognized that once a confession was written its use would prove divisive. If Southern Baptists ever really were a non-creedal people, they are not any longer.

People's Church or Preacher's Church?

Southern Baptists have long considered themselves a denomination of and for the laity. Congregational polity and local church autonomy are based on the belief that the authority of Christ is mediated, not through bishops, councils, or synods, but through the gathered congregation of believers. Most would agree with the seventeenth-century Baptist John Smyth who wrote "that the church of Christ has power delegated to themselves of announcing the Word, administering the sacraments, appointing ministers, disclaiming them and also excommunicating; but the last appeal is to the brethren or body of the church."[39] Perhaps the experience of evangelical conversion—warm, personal, and individual—was the great equalizer in Baptist churches. Conversion transcended economic, educational, or social status. In response to grace, the converted were called to convert others, and in this mandate informed a universal Christian ministry.

Through common spiritual experience, congregational government, and communal responsibility, nineteenth-century Baptists developed a "people's church," which asserted that the call to ministry was given to all Christians. Ultimate authority for the church came from Christ through the congregation of believers. J. M. Pendleton's "Church Manual," published in 1867, noted that "the governmental power is in the hands of the people." He went on to assert "the right of a majority of the members of a church to rule, in accordance with the law of Christ" and concluded "that the final power of a church cannot be transferred or alienated and that church action is final."[40] In

38. Shurden, "The Problem of Authority in the Southern Baptist Convention," p. 230.

39. William L. Lumpkin, *Baptist Confessions of Faith* (Valley Forge: Judson, 1959), p. 101.

40. Howard Grimes, "The United States," in *The Layman in Christian History*, ed. Stephen C. Neill and Hans Ruedi Weber (Philadelphia: Westminster, 1963), p. 246.

a similar work, T. M. McConnell wrote that a Baptist church "acts as a pure democracy, every member having a voice and all equal with each other." Clergy thus "derive their authority to preach and administer the ordinances *from* Christ, *through his churches.*"[41] At the same time, Baptists were never Quakers in their effort to create a community composed solely of the laity. They have always recognized that some individuals were called by God to carry out specific ministerial functions within the church. These persons were given authority to exercise leadership, proclaim the Word of God, and provide pastoral care within the community of faith.

The Regular Baptist churches in the South often reflected the influence of the Presbyterian-Reformed tradition in their view of the minister. They encouraged a high level of ministerial education, and their preachers often numbered among the gentlemen theologians of southern Protestantism. The Separate Baptist tradition was influenced by the model of the farmer-preacher on the American frontier. These individuals, often self-supporting and self-educated, provided preaching and pastoral care for the struggling frontier churches. The practice of licensing preachers was an early Baptist attempt to provide some official sanction and supervision to the work of these lay ministers. With congregational approval these preachers could perform all ministerial functions, with or without ordination. The farmer-preacher made it possible for Baptist churches to have ministers at a time when elaborate ministerial training was not available.

Southern Baptists administered ordination to two offices in the church: pastor and deacon, one clergy, the other laity. While pastors might come and go, deacons served as a group of ordained lay-ministers who provided continuity of leadership within the congregation. The deacon is normally asked to perform "an administrative and officiating ministry" in the local church.[42] In some churches deacons provide tangible ministry (diakonia) to members of the congregation; in others they serve as a spiritual board of trustees with ultimate administrative authority for the church.

Southern Baptists have invested great energy in educating and instructing the laity in their duty as Christian ministers. As William Clemmons writes, "The fact that Baptists have developed strong lay leaders, have staffed their church life for years, and have from time to time in denominational affairs raised their voices when they thought the clergy had erred is a tribute to the Sunday-after-Sunday study of the

41. Ibid.
42. J. B. McMinn, "Deacon," *Encyclopedia of Southern Baptists*, 1:352.

Bible and its devotional use both privately and in families."[43] Laity was instructed in the Bible, in doctrine, and in the techniques of "soul-winning." These training programs also contributed to the sense of Southern-Baptistness among the laity in the denomination.

Throughout the history of the SBC, however, the relationship between clergy and laity has been a tenuous one. Local autonomy and congregational democracy meant that churches voted on everything from the calling of a pastor to the color of the fellowship hall. And they frequently split over both. Power blocs of one sort or another exercise varying degrees of influence in almost every congregation. Ministers often bemoan the laity-led factions that control many Southern Baptist churches. Laypeople complain that some pastors demonstrate limited leadership skills while others are autocratic, seeking to control every aspect of church life. Recent studies indicate a significant increase in church conflicts and staff terminations.[44] Again it is amazing that the denomination avoided major schism so long, given the widespread fragmentation of local churches—often due to clergy-laity conflicts.

The Controversy in the SBC brings into focus several questions regarding the role of clergy and laity in the churches. Since the 1950s Southern Baptists have experienced the growing dominance of ordained professionals in denominational life. This trend has several causes. First, as church memberships increased and as congregational polity became more cumbersome, many have turned to the business world as a model for defining the administrative role of the pastor. Churches organize committees around a corporate structure with the senior minister as chief executive officer. Congregational involvement in fiscal affairs, if not other organizational aspects, is minimized. The business model is also shaping the self-identity of a new generation of SBC ministers.

Second, the increasing professionalization of the ministry has implications for the Baptist theology of the laity. In many congregations, positions once occupied by the laity are now held by seminary-trained, ordained professionals who provide specialized services to certain sub-groups—choirs, youth, senior adults, or children. While it may be helpful to have trained staff in such positions, the trend also fosters a view of laity as clients who hire professionals to perform specialized ministerial services.

Third, a growing number of Southern Baptists adhere to a view

43. William P. Clemmons, "The Contributions of the Sunday School to Southern Baptist Churches," *Baptist History and Heritage* 16 (1978), p. 41.

44. Jim Lowry, "Survey Shows 2,100 Pastors Fired During Past 18 Months," *Baptist Standard*, Nov. 30, 1988, p. 5.

of the ministry based on the ultimate authority of the pastoral office. This position, strongly advocated by fundamentalists, suggests that the only biblical model for pastoral leadership rests in the authoritative role of the pastor. The laity are to be guided by a benign chief executive or "undershepherd" who by virtue of divine enlightenment and spiritual responsibility retains primary authority in the congregation.

The fundamentalist leader Paige Patterson declares that the Bible teaches that the pastor is "clearly called the ruler" of the local church.[45] He suggests that "the first thing a congregation is responsible for doing is to listen to those who have the rule over you." Not only must the congregation listen to its pastor but also it should learn to "mimic, obey and submit to him."[46] The clergification of the SBC is another symptom of the fragmentation in the denomination. It undermines the role of the laity, creating a clerical elite who by virtue of call or training claim spiritual and functional authority over the church. These tendencies seem more compatible with the hierarchical establishment of medieval Roman Catholicism than the Free Church tradition of the Baptists.

Southern Baptists are again caught in a theological identity crisis. They continue to talk like congregationalists, promoting the priesthood of the laity, yet many act as though the denomination is controlled by the clergy.

Evangelism and Conversion: Dramatic Event or Nurturing Process

Evangelism is a hallmark of Southern Baptist life. The SBC is one of the most zealously conversionistic denominations in religious America. Conversion is required of all who would claim Christian faith and membership in the church. Denominational missionary efforts are aimed primarily at bringing the unconverted to a "saving faith" in Jesus Christ. Southern Baptist ecclesiology centers on a regenerate church membership, but the SBC is heir to a variety of theological traditions regarding conversion. While most congregations share a common concern for evangelism, many demonstrate diverse perspectives and methods regarding evangelism.

Southern Baptists have institutionalized and popularized the process of conversion in an effort evangelize the masses systematically. In so doing, they have created a kind of evangelical sacramentalism by

45. Larry E. High, "Bible Says Pastor Clearly the Church 'Ruler': Patterson," *Biblical Recorder*, Nov. 26, 1988, p. 6.
46. Ibid.

which an internal, subjective religious experience can be verified through certain objective criteria. While they proclaim conversion as an intensely personal experience, they have also developed elaborate plans, programs, and prayers for fulfilling the necessary salvific transaction. Not surprisingly, over time some confusion has developed over the relationship of saving faith and salvific event.

In their concern for evangelism and conversion Baptists were both biblicists and pietists. As biblicists they believed that the Holy Scriptures taught the necessity for and means of conversion. As pietists, they believed that salvation was a mysterious activity of divine grace experienced in the heart of the true believer. It was found, not in external works or dogmas, but in personal experience with God. Conversion involved a direct encounter with Christ, not merely intellectual assent to certain doctrines about him.

The denomination itself was founded for the evangelistic purpose of propagating the gospel in America and around the world. As the SBC evolved, it developed denominational programs, institutions, and literature to assist the churches in implementing the evangelistic mandate. It also fostered a way of "getting saved Southern Baptist" characteristic of the evangelistic intent and method evident in the churches. In weekly worship and seasonal revivals, preachers called sinners to repentance. Through witness training programs, laypeople were instructed in methods of personal evangelism and encouraged to "witness for Christ" at every opportunity.

Adult sinners were not the only ones in need of salvation, of course. Children were brought to faith through the loving nurture of the church. Indeed, a significant factor in the SBC's phenomenal evangelistic success was their ability to articulate a theology of conversion as both dramatic evangelical event and as nurturing process. This effort to convert both children and adults sometimes created serious theological confusion for a denomination based on the idea of a believers' church made up solely of those who were mature enough to accept the gospel for themselves. It raised many questions regarding Southern Baptist theology of conversion: What is the proper age of conversion? In a denomination that claims to take its baptismal tradition directly from Scripture, is the baptism of children consistent with the practice of the New Testament church? What is the nature of childhood faith? Is conversion through Christian nurture as valid as the dramatic adult experience? Are those nurtured into faith also required to have a dramatic conversion experience sometime in life? While affirming the biblical and personal nature of conversion, Southern Baptists have not always agreed on when and how a person is actually "saved." Naturally, they interpreted the Bible and their own experience in light of the varied historical traditions from which they came. The morphology of conversion in SBC life has not always been as homogenous as many seem to think.

Regular Baptist Tradition

As Calvinists, the Regular Baptists believed that all persons were totally depraved and therefore had no free will whereby to choose conversion. Only after receiving regeneration from the sovereign God was the human will free to experience repentance and faith. Conversion often involved a lengthy process of spiritual struggle prior to the infusion of divine grace. The idea that any person might freely choose to pray one prayer and immediately receive salvation was completely foreign to Regular Baptist evangelism. Since preachers did not know who was or was not among the elect, they preached as if everyone could be saved, believing that the Spirit would use the Word to awaken the hearts of the elect. Preachers could force no one to believe; only God could do that through the infusion of irresistible grace.

During the twentieth century, Southern Baptists generally moved away from this Calvinistic understanding of election and conversion. They have retained much of the language of Calvinism—election, depravity, sovereignty—but redefined it considerably with a greater emphasis on free will and human participation in the salvific process. In a sense, when they confront the issue of conversion, Southern Baptists talk like Calvinists but act like Arminians.

Separate Baptists

The Separates were revivalistic Baptists in whom Calvinism was thoroughly modified. They suggested that all people were potentially elected to salvation, but only those who accepted Christ freely through repentance and faith were actually numbered among the elect. God's sovereign grace and human free will cooperated together to accomplish salvation. Separate Baptists were given to bold, enthusiastic preaching which demanded a dramatic, often emotional, encounter with the living Christ. Yet even Separates described a conversion process which might extend over months, even years before the light of salvation broke through.[47] In spite of the emphasis on free will, Southern Baptists generally repudiated the more Arminian emphasis on falling from grace, the

---

47. William Warren Sweet, *Religion on the American Frontier: The Baptists* (New York: Henry Holt, 1931), p. 234.

idea that true believers could "lose" their salvation by turning from grace, and retained the Calvinist belief in the perseverance of the saints.

Landmarkists

Proponents of gospel Landmarkism insisted on the need for personal faith in Christ, but united the conversion experience with certain doctrines about baptism and the church. While everyone who accepted Christ through repentance and faith might be saved, they would receive true baptism and true church membership only in fellowship with the Baptists. Landmarkers rejected "alien immersion" and required rebaptism of all who were not of "like faith and order." Even today, non-Baptist Christians may be baptized alongside new converts in Southern Baptist churches, largely due to the influence of Landmarkism. To protect the integrity of their tradition, the Landmarkers modified, even changed, the New Testament practice of baptism as the profession of faith for new Christians to baptism as the way converts old and new could join a Baptist church. In so doing, they created two types of baptism: baptism into Christ and baptism into a Baptist church. External doctrines about baptism came to inform the way Baptists understood the internal experience of conversion. Today, many of the people counted in Southern Baptists' annual baptism statistics are not new converts, but Christians from other communions who received Baptist baptism.

Revivalism

Revivalism became the means by which many Southern Baptists carried their evangelical imperative to the masses. Through revivals, Baptists, with other American evangelicals, institutionalized the process of conversion. Revivals shortened the conversion process substantially. The lengthy struggles with sin and self that characterized earlier Regular and Separate Baptist conversions were reduced to sign posts on the way to instantaneous regeneration. Conversion became a simple matter of praying the "sinner's prayer" and inviting Jesus into the heart. One sincere prayer brought immediate salvation.

Revivals also produced a powerful set of symbols that dramatized the need for and possibility of immediate conversion. The invitation given at the end of every church service became an integral part of conversion in SBC life. It created what might be called the sacrament of walking the aisle, an outward and visible sign of an inward and evangelical grace. Converts soon described salvation in terms appropriate to the invitation—"when I went forward," or "when I shook the preacher's hand." Indeed, many testified that salvation seemed to come in the very act of moving from pew to aisle. The invitation thus became an almost essential element of the salvific process, an occasion for one's public profession of faith.

In some settings, revivalism also helped turn conversion from a process of experience with grace to a transaction that fulfills a salvific requirement. Today, many Southern Baptists live on the edge of doubt about their conversion experience. At every life crisis many return to repeat the transaction and reclaim salvation, hoping against hope that they will finally get it right. Christianity is less a life of spiritual growth and struggle than a perpetual return to the beginning.[48] The increase in the number of rebaptisms among Southern Baptist members is a dramatic phenomenon in SBC life. Some attribute it to the failure of revivalistic methods. Others suggest that, as the appeal of mass revivalism wanes, many Southern Baptist evangelists have concentrated on reconverting church members as a means to avoid changing their methods—or reducing their statistics.

The Sunday School Tradition

Sunday School represents the nurturing element of Southern Baptist conversionism. During the twentieth century Southern Baptists generally concluded that children were born, not with Adamic guilt, but with "a nature predisposed to sin" when faced with moral choice. Children who died before reaching the "age of [moral] accountability" were "covered by the atoning work of Christ."[49] Just when that mysterious age was attained was always a matter of some uncertainty. Baptist leader L. R. Scarborough concluded that "most children have a sense of sin between seven and ten years of age."[50] By the 1930s, therefore, denominational publications were urging the conversion of children in the elementary years. One manual suggested, "We cannot too earnestly insist that boys and girls should be won to Christ before they leave the Junior [elementary] department" in Sunday School.[51]

Today Southern Baptists continue to instruct children toward conversion through Sunday School and other programs of the church. Responding to that nurture, many children make faith their own less as

---

48. Norman Jameson, "We're Being Born Again . . . and Again," *The Baptist Messenger* (Oklahoma), Sept. 18, 1986, pp. 4-9.

49. L. R. Scarborough, *With Christ After the Lost* (Nashville: Broadman, 1952), p. 158.

50. Ibid.

51. P. E. Burroughs, *How to Win to Christ* (Nashville: Convention Press, 1934), p. 70.

a result of some profound personal crisis, but as a willing confirmation of what they have been taught. Several thousand preschoolers are baptized each year into the believers' churches of the SBC. For many years a majority of the candidates for baptism in the SBC churches were children age six to twelve.[52]

Southern Baptists have had some difficulty in helping these children move through various stages of faith. Many of the people now receiving rebaptism in SBC churches are those who were originally baptized as children. Many confront the moral dilemmas of adolescence or adulthood and conclude that their earlier experience was invalid because they did not "understand" what they were doing. The baptism of children has created significant theological confusion for many Southern Baptists. In reality, the practice of baptizing children and rebaptizing some of those same individuals after they have reached adulthood represents a kind of infant baptism and confirmation in Southern Baptist churches, a philosophy Southern Baptists reject theoretically yet implement in practice.

The Fundamentalist Tradition

One final conversion tradition involves the fundamentalism of the nineteenth and twentieth centuries. Fundamentalist rhetoric often sounds as if simple faith in Christ is not enough. Certain doctrines about his nature are prerequisite to conversion. Older conversion manuals warned the witness not to become entangled in theological debates and questions that would distract the sinner from the real issue, conversion. C. E. Autrey, a noted Baptist evangelist, wrote in 1961 that "soul winners" should not "argue questions like the virgin birth and related doctrines." Autrey suggested that, "Where the soul-winner finds a lost man who is confused about some doctrinal difficulty, if he will tell him that it is not required that he understand that particular problem in order to be saved, it will help greatly."[53]

This approach is in contrast to that of former convention president Adrian Rogers, who declared that "If you don't believe in the virgin birth of Christ, not only do you have difficulty with the character of Mary, . . . the character of Jesus, . . . the character of God, but you've got a big difficulty in your own character. And I'm gonna tell you something else, I would not give you half a hallelujah for your chance of heaven if you

---

52. Melvin Douglas Clark, "The Evangelism of Children: A Study in Southern Baptist Practice" (unpublished Th.D. thesis, Southern Baptist Theological Seminary, 1969).
53. C. E. Autrey, *You Can Win Souls* (Nashville: Broadman, 1961), pp. 33-34.

don't believe in the virgin birth of Jesus."[54] For Rogers, conversion seems dependent on assent to a particular fundamentalist dogma regarding the nature of Christ and the atonement. He insists: "No virgin birth, no deity; no deity, no sinlessness; no sinlessness, no atonement; no atonement, no hope."[55] The doctrine of Christ's virgin birth is affirmed by Southern Baptists, fundamentalist and moderate alike. The question here is whether knowledge of the doctrine is necessary in presenting the "plan of salvation." C. E. Autrey never doubted the virgin birth; he hesitated to make it an issue which might create debate and inhibit witness. Thus the fundamentalist agenda continues to shape Southern Baptist understanding of conversion less as dramatic, mystical experience than as assent to certain propositions regarding the nature and work of Christ.

Evangelism: Theological Confusion

Each of these traditions reflects the way in which a conversionist denomination has sought to objectify an essentially subjective, existential religious experience. Whether in nurture, as dramatic event, in revivalistic transactionalism, or propositional theology, some procedure for understanding and articulating the nature of conversion necessarily developed. In the present controversy, Southern Baptists seem unable to acknowledge the diversity of conversionist traditions that characterize SBC history, and this lack of historical perspective contributes to the serious theological confusion in the SBC regarding the nature of evangelism and conversion.

Both fundamentalists and moderates acknowledge an evangelistic identity crisis. Ed Young, the fundamentalist pastor of Second Baptist Church, Houston, noted in a 1988 address that Southern Baptists were failing to reach significant numbers of "unchurched" people with salvation. He reported that of 338,359 people baptized in 1987, 175,000 were children reared in SBC churches, 50,000 were from other denominations, and 26,000 were Southern Baptist church members who received "rebaptism." That left only 75,000 formerly unchurched persons who received baptism in SBC churches.[56] Ron Lewis, a former Sunday School Board staff member, noted in 1986 that "in 92 percent of your [SBC] churches, the only real growth you've had in the last five years has been from baptizing the children of your members and from transfers

---

54. Adrian Rogers, "The Virgin Birth," audio tape recording, Pastors' Conference of the SBC, June 8, 1986.

55. Ibid.

56. "Houston Pastor Urges 'Fishing for Lost,' " *Western Recorder,* Oct. 18, 1988, p. 4.

from other churches."[57] Overall baptismal statistics demonstrate the difficulty Southern Baptists seem to be having in evangelizing adults who have little previous religious background.

Moderates are often uncomfortable with older revivalistic, transactional methods of conversion, but are uncertain as to appropriate alternatives. Developing an appropriate theology and method for evangelism is a major challenge for SBC moderates. Fundamentalists claim to be the defenders of evangelism and cite certain statistical evidence as proof of their effectiveness. But they too acknowledge problems with the effectiveness of their conversion outreach, and the increasing rebaptisms of church members illustrates a widespread theological dilemma even among fundamentalists.

The current struggles regarding evangelism point up several issues for Southern Baptists. First, they reveal the theological difficulties created when a tradition founded on the idea of a regenerate church membership makes normative the baptism of children, even preschoolers. To baptize children within a context that demands a certain cognitive response to faith, an intense personal decision, and some degree of sense of self was bound to create confusion. While choosing to baptize both children and adults, Southern Baptists failed to develop a theology for two distinct approaches to conversion.

Second, the rebaptism of SBC church members in increasing numbers indicates several significant problems. Among other things, it reflects the inadequacy of many earlier evangelistic methods, the sense of doubt that troubles many active church members, and the inability of many Baptists to distinguish between justification (entering into faith) and sanctification (growing up in grace). In certain churches it may also reveal the inability of old revivalistic methods to reach many secularized persons who are unaccustomed to the language and practice of traditional evangelism. Unable to reach "the world" and to depart from orthodox forms, some Southern Baptists prefer to convert the already converted, or at least those who respond to traditional appeals.

Third, by placing so much emphasis on the cognitive, dogmatic elements of conversion, Southern Baptists may unwittingly have taken the life out of it. In a now classic analysis, H. Richard Niebuhr suggested that many evangelical churches so institutionalized conversion that

> regeneration, the dying to the self and the rising to new life, now apparently sudden, now so slow and painful, so confused, so real, . . .

57. Jim Newton, "Most Churches Grow because of Transfers of Memberships," *Western Recorder,* Feb. 18, 1986.

becomes conversion which takes place on Sunday morning during the singing of the last hymn or twice a year when the revival preacher comes to town. There is still some reality in it for some converts but, following a prescribed pattern for the most part in its inception and progress, the life has gone out of it.[58]

Southern Baptists would do well to hear those words as they evaluate their theology of evangelism toward the year 2000.

Dissenting Tradition—Establishment Status

The SBC is heir to the dissenting tradition of the Baptists with its opposition to all forms of religious establishment and its support for church-state separation. During the colonial period, Virginia Baptists were powerful proponents of religious liberty. Baptist clergy and laity distinguished themselves as advocates of dissent against those laws of conformity that favored the Anglican establishment. Baptist preachers would sooner endure fines and imprisonment rather than secure preaching licenses from the state. Later Southern Baptists pointed with pride to the legacy of Virginian John Leland and his influence on Madison, Jefferson, and other framers in securing the First Amendment to the Constitution. Denominationalists consistently called the convention to assert its dissenting role in opposing such issues as aid to parochial schools, ambassadors to the Vatican, tax-supported military chaplains, and state mandated prayer in public schools. In a 1939 address to the Baptist World Alliance, Southern Baptist statesman George W. Truett declared that Baptists "pleaded, and suffered, and kept on with their protests and remonstrances and memorials, until, thank God, forever, their contention was won in these United States and written into our country's Constitution that church and state must, in this land, be forever separate and free, and that neither must ever trespass upon the distinctive functions of the other."[59] He saw this as the great legacy Baptists offered to the world.

At the same time, the convention often demonstrates an approach to political and social concerns that reflects its establishment status in southern culture. At times, the denomination seems more comfortable in supporting the status quo than in promoting dissent. John Lee Eighmy

---

58. H. Richard Niebuhr, *The Kingdom of God in America* (New York: Harper Torchbooks, 1937), pp. 179-80.

59. George W. Truett, cited in J. M. Dawson, *Baptists and the American Republic* (Nashville: Broadman, 1956), p. 221.

observed that while Southern Baptists did give some attention to the dissenting heritage in matters of religious liberty, they consistently demonstrated a social conservatism which was "more Bourbon [establishment] than Populist."[60] Most Southern Baptist leaders in the late-nineteenth and early-twentieth centuries "accepted *laissez faire* economics without question and sided with employers in labor disputes."[61] Moreover they were willing to use secular means to maintain what they felt were important ethical standards within their culture. The response of the convention to social and political transitions—many related to questions of modernity—was less as a dissenting minority than as a religious establishment seeking to preserve certain traditional beliefs and practices. Eighmy concluded that in their opposition to alcohol, sabbath-breaking, gambling, and other issues, most Southern Baptist ministers "readily accepted the advantages that civil power would offer in achieving a religious goal they believed to be beneficial to society as a whole." Unconsciously, perhaps, they adopted "one of the basic methods of an established church where their numbers could significantly influence public policy."[62]

Again, Southern Baptist denominationalists sought to have it both ways. They claimed the tradition of dissent and the establishment ideal of social stability, accepting members who appealed to both positions. In recent years the dissenting perspective has been represented in such agencies as the Christian Life Commission and the Baptist Joint Committee on Public Affairs. During the 1960s the CLC and its director Foy Valentine led the denomination in supporting the civil rights movement in the South—an extremely controversial action within the convention and its churches. Some Southern Baptists never forgave the CLC for what they perceived as its militancy during the civil rights upheavals. Through the Baptist Joint Committee, the SBC united with other Baptists in lobbying against those actions that threatened certain Baptist positions on religious liberty. Fundamentalists who felt that the BJCPA does not reflect a more precise conservative agenda characteristic of the new religious-political right have worked since 1979 to move the SBC away from the Joint Committee and toward the establishment of a Southern Baptist agency in Washington.

The establishment side of the SBC influenced many convention leaders to avoid controversial political and social stands for the sake of

---

60. Eighmy, *Churches in Cultural Captivity*, p. 43.
61. Ibid.
62. Ibid., p. 49.

unity. As Samuel Hill notes, "At the very most [they] were gradualists in their desire for change in church and community."[63] When faced with such divisive issues, convention leaders called Southern Baptists to avoid any political controversy that would distract the denomination from its unified tasks: missions and evangelism. This kept the SBC from alienating large segments of its constituency over political issues. At the same time it was frustrating for those on both the left and the right who wanted their denomination to take a more prophetic stance on such issues as nuclear disarmament, the Vietnam War, abortion, and civil rights.

The ability of convention leaders to steer a middle course on controversial social and political issues helped the SBC avoid schism. But the fundamentalist dominance of the SBC has moved the convention toward more explicit identification with the agenda of the new religious-political right. After years of support for the 1962 Supreme Court ruling rejecting the use of prescribed prayers in public schools, Southern Baptists meeting in New Orleans in 1982 passed a resolution calling for a constitutional amendment stating that "Nothing in this Constitution shall be construed to prohibit individual or group prayer in public schools and other public institutions. No person shall be required by the United States or by any state to participate in prayer."[64] The same convention voted to "express our support for the teaching of Scientific Creationism in our public schools," but rejected the idea of tuition tax credits for families with children in private schools.[65]

Why the change in traditional Baptist positions on politics and public morality? Commenting on the 1982 school prayer resolution, social analyst Richard John Neuhaus suggested that the changes had less to do "with a change of mind than with a change of sociological circumstance. A religious community that no longer understands itself as an embattled minority begins to think more about influence than about tolerance."[66] Such changes reflect the tension between dissent and establishment in the SBC. Clearly, many fundamentalist leaders in the new SBC want the convention to take more affirmative positions toward a conservative political agenda, a response that would significantly reshape the denomination's approach to church-state issues. Sociologist James Guth notes that while many prominent Southern Baptists support the new religious-political right, the convention itself remains "badly

---

63. Samuel Hill, Jr., "Epilogue" in Eighmy, *Churches in Cultural Captivity*, p. 204.
64. SBC *Annual*, 1982, p. 58.
65. Ibid., pp. 59 and 62.
66. Richard John Neuhaus, *The Naked Public Square* (Grand Rapids: Eerdmans, 1984), p. 40.

split by Rightist politics."[67] He concludes that the active participation of many fundamentalists in right wing causes contributes to the public perception that ministerial political activism in the SBC is dominated by the Christian right.[68] In their analysis of the rightward drift of American religion, Samuel Hill and Dennis Owen suggest that right wing religionists tend to view America as a "religious society" from the beginning of its history, with Christianity as its primary religious influence. Christianity is seen as transcending mere religion to become the moral and spiritual "establishment" of the nation as intended by the founders of the republic.[69] Forrest E. Watson and former SBC president James T. Draper demonstrate just such views when they write: "It is obvious that the men who wrote the Constitution intended the United States to be a Christian union. Christianity was assumed in everything that was undertaken in the founding of our country. The United States was to have no established Church, but was to be Christian."[70] Draper and Watson also reveal their admiration for the Puritan religious establishment in colonial New England, a community where "the government was not ruled by the Church; it was, however, obedient to the Bible."[71] The Puritans did "not migrate to America to establish a community with many points of view, all tolerated." Rather, they established a holy commonwealth based solely on the Bible.[72] Contemporary SBC fundamentalists seem more comfortable with the Puritan establishment—which persecuted Baptists—than with the pluralism advocated by dissenter Roger Williams, long a hero of Baptist faith and politics.[73]

The fact is that most Southern Baptists have never been comfortable with dissent, perhaps because they were so closely aligned with the southern establishment over social, political, and racial issues. Fundamentalists continue to direct the convention toward a more establishment position regarding the role of religion in public life. Current revisionist trends, while rightly acknowledging the problems of religion and morality in an increasingly secular state, simply perpetuate frag-

67. James L. Guth, "The Politics of Preachers: Southern Ministers and Christian Right Activism," in *New Christian Politics*, ed. David G. Bromley and Anson Shupe (Macon: Mercer University Press, 1985), p. 236.

68. Ibid.

69. Samuel Hill, Jr., and Dennis Owen, *The New Religious Political Right in America* (Nashville: Abingdon, 1982), p. 45.

70. James T. Draper and Forrest E. Watson, *If the Foundations Be Destroyed* (Nashville: Nelson, 1984), pp. 86-88.

71. Ibid., p. 53.

72. Ibid., p. 42.

73. J. M. Dawson, *Baptists and the American Republic* (Nashville: Broadman, 1956), pp. 22-24.

mentation and division over the "correct" Baptist position. Fundamentalist efforts to create a new agency to represent Southern Baptist interests in Washington are further evidence of denominational fragmentation. In a sincere desire to respond to secularism, Southern Baptists must avoid fostering what Neuhaus calls a secular religion that translates "particularistic religious beliefs" into "more general terms."[74] This secularization of faith may create a generic religion devoid of pluralistic distinctiveness.

The Ordinances: Sacraments, Symbols, or Commands?

Southern Baptists refer to baptism and the Lord's Supper as the two "ordinances" of the church. Questions regarding the nature of baptism, its proper mode, candidates, and administrators have long divided local churches and associations throughout the SBC. Those issues, not debate over biblical inspiration, posed a threat to convention unity throughout much of this century. Differences concerning so-called "alien immersion" and "close communion" were particularly divisive. These practices, primarily related to the Landmark movement, shape the Southern Baptist theology of the ordinances to this day. Many who rejected antimissionary and antidenominational elements of the Landmark movement were staunch defenders of Landmark theology of the ordinances. Many congregations have been excluded from the local association for their acceptance of alien immersion, or for promoting an open baptism policy whereby varying forms of baptism are recognized as valid for those who confess faith in Christ. In recent decades, however, the enforcement of close communion practices has waned, and the widespread debate over alien immersion has been somewhat eclipsed by other debates.

The SBC never made a specific theological interpretation of the ordinances a test of fellowship for member churches. Thus a wide variety of attitudes toward the ordinances remains evident in SBC churches. Baptismal practices range across a wide spectrum. Some churches maintain a completely open policy, receiving members who were baptized as infants, children, or adults in any mode—sprinkling, pouring, immersion—practiced within the Christian tradition. They simply ask new members to confess personal faith in Christ at the time they join the church. Other congregations accept the baptism and specific mode of all who received baptism after an experience of faith. Still others accept all

74. Neuhaus, *The Naked Public Square*, p. 109.

those who received immersion following a profession of faith in any Christian communion, but they require immersion of all who have not previously received it. Other churches continue to require rebaptism of all who have not been immersed in a Baptist church. Some Southern Baptist congregations even require reimmersion of persons baptized in other Baptist traditions whose theology is "questionable." For example, the Southern Baptist association of churches in Evansville, Indiana, requires reimmersion of those who come from the General Baptist churches in the area. The General Baptists hold a more Arminian view of falling from grace. This doctrine is considered unacceptable by the SBC churches in the region, and thus they reject the baptism of General Baptists.

The theology and practice of the Lord's Supper among SBC churches is equally diverse. Many congregations invite to communion all who confess faith in Jesus Christ. Others extend an invitation to all "of like faith and order" to join in the supper. In some churches that nebulous phrase applies to anyone who professes an evangelical faith. In others it means all Baptists. In still others it refers to all Southern Baptists. Some congregations continue to practice close communion, permitting only members of their specific church to receive communion.

Theologically, some churches, particularly in the Southeast, reflect a more Calvinistic view of the ordinances as "means of grace" which bring a special, unique blessing and experience of Christ's presence. While eschewing transubstantiation, these congregations hold the Supper in high regard. They would not fear to refer to it as "an outward and visible sign of an inward and spiritual grace," a sacramental sign of God's presence. Many other SBC churches, perhaps a majority, look upon the Supper as a memorial, something akin to the theological interpretation set forth by Ulrich Zwingli, the sixteenth-century Protestant reformer. They emphasize Jesus' words, "Do this in memory of me." Still other churches and pastors use the language of memorial but qualify it even further. For them, the Supper and baptism are less symbols than commands, a "mere" observance ordered by Christ. Some pastors may frequently qualify the practice by saying "This is only a symbol which Jesus commands us to observe in his name." Thus the practice is minimized lest it appear to be salvific or too "Catholic."

The convention's official statements emphasize the symbolic nature of the ordinances. The Baptist Faith and Message calls baptism "an act of obedience symbolizing the believer's faith in a crucified, buried and risen Saviour."[75] The Lord's Supper is described as "a symbolic act of

---

75. Herschel Hobbs, *The Baptist Faith and Message* (Nashville: Convention Press, 1971), p. 83.

obedience whereby the members of the church, through partaking of the
bread and the fruit of the vine, memorialize the death of the Redeemer
and anticipate his second coming."[76] The phrase "the members of the
church" could apply to members of the local congregation or to the church
at large. Specific Landmark interpretations of the sacraments are therefore
acceptable but not required of all SBC churches. Nonetheless, Landmark
views, while not imposed on the entire convention, continue to influence
practices at denominationally supported institutions. Seminaries, Baptist
colleges, and other agencies do not practice the Lord's Supper in their
chapel services, largely in deference to the Landmark idea that only local
churches possess the authority to celebrate communion.

The variety of views on the Supper and baptism again illustrates
the diversity of the SBC itself. While most agree that the two ordinances
are symbols, there are many interpretations of the nature of such sym-
bolism. The fact that these questions have split innumerable churches
and associations but not the national convention is further testimony to
the success of the Grand Compromise that bound the denomination
together. Compromise over the nature of the sacraments was evident
early in the convention's history.

Theology and The Controversy

The Controversy clearly indicates that serious theological confusion exists throughout Southern Baptist life, in the seminaries and the churches,
among fundamentalists and moderates alike. Conclusions are tentative
at best. First, theology has been an important concern of Southern Baptists
from the beginning of the convention. Theological issues were at the heart
of most convention controversies throughout its history. Second, basic
theological positions regarding the great doctrines of the church were
interpreted from a distinctly Baptist perspective. Southern Baptists were
aware of theological boundaries from the time the convention was
founded. Third, doctrines were defined in terms broad enough to encom-
pass the diverse theological traditions and subgroups that composed the
SBC. Until 1979, attempts to define dogma in ways that would alienate
large segments of the constituency were resisted by the convention with
amazing success. Fourth, certain Baptist distinctives were held in an
uneasy tension with other ideals. For years, denominationalists sought to
maintain a balance that fostered compromise and inhibited the possibility

76. Ibid.

of schism. Fifth, within this delicate balance there existed a wide variety of theological attitudes and interpretations with roots in Calvinist, modified Calvinist, modified Arminian, and even occasional Arminian, Landmarkist, fundamentalist, neoorthodox, evangelical, charismatic, and social gospel interpretations of Christianity.

Many fundamentalists were never comfortable with what they viewed as doctrinal permissiveness for the sake of denominational unity. They sought to establish a more explicit theological identity for the denomination and insure conformity to those beliefs affirmed by the "majority" of Southern Baptists. Those who do not accept their formulas and definitions are excluded from representation on convention boards of trustees. Their efforts have narrowed the theological parameters of the SBC considerably and upset the delicate balance that the denomination had so long struggled, with amazing success, to maintain. The Controversy has simply accelerated the organizational dysfunction and theological confusion that existed in the denomination long before 1979. By 1989 the real question was: How narrowly can the denomination define itself and still remain intact?

CHAPTER 5

Piety, Populism, and Politics: A Denomination of Behavers

BEING SOUTHERN BAPTIST IS NOT ONLY A WAY OF BELIEVING, IT IS ALSO A WAY of behaving. Without doubt theology has been a significant ingredient of Southern Baptist identity throughout the convention's history. Denominational leaders warned their constituents that only through uncompromising loyalty to convention programs and policies could they be certain that Baptist doctrine and New Testament Christianity would be preserved. These same leaders also learned which doctrines would rally the troops and which, when defined too precisely, would fragment them. They knew which dogmas promoted consensus and which ones required a certain theological ambiguity for the sake of denominational unity. As we have seen, denominationalists scrupulously promoted adherence to basic doctrines of Christian and Baptist faith but hesitated to define those doctrines in ways that would alienate the diverse subgroups that coexisted throughout the convention. Yet the SBC not only promoted belief, it created a Southern Baptist way of acting in response to the faith and order, the life and work of the churches. In a real sense, believing was inseparable from behaving.

In the heat of anti-Catholic rhetoric prior to the election of John F. Kennedy in 1960, many Southern Baptists cited, with both envy and disdain, the supposed Romanist claim, "Give us a child for the first seven years of life and we will make that child a Catholic forever." The statement evidenced the power of Catholic indoctrination and its ability to implant an indelible Catholic identity in the hearts and minds of the young. It also provided one explanation for the difficulty of converting Catholics to Protestant Christianity. Catholics might have made a similar observation about the Southern Baptist Convention. For many southerners, instruction in the Southern Baptist way of believing and behaving originated in the Cradle Roll Department of the church and continued throughout the primary years. With subsequent baptism in childhood or adolescence, a lifelong commitment to the Southern Baptist Convention was established. While some ex-Southern Baptists did migrate to a variety of denominations ranging from Episcopalian to Pentecostal, there were generations of the faithful that could no more forsake their Southern Baptistness than they could relinquish their southernness. The SBC thus successfully created a surprising sense of loyalty within a constituency given to individualism, autonomy, and varying degrees of theological diversity.

Belief and Behavior

Denominational programs and practices fostered a basic pattern of behavior that became characteristically Southern Baptist. These programs were at once similar to and distinct from the activities of other evangelical Protestant denominations in the South. This Southern Baptist identity bound diverse churches and individuals together in one denomination while it also helped defer the impact of religious pluralism on many SBC institutions. This alleged unity-in-diversity reflects a powerful dialectic in SBC life. While there is diversity to the point of contradiction in belief and practice among SBC churches and individuals, there is also a patent uniformity, a genuinely Southern Baptist way of believing and behaving. As pluralism insinuated itself into program and doctrine, constituency and geography, Southern Baptist identity became both elusive and illusive throughout denominational life. For years, denominational programs shaped by piety and practice supplied a common identity for an individualized constituency. But as the programmatic formula faltered, traditional methods for maintaining unity-in-diversity became progressively obsolete.

Fundamentalists responded to this identity crisis by insisting that being a Southern Baptist was essentially a matter of correct belief. They maintained that the uniform affirmation of a clearly defined belief would preserve the convention and ultimately restore orthodoxy, the true source of denominational unity. Their strategy for compliance, however, called for a degree of conformity not easily accommodated by a highly independent constituency. In response to fundamentalist agendas, moderates seemed unable to structure an alternative Southern Baptist consciousness. Some simply clung to traditional programmatic methods and denominational slogans. Others sought to organize a rear guard action and reclaim lost influence. Many disagreed as to what form the responses to fundamentalism should take.

After a decade of contention, leaders of the two factions agreed that their differences were increasingly irreconcilable and that they were badly divided as to the nature of the denomination, if not the gospel itself. Neither party, however, would relinquish its claim to the Southern Baptist name or tradition. Many seemed willing to have either fundamentalists or moderates run the convention as long as the name Southern Baptist remained intact. So deep was the denominational identity that many members could not imagine being religious apart from the name Southern Baptist. After a decade of theological and political skirmishes, gradual fragmentation, rather than immediate schism, seemed the outlook for the future of the SBC. And in their confusion over what to believe, Southern Baptists also experienced considerable uncertainty over how to behave.

A Denomination of Behavers

In *A Nation of Behavers* (1976), Martin E. Marty proposed "a new map of religious America based on the visible loyalties of people as evidenced in their beliefs and social behavior and expressed in their public quests for group identity and social location."[1] His concern was with what people *do*, religiously, not merely with what they believe. Marty did not deny that beliefs were important; rather, he suggested that in most religious groups belief and behavior are inseparable. He noted that "while talking about behavior one is not denigrating belief but only holding it in some suspension while something else is being examined, all the while seeing the two to be profoundly and even integrally related."[2] No study of The Controversy in the Southern Baptist Convention can overlook the relationship between belief and behavior in the denomination.

Marty suggested that by the middle of the twentieth century membership in a denomination no longer provided an easy way of identifying religious behavior. To say, "I am a Methodist," said very little, since there might be "far more difference between two kinds of Methodists than between one kind of Methodist and another kind of Baptist."[3]

1. Martin E. Marty, *A Nation of Behavers* (Chicago: University of Chicago Press, 1978), p. 1.
2. Ibid., p. 45.
3. Ibid., p. 6.

He delineated a variety of subgroups that shaped the belief and behavior of religious America within and alongside traditional denominational alignments. These included evangelical-fundamentalist, mainline, pentecostal-charismatic, new religion, ethnic religion, and civil religion. Each was evidence of the effect of pluralism on the old denominational coalitions, creating new ways of "mapping" multiple subgroups within American religion.

The Southern Baptist Convention reflects similar patterns in its denominational life. As The Controversy spread throughout the denomination, divisions between theological subgroups, long present in the convention, became increasingly apparent. Throughout its history, the SBC combined elements of culture, theology and institutional program in ways that provided its constituency with important cues for believing and behaving. While doctrine has been important, elaborate doctrinal definitions probably had less to do with defining a Southern Baptist than did liturgical preference, congregational loyalty, geography, and personal spirituality.[4] In response to such issues Southern Baptists reflected substantial diversity. The denomination, "less focused on theology and belief than on intention and purpose," became a source of unity, identity, and security.[5] Subgroup loyalty and ideology were subordinated to institutional solidarity. As the cultural context changed and pluralism of belief and practice invaded both the region and the denomination, such unity became more difficult to sustain. In response to this dilemma some Southern Baptists sought to narrow the doctrinal parameters of the convention as a way of preserving unity. This effort simply increased the possibility of fragmentation, further illustrating the idea that, "paradoxical as it may seem, . . . the explicit affirmation of beliefs is the first step in their weakening."[6]

What behavior defined the life and faith of Southern Baptist people? Its name was legion. It included: the nature of salvation and personal spirituality; the use and meaning of religious language; the interpretation of Scripture; the practice of personal morality; the collection and appropriation of funds; the attitude toward other denominations and the outside world; and the rules for interpersonal relationships. A brief survey of the nature of Southern Baptist behavior suggests a profile of denominational loyalty and identity.

4. Ibid., p. 46.
5. Ibid., p. 5.
6. Ibid., p. 46.

Piety: Practicing the Presence of God

The need for and practice of personal piety lies at the heart of Southern Baptist religious behavior. An experiential faith requires a direct encounter with the divine, a relationship that begins at conversion and extends throughout a life of Christian discipleship. At their modified Arminian best Southern Baptists insisted that *every* human being could find salvation through a personal experience with Jesus Christ. Through this evangelical encounter, Christ himself became a living presence in the heart of the believing individual. Southern Baptist piety involves a direct experience with God and extensive personal devotion focused particularly on the Second Person of the Trinity. Many testify to an intimate relationship with Jesus Christ, whose presence is directly apprehended in daily life. Many Southern Baptists perceive Jesus as their constant companion and closest friend. To them he is not merely "Jesus Christ the Savior of the world," but "my Jesus," "my Savior," and "my Lord."

The concern for conversion and individual religious experience sometimes makes Southern Baptists sound as if they belong to the mystical tradition of the church. Most would no doubt agree with Quaker Rufus Jones's classic definition of mysticism as "the type of religion which puts the emphasis on immediate awareness of relation with God, on direct and intimate consciousness of the Divine Presence. It is religion in its most acute, intense and living stage."[7] Yet their tendency to suspect things "Catholic" or charismatic, as well as their fear that religious experience may get out of control, makes Southern Baptists generally hesitant to claim the mystical tradition too readily. Perhaps they are best described as heirs of classical pietism with its concern for heart religion and devotional study of the Scriptures, personal morality, and evangelistic witness to individual faith. In fact, one might suggest that the promotion of heart religion was a common cord that bound Southern Baptists together amid theological and historical diversity. Calvinists, modified Calvinists, Landmarkists, Arminians, and social gospelers in the SBC all often based their cooperation on the question, "Have you had a personal experience with Jesus Christ?" Such pietism moved beyond beliefs and theories *about* the Bible to the experience of biblical religion in the hearts and lives of believers. Many people initially joined Southern Baptist churches, not because they understood everything that Baptists believed, but because they had been "won to Christ" or drawn to faith within the context of a Southern Baptist church.

---

7. Rufus Jones, *Studies in Mystical Religion* (London: MacMillan, 1909), p. xv.

E. Glenn Hinson writes: "Broadly speaking, Baptists have exhibited a preference for a relatively simple and uncompromising piety both corporately and privately."[8] He finds the roots of that piety in Puritanism and Pietism with "remarkable affinities with late medieval monastic spirituality not only in thought and practice but even in style and language."[9] Southern Baptist piety, therefore, involved three important elements: the need for conversion, the responsibility to bring others to conversion, and the call to grow in Christian graces through private devotions, personal morality, and faithful participation in certain prescribed religious practices. The denomination shaped Southern Baptist identity by providing programs and organizational structures which guided people in spiritual formation, evangelism, and involvement in church life.

Evangelism: The Love for Souls

Southern Baptist piety was based on spiritual activism. Prayer, worship, and study were not ends in themselves but spiritual sustenance for carrying out service to God in the sinful world. Nowhere was this activism more evident than in the concern for evangelization. Salvation brought with it the responsibility to convert others. Like few other American denominations, the SBC succeeded in motivating its people to practice direct evangelism. From the moment of conversion, Christians received a Divine mandate to bring others to salvation. All believers were missionaries in the propagation of the faith.

The "love for souls" was a sure sign of genuine conversion. The Holy Spirit endued every true Christian with a desire to bring others to "a saving knowledge of Jesus Christ." The denomination, therefore, was one vehicle for promoting evangelistic zeal and training Christians in the techniques and strategy for evangelization. Denominational literature urged Southern Baptists to share their faith and provided instruction in the most effective methods. Believers were encouraged to give a witness for Christ wherever they went. Even the momentary, chance encounter could be an occasion for saving the lost. Witnesses were taught to abstract their own personal "testimonies" (the story of their conversion) in order to state them concisely in every encounter. The "Plan of Salvation" was reduced to a few brief statements and steps that could be

8. E. Glenn Hinson, "Baptists and Spirituality: A Community at Worship, *Review and Expositor* 84 (Fall 1987), p. 649.
    9. Ibid.

presented succinctly. When opportunities were limited Christians could leave tracts in restaurants, restrooms, and other public places so that lost persons might read them and believe. Denominational periodicals frequently included testimonies from persons converted through these methods.

The practice and promotion of personal evangelism had a major impact on the statistical growth of the denomination throughout the twentieth century. When problems arose and controversies divided the denomination, when baptisms lagged and conversions declined, Baptist jeremiads warned that it was due to spiritual indifference and the loss of evangelistic zeal, the true source of denominational unity and purpose. At a 1989 evangelism conference sponsored by Texas Baptists, several speakers evaluated the impact of The Controversy on evangelism. Chuck Swindoll, the popular evangelical preacher (and non-Southern Baptist), encouraged Baptists to pray more and stop "throwing rocks" at each other. He asked, "Could this explain why your soul winning has reached an all-time low?" "Could it be you're so busy throwing rocks?"[10] For Swindoll and others, The Controversy had distracted Baptists from their real task: evangelism.

Discipleship: Living the Faith

Along with their mandate to evangelize, Southern Baptists were also urged to cultivate the spiritual life for themselves. The center of this spiritual formation was Bible study, prayer, and church attendance. Denominational programs guided Christians old and new in spirituality. Worship, Sunday School classes, and daily devotions revolved around the study of the Bible. Believers were encouraged to "bring your Bibles" to every church service and to "follow along" when Scripture texts were read publicly. Diligent students of the Bible memorized as many passages as they possibly could.

While the doctrinal implications of the biblical text were given serious consideration, Southern Baptists placed a greater emphasis on the content of Scripture for its spiritual impact on daily living. Theological content was important primarily as it reinforced historic Baptist principles. So-called "problem texts" on such issues as predestination, apostasy, or eschatology were often sidestepped, ignored, or generalized in ways that would not offend or prove divisive. Southern Baptist beliefs and actions were presumed to be Bible doctrines. Like some other

10. "Thousands Pledge to 'Share Jesus Now,' " *Baptist Standard*, Jan. 18, 1989, p. 4.

American denominations, the SBC "tended to sanctify indiscriminately all the various elements of doctrine and practice that it adopted for whatever reason, under the supposition that it followed a blueprint revealed in the Word of God."[11]

Piety and Prayer

Prayer is also a significant element of Southern Baptist piety since it is the source of the ongoing encounter with the divine presence. Through prayer the individual and the believing community share common concerns and participate in the ministry of intercession. The midweek prayer meeting is one organizational expression of the Baptist concern for both corporate and individual prayer. Born on the frontier, prayer meetings provided opportunity for Christians to share personal and collective needs and to offer intercession for others. Here believers learned how to pray in public and were instructed in the language of Southern Baptist prayer. Although most contemporary SBC churches continue to hold a weekly prayer meeting, many members complain that it has become "another preaching service," a business session, or something other than a gathering devoted exclusively to prayer. Nonetheless, faithful attendance at prayer meeting remains an outward and visible sign of commitment to Christ and the church. Personal piety and church attendance go hand in hand in the SBC.

Piety and Ethics

A number of scholars have documented the relationship between piety and ethics in Southern Baptist life. All agree that the denomination and its churches generally gave greater attention to the personal rather than the corporate dimensions of ethical behavior. Stereotypes and caricatures of Southern Baptist morality and moralism abound. Though the ethical code seems less rigorous today—a fact lamented by many of the faithful—the list of prohibitions was formidable. For generations, Southern Baptist preachers denounced cussing, smoking, drinking, gambling, sexual promiscuity, short hair on women, long hair on men, pants on women, short pants on anybody, mixed swimming, stealing, lying, cheating, gossiping, gluttony, "sitting on the back row" at church, and

11. Sidney Mead, "Denominationalism: The Shape of Protestantism," in *Denominationalism*, ed. Russell Richey (Nashville: Abingdon, 1977), p. 80.

"backsliding," the failure to attend church services regularly. The distinction between venial and mortal sins was often difficult to determine. In God's sight one sin was as bad as another. Small sins were the seeds of larger ones. For example, temperance where alcohol was concerned really meant total abstinence. For many Southern Baptists there was no way to take just one drink and avoid the possibility of sin.

In spite of the caricatures of Baptist moralism, there were important social and communal implications behind the prohibitions. Some of the regulations were formulated on the American frontier when church discipline provided a basic form of law and order in many communities. Beyond the legalism there was a strong concern for promoting the stability of family and society. At the same time, most Southern Baptists gave the question of corporate morality only limited attention. As conversionists, they were convinced that society could be changed only by individuals born of the Spirit. Only through the infusion of divine grace would individuals be able to resist temptation and persevere ethically and spiritually.

Perhaps the hesitancy to focus on corporate ethics extensively was also related to the institutions of slavery and segregation in the South. Too much attention to corporate sinfulness would require a response to institutional racism in southern society. Racism was a major challenge to Southern Baptist piety. Indeed, the emphasis on personal piety and individual morality meant that preachers could urge believers to treat blacks with Christian kindness, while avoiding the question of racism perpetuated by the entire culture. Racism and piety coexisted throughout Southern Baptist life. Southern Baptists were encouraged to "love the souls" of their black neighbors and to respond to them with charity, but all within the limits of appropriate social segregation. It is one of the great paradoxes of Southern Baptist piety and ethics that a people who sought to follow the teachings of Jesus so closely and sincerely should have participated in racism, bigotry, and segregation so willingly. Will Campbell uses the term "racist Jesus" to describe this paradoxical piety.[12] It seems an appropriate appellation. Genuine piety and spiritual insight had its blind side in racial attitudes.

Piety and Program

Piety is also highly individualized in SBC life. For some it is quietistic and personal, evident in faithful church attendance, private spirituality,

12. Will D. Campbell, *Brother to a Dragonfly* (New York: Continuum, 1977), p. 151.

and a determination to live according to the teaching of Holy Scripture. Others reflect a similar orientation, but display their piety in greater activism, especially through aggressive personal evangelism. These are the "soul-winners" intent on giving a direct witness to every person they meet.

But all Southern Baptists are encouraged to be actively involved in the life of the Christian community, particularly the local congregation. Such persons often take great pride (in a humble sort of way) at being at church "every time the doors open." They represent the backbone of the local congregation—funding its budget, serving on its committees, and reflecting its witness in the community. One of the primary purposes of the denominational organization was to develop programs which encouraged the practice of piety in the lives of Christian believers. Through literature and organizational techniques the denomination shaped the nature and practice of Southern Baptist spirituality.

A Programmed Piety

Southern Baptist educator Linda Givens suggests that the denomination developed a "programmed piety," establishing an essentially programmatic approach toward the nurture of the spiritual life. Givens traces the evolution of that programmatic response to spirituality as it was evident during the years 1920-1959, the same period when elaborate denominational organization and bureaucracy took shape.[13] Instructional literature for Christian living was produced by various denominational agencies for use in the local church. Sunday School provided weekly, systematic instruction in the Scriptures. Through use of the Uniform Series of lessons Southern Baptists followed a cycle that periodically surveyed most of the Bible. These materials were written by Southern Baptist authors and published by the Sunday School Board.

Training Union (later called Church Training, now called Discipleship Training) was also a source of instruction in particular aspects of spirituality. Originally Training Union was intended to provide instruction in doctrine, history, ethics, and Christian citizenship, all with a biblical and Baptist base. In many churches it was held prior to the Sunday evening worship service. Weekly lessons were divided into

13. Linda Mays Givens, "A Programmed Piety: Education For Spirituality in Southern Baptist Study Course Literature 1908-1986" (unpublished Ed.D. dissertation, Southern Baptist Theological Seminary, 1988).

segments or "parts" to be presented by members of each specific age group; unlike Sunday School, members of both sexes participated in the Training Union experience. Generations of Southern Baptist laypeople testified to having first learned to speak publicly by giving a "part" in the weekly TU program. One of the clearest signs of spiritual slothfulness was "reading" your part—rather than telling it in your own words. Good programs were the result of diligent preparation throughout the week.

Short-term, intensive instruction in specific aspects of spiritual formation came through denominational "Study Courses," scheduled throughout the year. The convention published a diverse collection of training and devotional literature in study course books throughout this century. Members who completed the courses were rewarded with certificates in what was essentially a denominational form of continuing education. The titles of study course materials illustrate the type of spiritual instruction they provided: *Living Abundantly; The Growing Christian; Joy in Church Membership; Living in the Faith; Progress in the Christian Life; Deepening the Spiritual Life; Alcohol and Christian Influence; Growing in Christian Personality; God Calls Me;* and *Vital Problems of the Christian Life.*[14]

Givens's study provides significant insights into the relationship of denominational program to Southern Baptist piety. First, leaders insisted that Southern Baptist writers were the best resources for telling other Southern Baptists how to live as Christians. Again, the denomination sought to provide all the necessary resources for the spiritual pilgrimage of every Southern Baptist. Non-Southern Baptist literature might be helpful and offer a spiritual blessing, but only as a supplement to denominationally produced material. Too much reliance on other sources of spiritual instruction might dilute Baptist identity and doctrine, thereby undermining genuine biblical faith. Churches could be sure that SBC literature "excelled in regard to scriptural accuracy and doctrinal correctness."[15] Most Southern Baptist churches generally accepted this idea.

Through a series of organizational incentives, churches and church members validated their loyalty by support for and participation in denominational programs. These programs also provided uniform instructional materials that were inexpensive and readily available for congregational consumption, thus providing an important

14. Ibid., p. 92.
15. Ibid., p. 79, citing Arthur Flake, *Building a Standard Sunday School* (Nashville: Convention Press, 1911), p. 57.

service to the churches. Readers across the South were introduced to a common core of theological definitions that were distinctly Southern Baptist. Throughout most of the twentieth century, therefore, Southern Baptists avoided extensive involvement with other Christian denominations, even other evangelicals, lest such entanglements dilute their brand of Baptist identity and solidarity.

Second, Givens's study shows that the denomination builders increasingly followed a corporate model shaped by American business principles, not only in fiscal administration of the SBC but also in their approach to spiritual formation itself. The corporate approach reached its height in 1956 when the convention administrators engaged in an extensive self-study and reorganization. The firm of Booz, Allen, and Hamilton Management Consultants played a significant role in that reorganization and in promoting the business model for use in convention structures.[16] The influence of this approach contributed to the view that spirituality was something that could be quantified as well as qualified. Spiritual formation could be reduced to certain biblical "principles" that could then be outlined and circulated as systematic guides to personal piety. Givens writes that, "By the middle of the century, the truth which believers were competent and responsible to discover consisted in a specific divinely ordained life plan. Success for the Christian meant finding and then fulfilling God's divine purpose."[17] God had ordained certain "laws of growth" for the individual Christian and the church. When these were discovered and applied, successful Christian living and commensurate church growth were bound to occur.[18]

Third, Southern Baptist spirituality was closely linked to service in the local congregation as well as the denomination at large. At times, Southern Baptists seem to equate Christianity with church attendance. Implicitly or explicitly, the best Christians are thought to be those who demonstrate loyalty to the programs and activities of the church. Indeed, many Southern Bapists seem uncomfortable with or suspicious of contemplation and quietism. Rightly or wrongly, activism became a measure of genuine Christian devotion. Those who participated rigorously in the life of the church were often viewed as the most outstanding Christians. Preachers and laity alike acknowledged that activism did not guarantee genuineness of faith and warned of the dangers of equating church attendance with true Christianity. The fact that many of those "reconverted" and rebaptized in SBC life are often among the most active

16. Ibid., pp. 68-69.
17. Ibid., p. 72.
18. Ibid., p. 75.

church members gives at least some evidence of the continuing struggle with these two issues.

Activism in congregational and denominational life remains a major tenet of Southern Baptist faith. Churches and denominational programs continue to demand a high degree of participation. To this day many Southern Baptists affirm a significant correlation between the depth of Christian commitment and the extent of participation in church activities.

Meetings abound in Southern Baptist churches. In addition to the full day of Sunday activities, most SBC churches have a midweek prayer service and perhaps an additional evening for "visitation" when pastor and laity visit the homes of "prospects." Choirs, teachers, youth, Women's Missionary Union, Men's Brotherhood, and deacons also hold frequent meetings. Add church socials, revival meetings, study courses, Bible studies, and other special emphases and you have a brief and exhausting example of the programmed piety of SBC life. Such rabid activism accounts for much of the energy of the SBC as well as its statistical, financial, and evangelical success. The convention succeeded in inspiring a powerful sense of loyalty among its constituents. Theologically, however, such activism indicates that a people who talk a great deal about salvation by grace alone also maintain a strong sense of works-righteousness regarding the practice of Christianity.

Thus, a genuine and self-sacrificing piety permeates Southern Baptist life. The denomination nurtured that piety within the context of a peculiarly Southern Baptist ethos. Other Protestant denominations maintained similar organizations and programs, but not with the particular Southern Baptist touch. As the resources for spiritual formation became more pluralistic and less distinctively Southern Baptist, denominational identity and loyalty were difficult to sustain.

Populism

Much Southern Baptist behavior, identity, and practice has been shaped by a strong populist element. Alongside denominational programs and policies, there existed a sense of the SBC as a people's church, energized by the rhetoric of Southern Baptist preaching. Local church autonomy, individual conversion, and democratic polity created a context in which populist sentiments flourished. This spirit had the potential to enlist Southern Baptist multitudes in denominational crusades or to turn them away from denominational bureaucracy.

Populism and Early Denominationalism

Baptist individualism and a suspicion of denominational hierarchies made populism a force to be reckoned with from the very beginning. Such populism often pitted one segment of the clergy against another. Nineteenth-century religious populists deplored the clerical elitism of the South's "gentlemen theologians." As Brooks Holifield points out, these populists "complained of the power in the hands of the urban clergy."[19] Alexander Campbell, the nemesis of many Baptists, attracted many followers with his denunciation of "the extravagance, show, and pomp of city congregations."[20]

Historian Wayne Flynt notes that southern populism reflected a class consciousness that had both political and religious overtones. The leadership among southern Methodists and Baptists came from "the First Church elite, which dominated small towns and cities." This segment of the denomination was often at odds with "a subchurch dominated by poor whites."[21] This sense of insider against outsider in denominational life remains a powerful and divisive force in the SBC, one not overlooked by fundamentalists in their drive for dominance.

The early denomination builders were not all populists in their background and orientation. Many were Southern gentry, the products of elite economic and educational opportunities. Most, however, recognized the populist dimension in Southern Baptist life and used their powerful rhetorical skills to gain the support of the masses in the great cause of the new denomination.

James Pettigrew Boyce was such a leader. Born in 1827, Boyce was the son of Ker Boyce, "the wealthiest man in South Carolina."[22] His formal education included study at Brown University and Princeton Seminary. Yet when he took the lead in founding Southern Baptist's first theological seminary in 1859, Boyce was determined that it should not be an elitist institution. He proposed that students with and without formal educational backgrounds should be permitted to study at the new seminary. He also proposed that those students with outstanding scholarly abilities should be specially prepared as theological educators. The Southern Baptist Seminary was at once a school for both future

19. E. Brooks Holifield, *The Gentlemen Theologians* (Durham, N.C.: Duke University Press, 1978), p. 49.

20. Ibid.

21. J. Wayne Flynt, *Dixie's Forgotten People* (Bloomington: Indiana University Press, 1980), p. 53.

22. William A. Mueller, *A History of the Southern Baptist Theological Seminary* (Nashville: Broadman, 1959), p. 17.

preachers and teachers. Both kinds of ministers would aid the churches and the convention.[23] Boyce's patrician roots did not keep him from recognizing the populist character of the SBC. By promoting a more populist approach to theological education Boyce helped expand the base of support for the denomination and its fledgling seminary. It also stayed the fears of certain antieducation factions.

Populist Rhetoric

Whether populist or patrician, such individuals as Boyce, E. Y. Mullins, J. B. Gambrell, George W. Truett, Herschel Hobbs, and other denomination builders were master rhetoricians, able to articulate the denominational vision, not in bureaucratic procedures, but in biblical and spiritual imagery. By recognizing and responding to the populist dimension, SBC denominationalists were able to unite a diverse, restless, and sometimes unruly people in common endeavor. Those leaders had to learn how to appeal to the hearts and souls of Southern Baptist people.

Populist denominational preachers rallied opposition to antidenominational assaults on convention programs and unity. At no time was this more evident than in the response of George W. Truett and other denominationalists to an early fundamentalist attack on the convention led by J. Frank Norris, the pastor of First Baptist Church, Fort Worth, Texas. Norris was the consummate populist with an ability to sway multitudes through dynamic, colorful, and ironic rhetoric. He was also a rebel who refused to conform to the demands of the denominational "machine," as he called it, particularly in its elaborate financial programs for convention support. Norris loved nothing better than to bash the SBC bureaucracy for its supposed dictatorial mandates and its toleration of liberalism in schools and agencies. George Truett, the pastor of First Baptist Church, Dallas, was no friend of liberalism, yet neither would he permit the flamboyant Norris to control the destiny of the SBC. Truett was "the acknowledged leader of Texas Baptists," and he stood toe-to-toe with Norris, responding to his every challenge regarding the convention and its procedures.[24] Even the evangelist T. T. Martin, himself of populist sentiments, joined the fight against Norris and his "destructive work" which Martin charged was "turning thousands . . . from the

23. Ibid., pp. 22-27.
24. Bobby D. Compton, "J. Frank Norris and Southern Baptists," *Review and Expositor* 79 (Winter 1982), p. 67.

co-operative work of Baptists."[25] Ultimately, Norris took his congregation out of the SBC and would probably have precipitated a larger schism were it not for the work of Truett and other denominationalists whose rhetorical skills and populist appeal matched those of Norris. Truett thus retained the loyalties of persons who nonetheless were stirred by Norris's dynamic preaching and anti-institutional sentiments.

Historian W. W. Barnes recounts an event in the SBC that also illustrates the way in which denominationalists could turn their rhetoric against populist endeavors. At the 1949 annual meeting of the SBC, opponents of ecumenical alliances proposed an amendment to the convention's constitution that read: "No one who belongs to or is affiliated with any state or local council of churches which is connected with or sponsored by the Inter-council Field Department of the Federal Council [of churches of Christ] or any one or more of its six affiliated councils shall be eligible to serve on any board, agency, or institution of this Convention—either as an official, employee, or board member."[26] Barnes comments that the amendment would have penalized "any co-operating church by restricting for that church the privilege of full representation and opportunity for service by any or all of the messengers it might send to the convention."[27] It would also have had the convention itself dictating policies to local churches. The amendment was defeated, Barnes notes, largely due to the efforts of convention president R. G. Lee, a mastor orator and the pastor of Bellevue Baptist, Memphis. Lee was a rock-ribbed conservative who surely would have opposed ecumenical alliances with the liberal Federal Council of Churches. But he used his considerable power and rhetorical skills to defeat an amendment he felt was not consistent with the broader basis for denominational cooperation. Lee and other denominationalists could utilize or turn aside the populist appeal depending on whether it aided or threatened denominational unity and stability.

The Role of the Evangelist

Professional evangelists represent a colorful and influential source of Southern Baptist populism. Their charismatic personalities, populist

---

25. T. T. Martin, *The Inside of the Cup Turned Out* (Jackson, Tenn.: McCowat-Mercer, 1932), p. 1.

26. W. W. Barnes, *The Southern Baptist Convention, 1845-1953* (Nashville: Broadman, 1954), p. 119.

27. Ibid.

appeal, and "passion for souls" also makes them powerful interpreters of popular theology among grass-roots Southern Baptists. They claim a particular calling, not as local pastors, but as evangels to the world. Through seasonal revivals, protracted meetings, and mass crusades evangelists introduce multitudes of sinners to Christian faith. They also act as messengers to the church with jeremiads that prophetically warn of the dangers of worldliness, indifference, and liberalism among the people of God. Generations of Southern Baptists took their theological cues less from the writings of Boyce, Mullins, or other recognized theologians than from the sermons of professional evangelists preached in revivals and camp meetings across the South.

Professional evangelists had mobility. They were not tied to one local congregation but maintained an itineracy that spanned the region. They had the populist ability to take complex dogmas and make them simple, articulating the simple "plan of salvation" that any person could hear and understand. In the sermons of Southern Baptist evangelists the Calvinist idea of perseverance of the saints became "once saved, always saved," a doctrine that was transformed into a watchword for promoting the "eternal security of the believer" and refuting those who believed in "falling from grace."

Evangelists also maintained an uneasy relationship with the denomination. On one hand they were loyal supporters, insisting that the SBC was God's chosen vehicle for world evangelization. On the other hand, evangelists often found denominational bureaucracy a perfect target for denunciation and ridicule. When The Controversy in the SBC blossomed in 1979, many evangelists had sowed the seeds years before. In evangelistic conferences, pastors' gatherings, and local churches Southern Baptist evangelists denounced denominational compromise, corruption, and conformity. The work of James Robison provides a dramatic example of the power of the evangelist to shape both theology and popular opinion in the SBC.

During the 1970s and early 1980s Robison was one of the most popular evangelists on the Southern Baptist circuit. Based in Fort Worth, Texas, Robison traveled throughout the convention holding revivals in stadiums and local churches. A homiletical firebrand, Robison was the angry young man of SBC evangelists. In revival crusades and on syndicated radio and television programs Robison denounced the personal immoralities rampant in America, calling sinners to repentance and conversion. He also turned his skillful populist rhetoric on those institutions—government, churches, denominations, colleges, or seminaries—that appeared in his opinion to compromise with evil. Seminaries, Robinson believed, were particularly guilty of perpetuating liberalism.

At the SBC Pastors' Conference prior to the 1979 meeting of the convention, Robison let fly with a sermon denouncing liberal seminary professors and denominational bureaucrats while rhetorically preparing the way for the election of Adrian Rogers as SBC president. Warning of the danger of sowing seeds of doubt about the authority of the Scriptures, Robison told his listeners: "My friend, I wouldn't tolerate a rattlesnake in my house. . . . I wouldn't tolerate a cancer in my body. I want you to know that anyone who'd cast doubt on the Word of God is worse than cancer and worse than snakes."[28] He warned the pastors, "If you tolerate any form of liberalism, any form of skepticism of the Word of God, . . . if you belittle the importance of biblical, New Testament evangelism, you are the enemy of God."[29] The Bible, he declared, was the "infallible, inerrant Word of God." That meant that there is "no geographical error, no historical error, no scientific error, no religious error, no doctrinal error to be found in the Word of God, because God would not be party to deception by propagating error."[30] Defining academic freedom as the "search for Truth," Robison proclaimed that "the search for Truth has ended." Raising his Bible high above his head, Robison roared, "I hold Truth in my hand and it is the Word of God, the Bible."[31]

While he acknowledged that some of the denominational leaders were "great men," he warned that others were

> just like the government bureaucrats, they're ingrained and they're worse than cancer. Now listen to what I'm saying. You want to know what our leadership wants, that tries to turn their back on the truth? They want somebody to stand up at these meetings and put another coat of paint on the house. . . . The truth is, friend, that the house has a foundation that's eaten up with termites.

Southern Baptists, therefore, should "pray to God to send somebody to root those little devils out."[32] The applause was deafening.

Robison had a candidate: Memphis pastor Adrian Rogers. Not only should Southern Baptists elect a convention president who believed "the Bible is the infallible, inerrant Word of God," but they should also elect "a president who is totally committed to removing from this

28. James Robison, sermon. SBC Pastors' Conference, Houston, Texas, June 1979, audio cassette tape.
29. Ibid.
30. Ibid.
31. Ibid.
32. Ibid.

denomination anyone who does not believe that the Bible is the inerrant, infallible Word of the living God."[33] The crowd went wild.

Robison's powerful intimidating rhetoric was a major factor in the early success of the fundamentalist effort. By the mid 1980s, however, Robison's increasing association with the charismatic movement had led many of his Southern Baptist friends to distance themselves from him. He was no longer welcome in many fundamentalist Baptist churches or included on the program of the fundamentalist controlled Pastors' Conference. Robison himself had become somewhat more restrained. He confessed that he had been delivered from a "claw in the brain" and that God had given him a new ministry of reconciliation.[34] He even wrote letters of reconciliation to many of the denominational "bureaucrats" he had once attacked so vehemently. Nonetheless, Robison's power of persuasion illustrates the way in which evangelists have long interpreted theology and politics within the SBC.

Theology and Populism

Theology in the SBC has always reflected the influence of populism. Populist theology was reductionist theology, a way of simplifying more complex, laborious doctrines in order to communicate them more effectively and immediately from the pulpit. Populism no doubt accounts for much of the popular, people's theology in the SBC. Populist preachers, particularly evangelists, needed a theology that would "preach." The Regular Baptist preachers often mirrored their Puritan forebears and prepared elaborate discourses marked by theological precision and detailed biblical exposition. Not so for the farmer-preachers of the Separate Baptist tradition. They needed a theological shorthand suitable for the people in camp meetings and protracted revivals.

The Arminianization of much Southern Baptist theology of evangelism has its roots in democratic populism. Salvation was for all who would freely choose salvation. It was not limited to an "elitist" elect. The plan of salvation itself could be reduced to certain necessary but simple steps that any man, woman, or child could understand and accept. Greater emphasis on free will and human choice softened at least four of the classic five points of Calvinism. The only nonnegoti-

33. Ibid.

34. Toby Druin, "Robison-Green Seminars Draw Criticism, Cancellations," *Florida Baptist Witness*, Apr. 26, 1984.

able tenet was the perseverance of the saints or, as Southern Baptists call it, the security of the believer. As we have seen, the complexities of even that dogma were simplified in the slogan "once saved, always saved," yet another example of populist reductionism. Perseverance of the saints was a helpful idea, but for preaching purposes and debates with the Methodists, the phrase "once saved, always saved" said it all.

The doctrines of Landmarkism cut through the complexities of historical investigation to provide an easy and preachable "trail of blood" whose martyrs traced the unbroken Baptist lineage to Jesus and John the Baptist. Alien immersion and close communion not only provided Baptists with a simple guide for evaluating the validity of the ordinances but also promoted congregationalism as the only biblical form of church order.

Seminaries were particularly vulnerable to the vicissitudes of Southern Baptist populism. In the minds of many Southern Baptists, seminaries were established to promote a populist approach to doctrine, evangelism, and preaching. They were training schools where the people's preachers could be prepared for ministry. Yet they were also centers of learning where the complex issues of faith and doctrine were to be explored with integrity. While guided—and constrained—by confessional documents, they were also urged to pursue the highest degree of scholarship. This often meant that seminary professors raised issues and questions that created uneasiness and controversy among many of the churches. The methods of scholarly investigation did not lend themselves to populist slogans and easy generalizations, so SBC seminaries had to learn how to behave, how to walk the thin line between intellectual integrity and adherence to parochial dogma.

In 1859, John A. Broadus, one of the founding faculty of the Southern Baptist Theological Seminary wrote that

> in our seminary the student will not be required . . . to accept any given symbol or doctrine. The professors must accept a brief abstract of principles, as one safeguard against their teaching heresy; but they are supposed to be men [sic] who have already formed their leading opinions . . . and will therefore not be materially restricted in their inquiries, while the students will be perfectly at liberty and constantly encouraged to think for themselves.[35]

Not all SBC leaders have shared this view. In 1986, former SBC president Adrian Rogers stated:

35. A. T. Robertson, *Life and Letters of John A. Broadus* (Philadelphia: Judson, 1901), p. 2.

I do not believe it is the place of the seminary to "stretch us" and lead us into areas where we have never been before. Our theology needs to rise from our lay and pastor theologians, and this needs to be reflected in our seminaries. . . . A seminary is not a university in a quest for truth. Southern Baptists are a missionary organization spreading the truth that we hold in common.[36]

The history of Southern Baptist theological education is a history of skirmishes between the forces of populism and theological investigation. Given the difficulties in appealing to the diverse factions within the SBC, the amazing feat is that the seminaries maintained that uneasy tension as long as they did without major institutional collapse.

Fundamentalism and Populism

As demonstrated earlier, Southern Baptist fundamentalists are masters of pulpit rhetoric and populist appeal. At a time when the old denominational coalition seemed unable or unwilling to address the populist dimension of Southern Baptist life, fundamentalists had what seemed an unlimited array of pulpiteers who could motivate the multitudes in support of The Cause—the takeover crusade that would rescue the SBC from liberalism. Their rhetorical gifts were widely recognized on denominational platforms across the convention. Many were popular television preachers with large congregations, skilled at mass appeal and the use of the media. Their successes seemed proof that fundamentalism cultivated the gift of preaching while liberalism, seminaries, and bureaucracy represented the homiletical kiss of death. Fundamentalist theology itself often seemed more concise and clear than that of moderates whose complex and cumbersome qualifications were not conducive to the populist reductionism of public forums. Either the Bible was the inerrant, infallible Word of God or it was fraudulent. Any attempt at qualification was deemed liberal equivocation.

Populist preaching immediately put many moderates on the defensive. For years they had succeeded by being indirect and nonconfrontive. In fact, direct confrontation was anathema to many seasoned denominational campaigners. But the moderates were operating from an anachronistic game plan with rules that no longer applied. They seemed to defend the status quo in the face of a prophetic populism. Perhaps the greatest failure of the moderates early on in The Controversy

36. *Florida Baptist Witness*, May 29, 1986, p. 7.

was the loss of the pulpit—particularly at the national conventions—to the fundamentalist preachers.

Sometimes fundamentalist populism went too far, however. Their rhetorical techniques, honed in the sectarian environment of SBC churches, led to difficulties in the national arena. When SBC president Bailey Smith declared in a public forum in 1980 that "God Almighty does not hear the prayer of a Jew," he was probably repeating a statement made frequently to crowds of born-again Christians who echoed approving "amens" in faithful affirmation of the uniqueness of the Christian gospel. In the public arena, however, that simplistic confession resembled a dangerous racial slur, "the stuff of which holocausts are made," as one critic observed.[37] At least temporarily, fundamentalists were on the defensive. They had been caught on video tape crossing the line between religious conviction and bigotry.

Similarly, when fundamentalist leader Paige Patterson declares that his movement has succeeded in delivering the SBC from the hands of bureaucrats and placed it back into the hands of "the pastors and laity," he sounds like the populist crusader. When he then suggests that laypeople should be subject to their pastors, indeed, that they should "mimic, trust and obey them," he sounds like a new bureaucrat or an old demagogue.[38] Today's populism may become tomorrow's elitism.

Few can deny that populism is a powerful source of identity and motivation for the people called Southern Baptists. Throughout the convention's history such rhetoric has helped to unite a diverse people in common crusades and missionary endeavors. When the old denominational consensus prevailed rhetoric was a way of calling the group back to the unity of witness and mission. Today it merely exacerbates division. Today's convention is so badly fragmented that even the use of populist rhetoric is itself a divisive issue within the denomination, as a growing segment is turned off by what it sees as rhetorical manipulation in all convention affairs. In other words, the old rhetoric does not rally or unite the faithful as it once did. Cynicism in both theological camps has taken its toll.

37. E. Glenn Hinson, "An Open Letter to Dr. Bailey Smith," *Western Recorder*, Sept. 17, 1980, p. 7; *Newsweek*, Nov. 10, 1980, p. 76.

38. Larry E. High, "Bible Says Pastor Clearly the Church 'Ruler': Patterson," *Biblical Recorder*, Nov. 26, 1988, p. 6.

Convention Politics

In his monumental work *Democracy in America,* Alexis de Tocqueville observed of American religion in the early nineteenth century, "you meet with a politician where you expect to find a priest."[39] He might well have described the Southern Baptist Convention. Some acquaintance with the fine art of convention politics is necessary for those who wish to function in the denomination. It is no easy task. Individualism, congregational autonomy, and democratic populism often mean that the denomination, its agencies, and churches are ever at the mercy of the moment. Moderates and fundamentalists alike know well that majorities are difficult to sustain. Today's mandate quickly becomes tomorrow's mistake. Support for one position can falter from one annual meeting to the next. Such political realities are frustrating for many Southern Baptists, particularly those on both left and right who see politics as destructive to orthodoxy, integrity, and the sense of the prophetic. Yet most ministers soon realize that survival requires recognition of the realities of SBC politics.

Ministerial Politics

It begins at the local level. Congregational polity and diversity require ministers to confront issues of politics and compromise in each church they serve. Pastors and laity share a congregational "balance of power" that is always difficult to sustain. Ministers must choose among a variety of ministerial role models who are, in a sense, "creators" of certain types of ministerial identity. Will they be chief executive officers, directing every facet of congregational life? Will they be "enablers" or "equippers" who challenge and train the church in the work of the ministry? Will they be "partners" who share power and responsibility with the laity? Will they combine elements of those and other models to meet the needs of specific congregations? Congregations learn soon enough how to define the basic skills and emphases of their leaders. Sometimes labels can undermine ministers with faint praise. "Our pastor is more of a teacher than a preacher" can also mean, "He can't preach very well." "The pastor is a fine preacher, but not so good at counseling" may imply that the minister is unapproachable, or even unfriendly. Pastors who maintain the proper balance can usually stay for longer periods. But the average pastoral tenure in the SBC is ap-

39. Sidney Mead, "Denominationalism: The Shape of Protestantism," in Richey, *Denominationalism,* p. 82.

proximately two to four years, suggesting that the truly multitalented leader cannot realistically fulfill these goals.

Until recently, most southern communities featured a cluster of SBC churches that reflected the conservative middle and maintained generally strong support for denominational programs and policies. The community might also have a few "alternative" churches, which leaned more discernibly to the left or the right and were recognized as the "liberal" or the "fundamentalist" churches in town. These congregations often called pastors who expressly represented their more ideologically homogeneous identity. Ideological purity did not guarantee unity, however. Pastors who pushed too hard often had a major confrontation on their hands.

If the denomination has avoided a major split, many of its member congregations have not been so fortunate. Indeed, SBC churches give validity to the old saying that Baptists "multiply by dividing." Congregational schisms take many forms. Sometimes a controversial pastor leaves, taking a segment of the church along. Sometimes the pastor remains while a segment of the congregation pulls out. There are some significant indications that the spirit of compromise is becoming a lost art in the SBC. Recent studies suggest that clergy terminations are increasing at an alarming rate.[40] The Controversy also illustrates that the center is fast disintegrating in the SBC and that churches are being forced to choose between fundamentalist and moderate visions for the denomination. New political realities require new strategies for the present generation of ministers in the SBC.

Theological Education and Denominational Politics

Southern Baptist seminaries have long been places in which students were prepared for service in the convention and instructed, implicitly or explicitly, in the art of denominational politics. College and seminary professors were charged with introducing students to the diversity and complexity of theological issues while preparing them for ministry in a particular ecclesiastical context. Theological educators sought to promote the rigors of academic inquiry while affirming spiritual formation and preparation for ministry. It was no easy task. Thus professors often warned their classes not to tell their parishioners "everything you learned in seminary, at least not in the first month you are in a new

---

40. Jim Lowry, "Survey Shows 2,100 Pastors Fired During Past 18 Months," *Baptist Standard,* Nov. 30, 1988, p. 5.

church." One of the unspoken rules among some SBC ministers was that not all theological knowledge regarding the use of Scripture, dogma, ethics, and history could or should be transposed instantly in the parish setting. At the same time, ministers themselves were called to instruct their churches in theology, doctrine, and critical thinking. Applying theological education in the local congregation requires wisdom as well as knowledge. There is always the danger that professors and students will perpetuate a kind of sanctified duplicity, protecting the gnosis (secret knowledge) imparted in the seminary classroom. Even fundamentalists are not immune to this danger. They also acknowledge that certain ideas and doctrines are more complex than populist rhetoric implies. Thus denominational seminaries were to provide graduate education, within a crucible of spiritual development. They were to function on the cutting edge of theological investigation while preparing ministers to function according to certain expectations of the constituency. In order to function within the SBC, professors were compelled to be aware of denominational politics.

Many seminary graduates often sought to describe their educational experience in ways that would reassure their parishioners of their orthodoxy. Some felt compelled to make such confessions as "I spent three years in seminary, but it did not change me a bit," or something to that effect. They had run the gauntlet, secured the necessary credentials, but their orthodoxy had remained intact.

Pastors also learned how to say things so as to maintain the conservative middle. Many a pastor and denominational administrator lived by the adage: "You can say anything to your people, as long as you know how to say it." That idea became the watchword of denominationalists throughout much of this century. On one level, it was quite correct. Pastors had to earn the right to be prophetic with their congregations. They could speak freely because they had been with their people in the dark nights of the soul—death, sickness, and tragedy. At the same time, this approach perpetuated the idea that the prophetic could always be made palatable and that those who created controversy over doctrine or ethics were simply guilty of bad judgment or poor taste. Worst of all, perhaps, it implied that Southern Baptist people could be "handled," even manipulated, by the perceptive minister-politician. Compromise remains an essential element of SBC life. Since 1979, however, the old rules of compromise and confrontation have changed irrevocably at every level of SBC life.

Denominational Politics

In many ways, the art of denominational politics in the SBC is simply local church politics writ large. As noted earlier, denominationalists were forced to struggle with diverse churches and individuals who promoted innumerable methods and doctrines for fulfilling the gospel, Southern Baptist style. Essentially, denominational administrators learned how to wait out the fads and the occasional swing away from the conservative middle. They established particular bureaucratic machinery aimed at holding the denomination on course amid the vicissitudes of controversy, liberal professors, and crusading evangelists. The machinery was surprisingly efficient but bureaucratically inert, difficult to maneuver off its programmatic course, a course founded on compromise and a certain degree of theological ambiguity.

In his book *Trial as by Fire: Southern Baptists and the Religious Controversies of the 1920s,* James Thompson provides an illustration of the way in which SBC denominationalists sought to maintain their conservative credentials and opposition to modernism while distinguishing themselves from the fundamentalism of the 1920s. He writes that SBC conservatives "trod a treacherously narrow path, for in rejecting fundamentalism they had to avoid the appearance of endorsing modernism."[41] Thompson notes several reasons for the effort of conservatives to keep their distance from fundamentalism. First, they disliked the "frantic acrimony" of the fundamentalist movement. Second, fundamentalist fear of modernity created a reaction against learning and education that SBC conservatives—particularly educators like E. Y. Mullins—could not accept. Third, Thompson says, "many Southern Baptists resented the fundamentalist demand for adherence to a unique interpretation of Christian orthodoxy."[42] In other words, Southern Baptist denominationalists were not willing to have fundamentalist definitions of dogma imposed on the entire convention. Finally, Thompson's research illustrates that denominationalists rejected fundamentalism because it was divisive and detrimental to the Grand Compromise on which the SBC was built. Many feared that fundamentalist control of the convention would lead to fragmentation, even schism. Denominationalists insisted that they were for the fundamentals of Christian faith and that their beliefs were not very different from those of fundamentalists. Yet they determined not to act like

---

41. James J. Thompson, *Trial as by Fire: Southern Baptists and the Religious Controversies of the 1920s* (Macon: Mercer University Press, 1982), p. 80.
42. Ibid., p. 81.

fundamentalists in ways that would threaten the basis of denominational unity.

This refusal to narrow doctrinal definitions toward the right presented the convention with another major question: what were the doctrinal parameters toward the left? What scholarly pursuits were acceptable for orthodox Southern Baptists and what were not? Many convention leaders viewed the so-called Elliott and Broadman Commentary controversies as evidence of "course corrections" that established doctrinal safeguards on the left. They apparently did not recognize that the existence of any form of critical biblical studies in Southern Baptist schools and churches was unacceptable to many in the SBC. As fundamentalists saw it, the fact that such studies were pursued at all by people receiving Southern Baptist funds was evidence that the convention was turning away from orthodoxy. Denominationalists were no doubt naive in their belief that the SBC could continue to include advocates of both positions and still avoid major confrontation.

In the recent controversy fundamentalists appear to have been more successful in articulating their vision of the nature of the SBC than have moderates. The fact is, both elements could not have existed together indefinitely. The current success of the fundamentalists means that much of the earlier distinction between belief and action is now lost, that in the minds of the new establishment the SBC should both believe and behave like a fundamentalist denomination. Individuals who fail to combine those elements will no longer be appointed to convention boards of trustees or other denominational positions. By refusing to act like fundamentalists the early denominationalists opened the door to greater theological diversity—the very fact the fundamentalists feared. By creating a Southern Baptist way of acting that allowed room for fundamentalist and nonfundamentalist alike the denominationalists had sought to avoid schism over narrow definitions of dogma. One could be a fundamentalist or not a fundamentalist and still remain a Southern Baptist.

Today's Southern Baptist fundamentalists insist that a majority of persons in the convention acted and believed like fundamentalists all along. They declare that the denominational bureaucracy inhibited those beliefs and obscured the will of the people in their effort to retain control. In their minds, the fundamentalist movement is less a takeover than a restoration of the beliefs of the silent majority. Moderates say that fundamentalists are redefining the beliefs and behavior of the entire convention in ways that are exclusive, not inclusive, thereby repudiating years of Southern Baptist openness to diversity. Moderates who remain in the new SBC might not have to change their beliefs but they certainly would have to modify their behavior according to the fundamentalist model.

Religious Language: The Piety of Denial

For generations, a powerful source of denominational unity was found in "the language of Zion," a particular way of talking Southern Baptist. This pious language represented a kind of code that was acceptable to various ideological subgroups in the denomination. An important tactic for confronting controversy was "when in doubt, spiritualize." Pious rhetoric was a powerful tool for dealing with denominational politics. Whenever tensions reached the boiling point, whenever controversy seemed irreconcilable, preachers would restore order and unity with the language of spiritualization, an appeal to personal piety and heart religion, those ideals around which all Southern Baptists could agree and unite. This language represented an appeal to those spiritual truisms—"if we would all pray and dedicate ourselves completely to Christ we would not have these problems"—that no genuine believer could deny. Spiritualizing was a way of taking the edge off controversy and calling the convention to the spiritual dimension of its common life. It often grew out of deep piety and sincere spirituality. It was also one way in which a highly individualistic and pietistic people called themselves back to those spiritual foundations that transcended other differences.

Spiritualizing was also a way of avoidance. It fostered what might be called the piety of denial. By reverting to the language of Zion, Southern Baptists often covered over their real problems with pat answers, glib generalizations, and spiritual truisms. Hard questions, difficult decisions, corporate struggles, and personal disagreements were often concluded with an appeal to piety. Preachers might say the most terrible things about fellow Christians but attempt immediate reconciliation in the confession, "I love you, brother." While such rhetoric was often a genuine element of SBC piety, it also became a way of manipulating issues and people, a convenient method for tying up every crisis in order to end on an overtly spiritual and at least *publicly* harmonious note.

Genuine piety, callous manipulation, and populist rhetoric are often linked inseparably at SBC gatherings. The 1988 annual meeting of the SBC illustrates the point. At the preconvention Pastors' Conference fundamentalist patriarch W. A. Criswell told cheering pastors that today's liberals "call themselves moderates. However, a skunk by any other name still stinks."[43] Two days later, moderates and fundamentalists played political hardball over the election of the convention president. Two prominent SBC pastors, Richard Jackson and Jerry Vines, both acknowledged inerrantists, were the candidates. Vines, the fundamentalist-supported candidate, was elected by a margin of 692 votes out of 31,291 votes cast. Two days later, in the annual convention sermon, Joel Gregory, a popular convention preacher and conservative Texas pastor, warned messengers that "we are at a flashpoint. Southern Baptists cannot survive many more months of personal animosity in our midst."[44] His sermon calling for prayer and reconciliation was a dramatic presentation, praised by moderates and fundamentalists alike as a spiritual highlight of the annual meeting. Yet most people knew that nothing had changed, that the game would still be played, the intrigues would be perpetrated, and the hard questions would remain unsolved. Some of the same people who earlier in the week applauded uproariously when W. A. Criswell denounced SBC moderates as "skunks" amened Gregory's call for spiritual reconciliation—and apparently saw no contradiction in their actions. The convention ended on a "spiritual high," but The Controversy continued. The piety of denial made everyone feel better, but it changed little.

The language of Zion is endemic to SBC life. It simply becomes second nature for functioning in the SBC. It expresses genuine piety, orthodoxy, and community. It is a language of faith, but like any language it can also become a way of avoiding the hard questions of individual and institutional life. The issue here is not whether these spiritual truisms are appropriate but that they are an inseparable element of denominational rhetoric and populism. They illustrate that being a Southern Baptist is at once a way of believing, acting, and talking. Religious language can become a kind of spiritual "doublespeak" that covers a multitude of hidden agendas and corporate policies.

Moderates and fundamentalists alike are well schooled in the art of spiritualization. They know how to speak the language of Zion when necessary—some are simply better at it than others. The language is a way of assuring the listener that the speaker is a person of faith whose heart religion is genuine and sincere. Thus the suggestion that both sides in The Controversy use the same (pious) language but with different definitions is at least partially correct. To require elaborate definitions for the language of piety is to destroy something of its use as a tool for

43. Barbara Stewart, "Soul Searching," *Florida Magazine*, Sept. 11, 1988, p. 11.
44. Bill J. Leonard, "The Future is Now for Southern Baptists," *The Christian Century*, July 6-13, 1988, pp. 628-30.

consensus, trust, compromise, and, above all, spirituality itself. Such a way of talking may also involve the language of sanctified duplicity, whereby the masses are swayed, policies are established, and the game of denominational politics is played. Participation in the Southern Baptist Convention, like participation in any religious institution, is not one dimensional. It is a complex way of believing and behaving in which piety, populism, and politics are inseparably related. If nothing else, the fundamentalist dominance has thrown traditional behavior patterns into an uproar. Old rules no longer apply. Learning how to behave in the new SBC may be the most disconcerting aspect of The Controversy.

CHAPTER 6

The Controversy: An Overview

IN 1925, THE SOUTHERN BAPTIST EDUCATIONAL ASSOCIATION, AN ORGANIZA-
tion composed of professors from denominational schools, declared that
the "Bible cannot be taken literally and never was meant to be."[1] The
members called upon their colleagues to "avoid alliance with either
Fundamentalism or Modernism and strive to bring them together on a
working basis."[2] These teachers feared that religious dogmatism would
inhibit scientific inquiry, particularly regarding the question of human
origins raised by Charles Darwin's *Origin of Species*. T. T. Martin, a well-
known Southern Baptist evangelist, was infuriated by the educators'
remarks. He insisted that "a college that will 'avoid alliance' with the
teaching that the Bible is the Word of God . . . has no right to go to honest
Baptists for their money."[3] Martin adamantly opposed the teaching of
evolution in Southern Baptist schools. He was convinced that the theory
of evolution undermined the veracity of Holy Scripture, and teaching it
created a context for skepticism and unbelief. He was more willing to split
the convention than to accommodate Darwinism.

In response to the Educational Association controversy, Martin
presented "A Proposal to Divide the Southern Baptist Convention." He
urged the denomination to "agree to divide peaceably" with supporters
of the Educational Association constituting one convention and conservatives forming another. If such an arrangement did not occur, Martin
warned, "there is going to be fearful division and strife."[4] Historian
Kenneth Bailey notes that the convention's hard line statement against

1. Kenneth K. Bailey, *Southern White Protestantism in the Twentieth Century* (New
York: Harper & Row, 1964), p. 65.
2. Ibid.
3. Ibid.
4. Ibid., p. 66

evolution, approved in 1926 and imposed on all SBC employees, apparently "mollified" many fundamentalists like T. T. Martin.[5] Schism was avoided, even though the anti-evolution rule for SBC staff was never really enforced.

Controversies Aplenty

Theological controversy and the threat of schism are nothing new in the Southern Baptist Convention. The history of the denomination records a succession of doctrinal debates, each related in some way to the question of biblical authority. When the SBC was formed in 1845, southerners insisted that the issues of slavery and biblical authority were inseparably related. Either the Bible approved of slavery or it did not. In the minds of many Southern Baptists, biblical literalism required acceptance of the validity of human slavery.[6]

The Landmark controversy also threatened to split the fledgling denomination both before and after the Civil War. Cultivated in the denominationally competitive environment of the American frontier, Landmarkism was a ready-made history that soon became a nonnegotiable theological position on the nature of the church. It suggested that the Baptist tradition alone had preserved the true church and its ordinances since the New Testament era. As noted earlier, William Whitsitt's historical investigations were unacceptable not simply because they undermined Landmark historiography but also because they denied the New Testament principles on which Landmark Baptist churches claimed to be founded. Whitsitt's discovery that seventeenth-century Baptists did not initially practice immersion was much more than a matter of simply reporting the results of scholarly research; it was a denial of orthodox faith. Whitsitt and his supporters were "infidels" who denied biblical authority, in the eyes of the Landmarkists.[7] Landmark patriarch J. R. Graves denounced Whitsitt and the Southern Baptist Seminary that allowed him to continue in its employ. He concluded, "We do not want German Rationalism and infidelity taught to our young ministers."[8] When conservatives threatened to cut off funds to the seminary Whitsitt resigned and the possibility of schism was avoided. Yet Whitsitt's sup-

5. Ibid.
6. Richard Furman and Francis Wayland, *Domestic Slavery Considered as a Scriptural Institution* (New York: Lewis Colby, 1845), p. 9.
7. Bailey, *Southern White Protestantism in the Twentieth Century*, p. 16.
8. Ibid., p. 14

porters and opponents alike remained in the denomination. The coalition prevailed, and Landmarkists were unsuccessful in seeking to impose their theological position on the entire SBC. Southern Baptist doctrine was not to be limited to Landmark definitions, though Landmarkists themselves were encouraged to remain Southern Baptist.

Sociologists Larry McSwain and Tom Wilkerson suggest that during the twentieth century, three major events "threatened the increasingly bureaucratic approach to internal cohesion within the SBC."[9] These conflicts were "essentially theological" and in each "the bureaucratic approach failed with a fundamentalist theological perspective prevailing by vote of the convention."[10] The first controversy involved the issue of evolution, the second concerned the use of the historical-critical method of biblical studies, and the third is the present inerrancy controversy. Only the current controversy has featured an attempt to appoint people of a single ideological persuasion to convention boards and agencies. Until now, convention appointments reflected a wide diversity of perspectives and representation. Fundamentalists were not excluded from service on boards of trustees and other convention offices. In fact, the 1960s and 1970s witnessed the election of a series of well-known conservatives to the SBC presidency, among them fundamentalists W. A. Criswell and K. O. White.

In addition to these internal controversies, the denomination was not immune to the impact of external social and political debates, particularly those related to the civil rights movement and the Vietnam War. The response of the SBC to the tumultuous times was not lost on fundamentalists. Many opposed what they felt was the social liberalism evidenced by the denomination's Christian Life Commission in its response to the civil rights struggles in the nation. Many conservatives equated a positive response to civil rights with encouragement to civil disobedience, left-wing politics, and theological liberalism attributed to Martin Luther King, Jr., the National Council of Churches, and other advocates of racial reform.

Having won on the controversies over evolution and biblical criticism, many fundamentalists wanted to remove all vestiges of liberalism from the convention. They had been less successful in challenging the convention's stand on social and political affairs. So while the fundamentalists spoke out strongly on the issue of inerrancy and biblical interpretation, many also hoped that in winning that battle they

---

9. Larry L. McSwain and Tom Wilkerson, "Negotiating Religious Values: Dilemmas of the SBC 'Peace Committee' in Resolving Denominational Conflict," typescript, nd.

10. Ibid.

might be able to reshape the convention's response to social and political issues.

The present controversy, therefore, cannot be considered apart from earlier denominational debates. Each of these controversies flirted with schism, but avoided a major split for the reasons already outlined: (1) the unity of southern culture; (2) the power of denominational identity; (3) the hesitancy to appear too creedal; (4) the pietistic concern for heart religion; (5) the commitment to missions and evangelism; (6) a reliance on certain basic doctrinal statements that were defined broadly enough to allow for a variety of diverse theological outlooks; (7) an almost obsessive concern to avoid schism at all costs; and (8) a strategy for resolving disputes that retained the loyalty of adherents on both sides of an issue.

A Fundamentalist Agenda

For many fundamentalists, the compromise necessary for holding the denomination together was often achieved at the expense of truth. Compromise was little more than equivocation. The truth of unchanging dogma could not be sacrificed for the sake of institutional unity, and bureaucrats were as guilty as liberals in leading the denomination toward heresy. Since the denominational organization itself worked against orthodoxy by tolerating theological deviance, the denomination itself had to be changed. As many saw it, the convention was infected by a "cancer," removal of which required radical, perhaps even life-threatening, surgery.[11]

The Gathering Storm

With their victories in the earlier controversies under their belt, fundamentalists doubled their efforts at changing the overall direction of the denomination. Throughout the 1970s fundamentalism promoted not only a theological outlook but also a political agenda for gaining control. By 1979 fundamentalist dogma was articulated through a fundamentalist power bloc with a political game plan.

---

11. A variety of fundamentalists use the term "cancer" to refer to liberalism in the SBC. See James Robison, sermon, SBC Pastors' Conference, Houston, Texas, June 1979, audio cassette; and Claude L. Howe, Jr., "From Houston to Dallas: Recent Controversy in the Southern Baptist Convention," *Theological Educator,* 1985, p. 33. Howe cites William A. Powell's reference to the "cancer of liberalism."

In 1973 a group of fundamentalists formed the Baptist Faith and Message Fellowship to monitor SBC agencies for compliance to the 1963 Confession of Faith. They were particularly opposed to the use of the historical-critical method in Baptist schools. Through its periodical, the *Southern Baptist Journal* edited by William Powell, this organization sought to awaken Southern Baptists to the dangers of liberalism. Its members insisted that convention funds should not be used to support any teachers or writers who "believe that the Bible contains errors."[12] They were becoming convinced it was time for a purge.

The publication of two books by Harold Lindsell, a leading inerrantist among American evangelicals, also focused attention on the issue of biblical inerrancy. Lindsell's *The Battle for the Bible* (1976) examined the question of inerrancy in the SBC and in other evangelical communions. The section on the SBC identified numerous "liberals" including William Hull, a former provost at Southern Baptist Seminary. In a later work, *The Bible in the Balance*, Lindsell responded to his critics and continued to describe inerrancy as *the* decisive issue for the SBC. Lindsell was particularly critical of SBC seminaries, noting that the presence of strong inerrantist institutions like Criswell Center for Biblical Studies (later Criswell College) in Dallas and Mid-America Baptist Seminary in Memphis—institutions organized by and for Southern Baptists but not officially funded by the SBC—was further proof of the failure of SBC schools to fulfill their appointed task.[13]

By 1977 the Pastors' Conference of the SBC was dominated by fundamentalists who utilized it as a forum to extend their attack on liberalism and the tolerance of convention leaders toward noninerrantists in the employ of the SBC. At the 1977 Pastors' Conference held just prior to the annual SBC meeting in Kansas City, Missouri, W. A. Criswell and Adrian Rogers were among the speakers who denounced the growing influence of noninerrantists in the convention. In a sermon entitled "The Infallible Word of God," Criswell declared that the Bible contained no scientific errors and those who said it did were "false teachers."[14] The Pastors' Conference became an important vehicle for fundamentalists in

12. William Powell, *The SBC Issue and Question* (Buchanan, Ga.: Baptist Missionary Service, 1977), p. 25; and A. Christopher Hammon, "Biblical Controversy and the 1979 Southern Baptist Convention," unpublished paper submitted at Southern Baptist Theological Seminary, May 13, 1980. I am indebted to Mr. Hammon for his fine research carried out in the early years of The Controversy.

13. Harold Lindsell, *The Bible in the Balance* (Grand Rapids: Zondervan, 1979), p. 126; and Hammon, "Biblical Controversy and the 1979 Southern Baptist Convention," p. 10.

14. W. A. Criswell, audio tape by the SBC Radio-Television Commission, June 13, 1977; Hammon, "Biblical Controversy and the 1979 Southern Baptist Convention," p. 11.

denouncing liberalism and promoting possible candidates for the SBC presidency.

The Annual Meeting, 1979

Thus the stage was set for the 1979 SBC meeting at the Summit in Houston, Texas. By the time the convention convened in June, the ten-year plan orchestrated by Paul Pressler, a Houston Appeals Court judge, and Paige Patterson, the president of the Criswell Center (now Criswell College), was already set in motion. Meetings were held in at least fifteen states across the convention for the purpose of organizing to elect an inerrantist candidate. The candidate was Adrian Rogers, the pastor of Bellevue Baptist Church, Memphis. Just when Rogers decided to become a candidate is uncertain; he claims that he had made no decision on the matter until a late night prayer meeting the day before the presidential election.[15]

Paige Patterson acknowledged that he and Pressler had attended "a number of those [preconvention] meetings," and outlined two priorities of the gatherings. First, they sought "to meet together with fellow Baptists who were greatly concerned about some of the things happening in the Southern Baptist convention with a view to discussing how we could help those in leadership know what we feel the majority view point really is, and especially as it concerns the reliability of the scriptures." Second, they wanted "to discuss ways by which we might be able to secure the elected leadership of the convention from among those we know are committed to Biblical inerrancy."[16]

Paul Pressler claimed that his efforts to reshape the SBC began in 1977 after he became aware of the theological liberalism taught at Baylor University, the largest Southern Baptist-supported school in Texas. When he discovered the "garbage" perpetuated by Baylor religion professors, he began studying how the "system could be retaken" by the "grassroots constituency."[17] Pressler noted that he and Patterson made "a good team." Patterson was the theologian while Pressler understood the legal structure. They determined not to begin a movement that had no possibility of "success." By 1979 they recognized that by electing a series of SBC presidents who "know what's coming off and are deter-

15. Howe, "From Houston to Dallas," p. 36.

16. Toby Druin, "Texans Push for SBC Head Favoring Biblical Inerrancy in Campaigns in 15 States," *Western Recorder,* May 16, 1979, p. 1; and Hammon, p. 13.

17. Paul Pressler, interview with Gary North, "Firestorm Tapes," audio cassette.

mined to redirect the energies of the convention into a line that is consistent with their constituency," their efforts would succeed.[18]

By 1979, they had their first candidate in Adrian Rogers. Rogers, Pressler recalls, was in "complete sympathy" with their efforts to change the direction of the convention.[19] The fundamentalist-controlled Pastors' Conference prepared the way with sermons exalting inerrantist churches and pastors while condemning seminary professors, denominational bureaucrats, and all who would sacrifice conviction for the sake of unity. Adrian Rogers's sermon warned that liberalism was dominating Baptist schools. He proclaimed that evangelism and inerrancy were inseparable doctrines, insisting that a church with a large number of baptisms is "a conservative Bible-believing church with a pastor who believes in the inerrant, infallible Word of God."[20] W. A. Criswell followed Rogers on the program. He brought down the house when he proclaimed, "We will have a big time here, if for no other reason than to elect Adrian Rogers as president of the Southern Baptist Convention."[21] Denominational statesmen, in a gentlemen's agreement, had previously considered it unbecoming for a former SBC president formally to endorse a candidate for the office. Criswell's action not only solidified popular support for Rogers but it also signaled that things had changed in the SBC. As noted earlier, however, it was evangelist James Robison whose fire-breathing rhetoric raised the intensity of fundamentalist sympathizers to fever pitch. Liberal "rattlesnakes" and "termites" could not be tolerated in the Baptist house.[22]

On the day of the presidential election, the plan was put into action. Busloads of fundamentalist supporters appeared in time to register as messengers and vote for the president. Adrian Rogers was elected on the first ballot with 51.4 percent of the vote as divided among six candidates, some conservative, some moderate. The takeover had begun. Complaints alleging irregularities in the voting procedures simply heightened tensions, and in the long run they had little impact on the extension of fundamentalist influence.

What did matter was that fundamentalists had elected a president who would follow Pressler's plan to secure the appointment of agency

---

18. Ibid.

19. Ibid.

20. Adrian Rogers, sermon to the SBC Pastors' Conference, June 10, 1979, audio cassette; and Hammon, p. 14.

21. W. A. Criswell, sermon ɪo the SBC Pastors' Conference, June 10, 1979, audio cassette; and Hammon, p. 13.

22. James Robison, Sermon to the SBC Pastors' Conference, June 10, 1979, audio cassette.

trustees who were committed to the twin agendas of biblical inerrancy and denominational control. The plan worked something like this. The SBC president, in consultation with the two convention vice presidents, was to appoint a committee on committees. That group would in turn name a committee on boards, which would then make specific appointments to each of the boards of trustees of every national convention agency or institution.[23]

After the election of Rogers the attendance at the 1979 convention dropped off noticeably, especially from the fundamentalist side, with the result that Abner McCall, the president of Baylor University and an obvious moderate, was elected first vice president. During the next few years the fundamentalists would learn to remain for later ballots.

Nonfundamentalists (the name "moderate" had not yet evolved for this group) responded to Rogers's election with anger, shock, and disbelief. Many old convention "pros" insisted that this was merely another rightward swing of the denomination that would wear itself out in five to seven years, a familiar pattern in the SBC. Convention insiders also believed that the movement could be brought to heel by bringing the leaders into convention life thereby defusing their agenda. When the fundamentalists understood how the convention really worked, they would moderate their criticisms of the denominational system. In an attempt to extend the olive branch and introduce fundamentalists to seminary campuses and professors, three seminary presidents proposed to sponsor a series of Bible conferences presented jointly with the James Robison Evangelistic Association. The first, cosponsored by Robison and Milton Ferguson of Midwestern Baptist Seminary, was held in St. Louis, Missouri, and a second was held at Southern Seminary in Louisville. The third conference, scheduled for Southwestern Seminary in Fort Worth, was canceled by seminary president Russell Dilday because of some dispute over program personnel. The Bible conferences produced mixed results. Moderates had responded to the new denominational power bloc by showing the fundamentalists that the seminary campuses, the supposed seedbeds of liberalism, were benignly orthodox. But little real dialogue between the fundamentalists and seminary moderates actually took place. The old formulas for returning the denomination toward the institutional center were proving to be almost entirely ineffective.

In many respects 1979 was the culmination of a century of doctrinal debate and the beginning of a new denominational coalition. The first decade of The Controversy has been marked by issues and events so complex as to defy hasty or easy analysis. We can, however, trace the

---

23. Pressler, interview with Gary North, "Firestorm Tapes," audio cassette.

history of the basic events that have contributed to a decade of controversy and fragmentation in the SBC.

The Election of Presidents

The Controversy formally began with the attempt to elect fundamentalist candidates to the presidency of the Southern Baptist Convention. In that effort the fundamentalist party has scored a decade-long victory. Following his election in 1979, Adrian Rogers chose not to seek a second consecutive term. He was succeeded by Bailey Smith, then pastor of First Baptist Church, Del City, Oklahoma, who served two terms from 1980 to 1982. Smith later resigned the church to enter full-time evangelistic work. Smith was succeeded by James T. Draper, the pastor of First Baptist Church, Euless, Texas, who was considered by many to be the most denominationally "centrist" of the fundamentalist presidents. After he had served two terms, through 1984, he was followed by Charles Stanley, the pastor of First Baptist Church, Atlanta, well-known to many through his syndicated television programs. Stanley's presidency also ran for two terms, from 1984 to 1986; the second term included a major showdown in which Stanley's reelection was publicly opposed by numerous leaders of convention seminaries and agencies. Following Stanley's tenure, Adrian Rogers was reelected for two more terms, from 1986 to 1988. Rogers's successor, Jerry Vines of Jacksonville, Florida, completed the ten-year cycle that the fundamentalists had projected in 1979. While his election in 1988 was close—barely a 600 vote margin out of 31,000 votes cast—it solidified fundamentalist control. Vines was reelected by a substantial margin in 1989 as The Controversy entered its second decade.

Each of the presidents has continued to oversee the appointment of inerrantists to convention boards of trustees who, to varying degrees of commitment, agree with the fundamentalist agenda for the convention. Out of this general pattern, each board has exercised its prerogatives in various ways, some involving more controversy than others. The moderates by now are facing a new dilemma. Should they continue to oppose fundamentalist presidential candidates after ten years of failure, invest that energy elsewhere, or accept defeat and adjust to new denominational realities?

Moderates and the SBC Presidency: A Search for Candidates

Moderates were slow in developing a strategy or an agenda around which to unite. Early in The Controversy they had difficulty deciding on candidates to run against the fundamentalists. In fact, there were often several identifiably "moderate" candidates nominated at the same convention, thereby enhancing the electability of the lone fundamentalist. For a time moderates turned to denominational statesmen, individuals whose lifetime service to the convention made them highly respected and widely known. These included Grady Cauthen, the executive director of the Sunday School Board, and Duke K. McCall, the president of Southern Seminary. Neither candidate was able to overcome the fundamentalist machine. It was the day of the preachers, not the "bureaucrats," as fundamentalists called convention leaders.

That is not to suggest that moderates were slow to speak out against the fundamentalist activities. Duke McCall insisted that Baptists affirmed biblical authority and that the issue of inerrancy was divisive and unnecessary. In May 1979, in a sermon preached in the chapel of Southern Seminary, he denounced those who accused the school of liberalism. The sermon became a red flag for those fundamentalists who preached at the 1979 Pastors' Conference a few weeks later. McCall's rhetoric simply sharpened the attack of fundamentalists who claimed they were being persecuted by the denominational establishment. Moderate Houston pastor Kenneth Chafin and North Carolina pastor Cecil Sherman were also quick to denounce fundamentalist methods and actions, but many denominationalists were uncomfortable with their outspoken response.

It took almost five years of The Controversy before those who opposed the fundamentalist takeover could establish anything resembling a united front and focus their energy on a specific candidate. In 1984, a significant number of denomination executives decided that it was time to make a stand. They declared their opposition to the takeover movement and the reelection of Charles Stanley as SBC president. By this time five years of fundamentalist appointments to trustee boards was beginning to make its impact known.

Seminary presidents Russell Dilday (Southwestern), Roy Honeycutt (Southern), Randall Lolley (Southeastern), and Landrum Levell (New Orleans) led the opposition, warning that irrevocable changes would occur in denominational life if the takeover continued. It was Honeycutt, however, who aroused the greatest furor with a sermon officially entitled "To Your Tents, O Israel," but which was soon dubbed the "Holy War" sermon.

Honeycutt acknowledged that he had waited for five years before making a public challenge to the fundamentalist movement. The term "Holy War" was appropriate he said, because of "my conviction that unholy forces are at work in our midst—forces which, if left unchecked, will destroy the essential qualities of both our convention and this seminary."[24] Fundamentalism itself was a threat to various Baptist ideals including "freedom of conscience, pluralism in worship and witness, . . . and separation of church and state."[25] Soon fundamentalists—and numerous moderates—were denouncing Honeycutt for having gone too far, charging that he was escalating the conflict and that as a "hireling" of the denomination he was guilty of gross insubordination. In an interview broadcast on a Louisville television station, Charles Stanley suggested that Roy Honeycutt "should be man enough to resign [as seminary president], and if he won't then the trustees should be men enough to fire him."[26]

In April 1985, Keith Parks, the head of the SBC's Foreign Mission Board, also entered the debate with an address entitled "Will Missionaries Be Hostages of Convention Conflict?" He noted that numerous SBC churches were limiting their Cooperative Program giving because of the spreading fear of "liberalism" in convention agencies. He observed that "the missionaries are the ones becoming hostage to the conflict, and the lost of the world are the losers."[27] Parks also insisted that the fundamentalist takeover movement was pushing the SBC toward (1) "a more rigid creedal concept of dogma"; (2) "an independent local church mission program rather than a convention wide cooperative mission effort"; (3) "supplanting" the doctrinal autonomy of local churches; (4) demanding "creedal conformity"; (5) replacing the biblical concept of separation of church and state with a "civil religion"; and (6) "a carefully defined biblical view as dominant rather than trusting each individual to live under the authority of the Bible."[28] Parks thus urged that Charles Stanley not be elected president of the SBC because he and his congregation gave minimal support to the Cooperative Program and other convention causes.

Fundamentalist leaders were furious that agency heads were offering insubordinate opposition. Paige Patterson charged that Parks

24. John C. Long, "Seminary President Declares a 'Holy War' on Fundamentalists," *Louisville Courier-Journal* (Indiana edition), Aug. 29, 1984.

25. Ibid.

26. Charles Stanley, videotape interview, WHAS, Louisville, Ky.

27. Keith Parks, "Will Missionaries Be Hostages of Convention Conflict?" typescript, Apr. 19, 1985.

28. Ibid.

was trying to "impose monetary creedalism on the convention rather than doctrinal creedalism."[29] Patterson suggested that Roy Honeycutt's writing on certain texts of the Old Testament were clearly detrimental to the doctrine of biblical authority. "Honeycutt does not believe all that the Bible says," Patterson stated, "and when another denominational executive like Dr. Parks says all agency heads believe the Bible it makes him suspect, too."[30] Defending an accused liberal was as dangerous as being liberal oneself.

The charges and countercharges continued until the June 1985 meeting of the SBC in Dallas. With over 45,000 messengers in attendance it became the largest SBC meeting ever convened. Charles Stanley was reelected over the moderate candidate, Winfred Moore, the longtime pastor of First Baptist Church, Amarillo, Texas. In Moore the moderates finally seemed to have found an electable candidate. Moore was a man of impeccable conservative credentials. In any other era, his presence on a convention board of trustees might have been considered fundamentalist representation. His candidacy did cause a momentary problem for fundamentalists who had insisted that only the liberal fringe of the convention was opposing the denominational "course correction." All they could say was that Moore had been duped by liberals who were simply using him to retake control.

By 1985, therefore, the fragmentation of the SBC was indisputable. Moderates and fundamentalists were locked in head-to-head combat. This kind of public confrontation "frightened the long time advocates of the bureaucratic approach to conflict," sociologists McSwain and Wilkerson observe.[31] After five years of struggle, "there was no longer a middle to claim as the power base of the traditional convention leadership."[32] A new coalition took shape, made up of people from diverse theological and regional orientations, who agreed that they would work together to oppose the fundamentalist takeover. This loosely organized coalition is the group that came to be called the "moderates."

---

29. Ed Briggs, "Mission Board Chief Opposes Stanley Re-election," *Richmond Times-Dispatch,* Apr. 20, 1985.
30. Ibid.
31. McSwain and Wilkerson, "Negotiating Religious Values," p. 6.
32. Ibid.

A "Peace Committee" Is Formed

Meanwhile, there were still those denominational leaders who refused to believe that the divisions were irreconcilable and that the old art of compromise no longer prevailed. These consensus seekers called for the formation of some type of "peace committee" that would work out a compromise and avoid further fragmentation. In late 1984, Franklin Paschall, former pastor of First Baptist Church, Nashville, and a past SBC president, and Charles Pickering, president of the Mississippi Baptist State Convention, began separate efforts to get the two sides to the bargaining table. Pickering invited state convention presidents to a gathering to chart a process for peace. Such a meeting was convened April 11 and 12, 1985, and the procedures leading to the establishment of a Peace Committee were set in motion.[33] On May 14, 1985, the presidents offered a recommendation calling for a committee of fifteen persons made up of leaders from both sides in The Controversy as well as persons "we consider bridge-builders and middle-of-the-road people."[34] As the proposal evolved, the committee was set up to include people who were clearly identified with the two sides. The Peace Committee, both its machinations and its impact on The Controversy, merits a separate study. Here I attempt only a brief summary of its activities.

The committee held its first meeting on August 5 and 6, 1985. Twenty-two members had been appointed, including people from both ends of the theological and denominational spectrum. Many were outspoken protagonists in The Controversy. These included such well-known fundamentalists as Adrian Rogers, Jerry Vines, and Charles Stanley, and such prominent moderates as Winfred Moore, Cecil Sherman, the pastor of First Baptist Church, Asheville, North Carolina, and William E. Hull, the pastor of First Baptist Church, Shreveport, Louisiana. Denominational statesmen such as Herschel Hobbs and Albert McClellan were also included. In response to criticism regarding the omission of women on the original committee, two women were added: moderate Christine Gregory and fundamentalist Jodi Chapman. Gregory observed that the failure to add women to the initial committee was not surprising. Given our "cultural situation," she said, men simply do not think about including women in leadership positions.[35] Charles

33. Ibid., citing *Baptist Press*, Apr. 26, 1985.
34. Ibid., citing *Baptist Press*, May 17, 1985.
35. Bill J. Leonard, "Southern Baptists: In Search of a Century," *The Christian Century*, July 17-24, 1985, p. 683.

Fuller, the conservative pastor of First Baptist Church, Roanoke, Virginia, was selected as chair.

The Peace Committee met for the better part of two years, presenting its final report to the SBC annual meeting in St. Louis in June 1987. From the beginning, the committee mirrored the fragmentation of the SBC itself. Members disagreed as to the nature of The Controversy. Fundamentalists saw it as a quest for theological orthodoxy; moderates insisted that it was a political power struggle. Committee members often seemed to operate from completely different perspectives in their approach to problem solving, conflict management, and organizational dynamics. At times it seems that they could not agree on the nature of reality itself. Consensus was elusive and compromise was tenuous.

Subcommittees were dispatched to SBC agencies to conduct interviews and investigate "concerns," particularly about the seminaries. Faculty members at several institutions were asked to make written responses to questions regarding their teaching and writing. After these investigations were completed, the committee issued a statement on theological diversity in the SBC. The committee listed several examples that were "illustrative but not exhaustive," including:

1. Some accept and affirm the direct creation and historicity of Adam and Eve while others view them instead as representative of the human race in its creation and fall.
2. Some understand the historicity of every event in Scripture as reported by the original source while others hold that the historicity can be clarified and revised by the findings of modern historical scholarship.
3. Some hold to the stated authorship of every book in the Bible while others hold that in some cases such attribution may not refer to the final author or may be pseudonymous.
4. Some hold that every miracle in the Bible is intended to be taken as an historical event while others hold that some miracles are intended to be taken as parabolic.[36]

When these conclusions were made public fundamentalists were ecstatic. The Peace Committee had shown that "some" Southern Baptists held what fundamentalists considered heretical positions on a variety of theological matters. What the Peace Committee called diversity was

---

36. "Report of the Southern Baptist Convention Peace Committee," *Convention Bulletin*, June 16, 1987, p. 11.

what the fundamentalists called heresy, and the indisputable evidence seemed to vindicate their actions.

The Glorietta Statement: Compromise or Capitulation?

In response to these theological investigations, the six seminary presidents produced a document they hoped would relieve some of the pressure on their institutions and the entire denomination. The document was presented at a joint meeting of SBC agency executives and the Peace Committee held at the Glorietta Baptist Conference Center near Santa Fe, New Mexico, in October 1986. The "Glorietta Statement," as it came to be called, represented an effort by the seminary presidents to seize the initiative in the controversy by promising to provide a more intentionally positive response to inerrancy and other fundamentalist concerns in the faculties, classrooms, and curricula of their respective institutions. The statement was at once a confession of faith and a pledge to reform institutional policy. The presidents affirmed the supernatural origins of Christianity, repudiating all religious theories that deny such supernatural elements of faith. They agreed that "the miracles of the Old and New Testaments are historical evidences of God's judgment, love and redemption."[37] In perhaps the most significant and controversial segment of the document, the presidents declared that "The sixty-six books of the Bible are not errant in any area of reality."[38] The meaning of that phrase and the wisdom of including it would be debated extensively throughout the SBC. Its inclusion meant that fundamentalists had won and that the seminary presidents knew it.

The Glorietta Statement also reaffirmed the basic confessional statements used by each institution and promised a "balanced, scholarly frame of reference" that presented "the entire spectrum of scriptural interpretations represented by our constituency."[39] The presidents pledged to respect "the convictions of all Southern Baptists" and avoid "caricature and intimidation" of persons for their theological views.

Whatever else it may have been, the Glorietta Statement was another attempt by denominationalists to find some ground for compromise in The Controversy and, if possible, to slow the fundamentalist momentum. The presidents no doubt believed that it did promise some balance—that seminary faculties would be drawn from various seg-

37. Ibid.
38. Ibid.
39. Ibid.

ments of the denomination, but that a greater effort would have to be made to secure faculty who were distinctly inerrantist in their view of Scripture. The presidents even promised to sponsor three national conferences: on biblical inerrancy (1987), biblical interpretation (1988), and biblical imperatives (1989). Speakers would come largely from evangelical circles outside the SBC. The first two were held as scheduled; the third was "postponed" when only a handful of persons registered to attend.

Denominationalists around the SBC were generally pleased with the Glorietta Statement. Again, most hoped that it would take some of the edge off The Controversy, soften the rhetoric, and delay the continued talk of purges. At best, it was at least a promise of balance rather than a guarantee to secure only inerrantists for vacancies on seminary faculties. Fundamentalists, however, saw it as an admission by the seminary presidents that The Controversy was indeed theological, not political, and that the Bible was indeed inerrant in all its subject matter. Adrian Rogers called the Glorietta Statement "a significant breakthrough," while an elated Paul Pressler observed, "I'm extremely grateful for the seminary presidents finally admitting the legitimacy of the concerns which we have been expressing these eight years."[40] For Pressler, it was a vindication.

Many moderates were shocked and angered by the presidents' action. Cecil Sherman, a member of the Peace Committee and a determined foe of the takeover movement, resigned from the committee immediately upon the adoption of the Glorietta Statement. For Sherman and others, the Glorietta Statement represented the final capitulation to fundamentalism. "We will have peace," he wrote, but "moderates will no longer function as any recognizable force in the politics of the Southern Baptist Convention."[41] He resigned, he said, because he could no longer see any credibility in a Peace Committee dominated by the fundamentalist agenda. In a statement to his congregation, the Broadway Baptist Church of Fort Worth, Sherman charged that "the Peace Committee has become an agent for the work of the Fundamentalists."[42] The seminary presidents did win a reprieve of sorts. The theological "concerns" still maintained against three of the seminaries—Southern, Southeastern, and Midwestern—were dropped and the presidents

---

40. Steve Maynard and Julia Duin, "SBC Fundamentalists Win Victory in Statement on Bible's Inerrancy," *Houston Chronicle*, Oct. 24, 1986, sec. 1, p. 13.

41. Jim Jones, "Baptist Says Moderates Defeated," *Fort Worth Star-Telegram*, Nov. 4, 1986.

42. Cecil Sherman, "What About the Peace Committee?" *The Window*, Oct. 30, 1986.

themselves were charged with evaluating their respective faculties on such matters, a responsibility that was theirs all along.

Even after the Glorietta Statement and Sherman's resignation, the Peace Committee itself remained fragmented, almost to the very moment its report was submitted in St. Louis in 1987. The report included two sections. The first involved a report on the activities and findings of the committee, with particular attention to the theological and political aspects of The Controversy. The statement on political activities began with the assertion that "in the opinion of the Peace Committee, the controversy of the last decade began as a theological concern. When people of good intention became frustrated because they felt their convictions on Scripture were not seriously dealt with they organized themselves politically to make themselves heard."[43] That statement in itself demonstrates fundamentalist dominance of the Peace Committee process. The committee simply accepted reality as articulated by the fundamentalists and verified it.

Concerning theological issues in the SBC the document suggested that "most Southern Baptists" accept Adam and Eve as "real persons"; believe all biblical books were written by the authors whose names they bear; believe that the supernatural events described in Scripture are historically accurate; and believe that historical narratives of biblical writers are "accurate and reliable."[44] Not all committee members would accept this assertion, however, and that factor threatened the committee's entire report until only a few hours before it was submitted. In a last-ditch compromise measure the committee included the following minority statement in its report:

> However, some members of the Peace Committee differ from this viewpoint. They would hold that "truth without mixture of error" relates only to faith and practice. They would also prefer a broader theological perspective. Yet, we have learned to live together on the Peace Committee in mutual charity and commitment to each other. We pledge our mutual efforts to fulfill the Great Commission and we call on others within our convention to make the same pledge.[45]

When the fundamentalists agreed that this brief minority disclaimer could be added, the entire Peace Committee was able to submit the report. But while the fundamentalists were willing to participate on the Peace Committee with people who did not share their inerrantist inter-

---

43. "Report of the Southern Baptist Convention Peace Committee," p. 11.
44. Ibid., p. 12.
45. Ibid.

pretation of Holy Scripture, they were not willing, under any circumstances, to appoint such people to trusteeships on convention boards and agencies. Compromise on the Peace Committee did not mean that moderates would be allowed to participate in the trustee leadership of convention agencies.

The report also urged an end to political activity on both sides of The Controversy, specifically calling for independent newspapers and Baptist state papers to avoid inflammatory language and subject matter. The committee even advised that the terms "fundamentalist," "liberal," "fundamentalist-conservative," or "moderate-conservative" no longer be used. Unfortunately, they did not suggest new labels to replace these divisive ones. It was almost as if they hoped that The Controversy would go away if the labels were eliminated.

The Peace Committee also made a number of specific recommendations stressing denominational unity, support for the Cooperative Program, and avoidance of "unwanted extremes."[46] Seminary trustees were urged to "determine the theological position of seminary administrators and faculty members in order to guide them in renewing their determination to affirm the Baptist Faith and Message Statement of 1963," the Glorietta Statement, and their "institutional declarations of faith."[47] SBC institutions were encouraged "to build their professional staffs and faculties from those who clearly reflect such dominant convictions and beliefs held by Southern Baptists at large."[48] The committee also requested "all organized political factions to discontinue the organized political activity in which they are now engaged."[49] The report made no mention of the appointment of persons to denominational boards and agencies. Fundamentalists could infer, however, that trustee appointments, like denominational faculties and staffs, should reflect the "dominant convictions and beliefs" of the SBC as defined by the Peace Committee.

The Peace Committee Report was approved by majority vote of the convention messengers in St. Louis on June 16, 1987. Discussion was kept to a minimum, and there was limited debate over the recommendations. The Peace Committee itself remained in service for one more year, charged with overseeing the implementation of its recommendations. Many feared that it would become a watchdog agency, and there was considerable debate about its continuation. The committee was officially abolished at the annual SBC meeting in San Antonio in June 1988.

46. Ibid., p. 14.
47. Ibid.
48. Ibid.
49. Ibid.

"Peace," but No Peace

In terms of its impact on the continuing fragmentation of the SBC the Peace Committee was too little too late. By the time its work was completed the fundamentalist faction had so solidified its control of the machinery of the convention that there was little need for them to seek a compromise with moderates. They operated from a position of strength, a fact that influenced both the initial Peace Committee report and its application in convention life. The Peace Committee failed to address the appointment of only inerrantist trustees to convention boards and agencies, and the fundamentalists had no intention of changing that policy. The moderates, thus, had made numerous compromises that simply had no real effect on creating a new denominational coalition or fostering a spirit of compromise.

Many fundamentalists and not a few denominationalists suggested that if the moderates had shown greater intentionality in including inerrantists on seminary faculties and other convention agencies, The Controversy might never have occurred. They note that it is the political control exerted by the fundamentalists that led the seminary presidents to issue the Glorietta Statement, something they otherwise would never have accepted. That argument again illustrates how fundamentalists set the agenda for defining the issues and the terms throughout The Controversy.

Through their dominance of the convention the fundamentalists were able to make inerrancy an issue for the hiring and evaluation of seminary faculty where it had not been before. Before the fundamentalist takeover, seminary faculty members were asked to affirm the authority of Holy Scripture as the Word of God. After the fundamentalists had gained control, biblical authority was defined in terms of biblical inerrancy. The fact is that the seminary faculties were composed exclusively of men and women who were certainly conservative, if not always inerrantist, in their attitudes toward Scriptures. For fundamentalists, however, the question of inerrancy was nonnegotiable. At the beginning of the Peace Committee process, Adrian Rogers insisted that,

> The issue with me is almost one issue: What is scripture? There are a lot of side issues, but frankly I believe that if we can settle that one issue, that's the log causing the logjam. . . . Because I believe so much in the priesthood of the believer and our accountability to God alone, I would never, I hope till I die, compromise conviction on the altar of cooperation. This is not to say I do not believe in cooperation, but there are certain things in my life that are non-negotiable.[50]

50. McSwain and Wilkerson, "Negotiating Religious Values," p. 18.

Likewise, Rogers rejected even the occasional appointment of conservative but noninerrantist professors in denominational seminaries. "The seminaries say that they may hire one inerrantist—that's just like throwing us a bone," he insisted. "That's not reversing the trend which is what conservatives are really after. We want to see the pendulum swinging back to the right."[51] Jerry Vines, another Peace Committee member, agreed and again raised the issue of paying the salaries of noninerrantists. Professors at denominational schools were not free to teach variant interpretations of inerrancy. "Those who are deriving financial support from us should teach what we're paying them to teach," Vines concluded. "Why should we be forced to pay people to teach things that are morally repugnant to us?"[52] Vines's church gave barely two percent of its annual income to the Cooperative Program in 1987, the year Vines made that statement.

Such comments serve to illustrate why the Peace Committee report had limited success in alleviating the fragmentation of the SBC. For fundamentalists, The Controversy was primarily theological and centered on the issue of inerrancy, an issue on which no compromise was acceptable. In any areas where some negotiation was possible, the fundamentalists were the ones who by 1987 were able to negotiate from a position of strength. McSwain and Wilkerson, evaluating the Peace Committee process shortly before the report was submitted, concluded that the committee essentially accepted the "fundamentalist definition of the [SBC] problem as ideological and value-laden."[53] Thus fundamentalist solutions were the only possible conclusions for the committee to come to, since anything else would compel fundamentalists "to abandon their belief system and power base within the committee."[54] In short, the only members of the Peace Committee who could compromise were the moderates. Since their power base was eroded, the moderates were compelled to compromise in an attempt to retain at least something of their place in the denomination.

At best, the Peace Committee was a last-ditch effort to preserve the old denominational art of compromise, avoid schism, and retain a semblance of cooperation among diverse factions in the convention. What had already occurred, however, was the accumulation of power and control by a group that wanted to narrow the theological parameters of the denomination, a faction that was well on its way to accomplishing

51. Diane Winston, "Panel Seeking Southern Baptist Unity Called Deadlocked," Raleigh, N.C., *The News and Observer,* Jan. 25, 1987.
52. Ibid.
53. McSwain and Wilkerson, "Negotiating Religious Values," p. 18.
54. Ibid.

that goal. The selective implementation of the Peace Committee recommendations merely hastened the inevitable fragmentation.

Inerrancy and Authority: The Broader Issues

During the early stages of The Controversy, fundamentalists insisted that their primary concern was to preserve the integrity of Holy Scripture by making inerrancy the normative hermeneutic for biblical interpretation in the SBC. Paul Pressler continually asserted that the authority of the Bible was his primary—if not his only—goal. For the fundamentalists, that portion of the Glorietta Statement that affirmed that "the sixty-six books of the Bible are not errant in any area of reality" represented the victory of their efforts.

The line between inerrant Scripture and inerrant dogma is a thin one, however. Throughout The Controversy fundamentalists promoted a number of doctrines that they viewed as the only correct interpretation of Scripture possible for "Bible-believing" Christians. These doctrines were based on, if not inseparable from, biblical inerrancy. They included the role of women, the nature of the ministry, and the Christian response to social issues. Debate and division over these issues further accelerated denominational fragmentation.

The Role of Women

The question of women's role in church and society was the first to surface; indeed, many feared it might be more divisive than the inerrancy question. At the 1984 SBC meeting, 58 percent of the messengers voted in favor of a controversial resolution regarding the role of women in the church. Presented by the prominent evangelical theologian (and Southern Baptist) Carl F. H. Henry, the document noted that "the New Testament emphasizes the equal dignity of men and women," that both sexes received the Spirit at Pentecost, and that New Testament women "fulfilled special church service-ministries."[55] Yet it also delineated "God's delegated order of authority (God the head of Christ, Christ the head of man, man the head of woman, man and woman dependent one upon the other to the glory of God)."[56] Thus, "while Paul commends

55. SBC *Annual*, 1984, p. 65.
56. Ibid.

women and men alike in other roles of ministry and service (Titus 2:1-10), he excludes women from pastoral leadership (I Tim. 2:12) to preserve a submission God requires because the man was first in creation and the woman was first in the Edenic fall (I Tim. 2:13ff)."[57] The conclusion stated:

> Be it resolved, that we not decide concerns of Christian doctrine and practice by modern cultural, sociological, and ecclesiastical trends or by emotional factors; that we remind ourselves of the dearly bought Baptist principle of the final authority of Scripture in matters of faith and conduct; and that we encourage the service of women in all aspects of church life and work other than pastoral functions and leadership roles entailing ordination.[58]

Few people apparently noticed that a similar literalistic hermeneutic was operative in 1845 in the "biblical" defense of human slavery.[59]

In spite of the fact that resolutions at SBC meetings are accepted only as the opinion of the messengers who happen to be present in the hall at the time of the vote and are not a mandate to be imposed on churches or individuals, this particular resolution was a powerful statement of fundamentalist biblical interpretation regarding the role of women. Fundamentalists had long been disturbed by the growing number of women ordained as pastors and deacons in Southern Baptist churches. Denominationalists, even those who personally opposed women's ordination, usually tried to leave this matter to the local church. The autonomous, congregationally governed churches of the SBC were free to ordain or call whom they pleased. Yet many fundamentalists saw such actions as a direct contradiction of biblical teaching regarding the subordinate role of women, not only in the church but also in the divine order itself. It was not that women were inferior or were to be treated as second class members of the kingdom of God; it was just that they, like every creature, had a particular "place" in the divine scheme of things. Ordination, or any leadership status outside the divinely established parameters, violated the teaching of Holy Scripture and upset the order of creation. For W. A. Criswell and others, the biblical description of the qualifications for the pastoral office answered the question of ordination incontrovertibly. A pastor was to be "the husband of one wife" (I Tim. 3:2). Since women could not meet that qualification, they were ineligible.

---

57. Ibid.
58. Ibid.
59. Richard Furman, "An Exposition," in Bill J. Leonard, *Early American Christianity* (Nashville: Broadman, 1983), pp. 381-83.

If women thought that God had "called" them, they were simply mistaken, since God would not violate his inerrant and infallible Word as fundamentalists interpreted it.

Many fundamentalist women agreed, insisting that the desire of some women to be ordained and serve as pastors was not only a contradiction of the teaching of Scripture but was also another way of confusing sex roles and undermining the work of women as nurturers, wives, and mothers. The disintegration of the modern home was due, at least in part, to the efforts of women to move outside their divinely ordained role. Fundamentalist Charlene Kaemmerling observed that "some women want to take over the ruling aspect of the home, and do not want to be bothered with the bearing and nurturing of children. Often this is turned over to someone else. This is open rebellion against God's design for women."[60] Fundamentalist men generally agreed. Bailey Smith's comments on the issue reflect that blend of popular rhetoric and popular theology characteristic of much fundamentalist preaching: "I believe the highest calling possible for a Christian woman is to marry a good Christian man, have his children, help him build a Christian home, and hear God speak to her through her husband."[61]

While the 1984 SBC resolution on women was not a mandate to be obeyed in the churches, it apparently served as a guide for the trustees of the denomination's Home Mission Board. The agency approved new regulations regarding financial aid to those churches which had women ministers. The trustees ruled that no Home Mission Board money would be given to such congregations. Women could continue to work for the HMB, but not as pastors of churches that received home mission funds. That HMB action was a powerful indication that the fundamentalist dominance was indeed effecting policy in the SBC. It contributed to the first real signs of fragmentation in the denomination. In response to that decision, many moderate congregations began to reassess their financial response to the HMB and to consider alternate ways of funding mission churches that chose to call women pastors. Southern Baptist seminaries continue to train significant numbers of women, many of whom eventually pursue formal ordination to Christian ministry. Women serve in various capacities as counselors, chaplains, church staff members, Baptist college and seminary professors, and pastors. So far, however, the number of Southern Baptist women serving as pastors has remained relatively low.

60. Charlene Kaemmerling, "Ordination of Women: Wrong or Right?" *Theological Educator* (Spring 1988), p. 99.
61. Terry Mattingly, "Old Baptists, New Baptists: A Reporter Looks at the Battle to Control the SBC," *Southwestern Journal of Theology* 28 (Summer 1986), p. 9.

One of the most publicized incidents related to this issue involved the call of Nancy Sehested as pastor of Prescott Memorial Baptist Church in Memphis in 1987. A native Texan, Sehested's father and grandfather were both Southern Baptist ministers. Before moving to Memphis she had served as associate pastor at Oakhurst Baptist Church, Atlanta. No sooner had Sehested accepted the position than the Shelby (County) Baptist Association, the fraternity of Southern Baptist churches in the Memphis area, voted to "disfellowship" Prescott Memorial church from its organization. At issue was ordination and the question of a woman serving as pastor of a local congregation.[62] In response to the association's action, the congregation of Prescott Memorial Baptist Church reaffirmed its decision to call Sehested and presented its own interpretation of the nature of Christian ministry in light of Scripture, history, and the Baptist Faith and Message. They declared of Reverend Sehested, "we will receive her and her family with joy and gratitude to God for sending our way this most gifted and dedicated Christian servant."[63]

The increasing involvement of Southern Baptist women in all facets of Christian ministry is less a sign of rabid liberalism in the SBC than it is a testimony to the deep spirituality of the Southern Baptist people. For generations, girls and boys have been told in Sunday School classes, summer camps, and revival services: "Do whatever God calls you to do"; "Follow the leadership of the Spirit wherever it takes you." It was inevitable that women would someday carry that spiritual command to its logical conclusion. Some Southern Baptist women are simply responding to the call to surrender all their lives to God, wherever it may take them, even into the male-dominated bastions of the pulpit and the pastorate. If Southern Baptists want to stop that movement they will have to readjust their spirituality considerably and qualify the movement of the Spirit for men and women alike.

Meanwhile, the question of women's ordination and the role of women in the church continues to divide churches, associations, and families within the SBC. It is a major source of fragmentation for the denomination with no sign of resolution in sight.

62. "Baptist Congregation Ousted for Hiring a Woman," *Fort Worth Star-Telegram,* Oct. 20, 1987, sec. 1, p. 4.
63. "Response of the Prescott Memorial Baptist Church to the Request of the Credentials Committee of the Shelby County Baptist Association," Oct. 12, 1987, typescript.

Ministerial Authority

Regarding ministerial authority itself, SBC fundamentalists continue to press the authoritarian model as normative for Bible-believing Baptist congregations.[64] Fundamentalist theology was behind the divisive 1988 convention resolution regarding the priesthood of believers. The resolution placed the priesthood of all believers within the context of ministerial authority, declaring that

> the doctrine of the Priesthood of the Believer in no way contradicts the biblical understanding of the role, responsibility, and authority of the pastor which is seen in the command to the local church in Hebrews 13:17, "Obey your leaders, and submit to them; for they keep watch over your souls, as those who will give an account;" and . . . that we affirm the truth that elders, or pastors, are called of God to lead the local church (Acts 20:28).[65]

In commenting on the Hebrews 13 text, fundamentalist Paige Patterson insisted that the congregation is to listen, "mimic, obey and submit" to its pastor. The congregation are like sheep, Patterson observed, "who voluntarily and willingly follow the shepherd of the sheep. They are following the leadership role of the pastor."[66] Some congregations have accepted such a model while others find it incompatible with traditional Baptist congregationalism. Clearly, it has had significant impact on congregation-clergy confrontations throughout the convention. It also influences the attitudes of a new generation of young ministers in the convention. For many, the doctrine of biblical inerrancy requires acceptance of the authoritarian role of the pastor.

Theological Education and The Controversy

Southern Baptist denominational seminaries and numerous state Baptist colleges and universities have been at the center of The Controversy from the beginning. In a sense, the entire controversy began as an attack on liberalism generally in the six SBC seminaries. Fundamentalist leaders also insisted that none of the seminaries gave sufficient attention to the doctrine of biblical inerrancy. The "concerns" cited by various

64. Richard Land, "Pastoral Leadership: Authoritarian or Persuasive?" *Theological Educator* (Spring 1988), pp. 75-82. Land prefers the term "authoritative" when describing the pastor's authority.
65. *Convention Bulletin*, June 15, 1988, p. 5.
66. Ibid.

members of the Peace Committee were directed toward certain ideas set forth in the writings of specific professors. Early in The Controversy an unsigned typescript entitled simply "Evidences" was circulated among fundamentalists. It was a collection of excerpts from the published works of various seminary and college teachers including E. Glenn Hinson, Frank Stagg, Eric Rust, and Roy Honeycutt (Southern Seminary); Fisher Humphreys (New Orleans); Robert Crapps and David Smith (Furman University); H. J. Flanders and C. W. Christian (Baylor University); and Temp Sparkman (Midwestern Seminary).

Temp Sparkman

Sparkman's views on conversion and Christian nurture were particularly disturbing to fundamentalists who charged him with "universalism," in this case the idea that persons could be saved apart from an experience with Jesus Christ. Fundamentalists charged that several of Sparkman's books—particularly *The Salvation and Nurture of God: The Story of Emma* (1983)—undermined the significance of human sin and the need for evangelical conversion, thereby implying that there were other possibilities for salvation apart from regeneration through Christ. Sparkman denied the charges, insisting that he was indeed a "conversionist" but that his aim was to show that saving faith is sometimes nurtured through various developmental stages within the environment of home and church.

In October 1986, the board of trustees of Midwestern Baptist Seminary voted 21-11 that Sparkman was teaching within the boundaries of the seminary confession of faith.[67] Fundamentalists said that Sparkman's views were evidence of liberalism in the seminaries. Moderates insisted that his case was merely a political effort on the part of fundamentalists to dictate biblical interpretation and increase their control. Sparkman's acquittal was one of the few genuine victories for SBC moderates during the first decade of The Controversy. It also revealed that firing a professor was an extremely difficult task.

Farrar Patterson

A more complex encounter took place in 1985 at Southwestern Baptist Seminary, Fort Worth, when seminary President Russell Dilday sought

---

67. Bob Terry, "Midwestern Trustees Find Sparkman's Views Acceptable," *Western Recorder*, Oct. 28, 1986, p. 3; and Paul Wenske, "Critics Attack Seminary Professor," *Kansas City Times*, Oct. 11, 1986.

to dismiss Farrar Patterson (no relation to Paige Patterson), a professor of preaching at the school. Dilday charged Patterson with poor performance in his classroom and scholarly pursuits, demonstrating "a critical and negative attitude, disloyalty to the seminary president, meddling in administrative affairs and giving out inaccurate information about the Seminary."[68] Patterson denied all the charges. His supporters countered that Dilday was unhappy with Patterson's criticism of the antifundamentalist political activities of the seminary president. Whether the conflict was actually related to the fundamentalist-moderate debate, it soon became part of The Controversy. In March 1985, the seminary trustees voted 19-12 to dismiss Patterson, two votes short of the necessary two-thirds majority. The professor later resigned, but many fundamentalists interpreted it as a major defeat for Dilday. Presnall Wood, editor of the Texas *Baptist Standard*, observed after attending the deliberations, "If anyone doubted how politicized and polarized we are, they should have been at these meetings."[69] Every volatile issue in the SBC sooner or later relates to The Controversy.

Southeastern Baptist Theological Seminary

These encounters were merely skirmishes, however, compared to the effects of The Controversy on Southeastern Baptist Theological Seminary in Wake Forest, North Carolina. The situation at SEBTS is the most volatile at any SBC institution during the first ten years of The Controversy. In 1985, Randall Lolley, then president of SEBTS, joined with seminary presidents Dilday and Honeycutt and other convention executives in opposing the reelection of Charles Stanley as president of the SBC. He became an outspoken opponent of the fundamentalist takeover. At the time, fundamentalists charged that Southeastern was among the denomination's most "liberal" seminaries. As the fundamentalist segment on the Southeastern board of trustees increased, Lolley also joined with the other seminary presidents in proposing the Glorietta Statement. In defending his participation in that process, Lolley sought to distinguish between the idea that the Bible is "not errant in any area of reality" and the word "inerrant" as a means of defining the nature of Scripture. The latter term, he said, involved "a far more technical set of polarities."[70] He concluded that the "perfection of the sixty-six books of our Bible derive from their purpose as

---

68. Jim Jones, "Dilday Loses Bitter Feud at Seminary," *Fort Worth Star-Telegram*, Mar. 21, 1985, pp. 1-2.

69. Ibid.

70. Randall Lolley, "President's Message," *Southeastern Outlook* (Nov.-Dec. 1986).

books of redemption,"[71] implying that questions of science and history were not subject to the primary spiritual authority of Holy Scripture.

Within a year, Lolley resigned as president of Southeastern along with the school's dean, Morris Ashcraft. The resignations came as tensions escalated between the seminary administration and the board of trustees on which by 1987 fundamentalists had secured a majority. The two administrators resigned rather than carry out the policies set forth by the fundamentalist-dominated board, particularly the policies regarding the hiring of faculty who fit certain inerrantist criteria. The resignations marked the beginning of extended turmoil at Southeastern involving continued conflict between the fundamentalist-controlled board and the faculty represented by its chapter of the American Association of University Professors, one of only two chapters in the United States with 100 percent faculty membership.

Lewis Drummond, professor of evangelism at Southern Seminary and an internationally known evangelist, was chosen to succeed Lolley as president. In the fall of 1988 accreditation teams from the Southern Association of Colleges and Schools and the Association of Theological Schools raised numerous questions about the stability of the seminary and the new procedures for hiring faculty and administering the school. The report noted that "open and public conflict between the faculty and the trustees is adversely affecting the operation of the institution." "Confusion" over faculty appointments, declining enrollment, and the adoption of "an additional criterion" (inerrancy) for faculty recruitment were also cited as creating major problems. The latter procedure "has not been submitted to the Southern Baptist Convention for ratification." Only by informal consensus had trustees determined to interpret the seminary articles of faith as indicating an inerrantist interpretation of the nature of Scripture.[72] The ATS evaluation committee suggested that Southeastern was "a very troubled campus and divided institution."[73] The committee charged that trustees, without input from administration or faculty, changed policies regarding the faculty's role in the process of appointments and used nonofficial confessional documents as criteria for interviewing potential faculty.[74] The report concluded "reluctantly" that "institutional effectiveness is low." So, too, was faculty morale. "In fact," the

71. Ibid.

72. R. G. Puckett, "Accrediting Committee Cites Problems at Southeastern," *Biblical Recorder,* Dec. 17, 1988, pp. 3 and 8.

73. R. G. Puckett, "Report Says Seminary is 'Troubled, Divided,'" *Baptist Standard,* Aug. 31, 1988, p. 5; and *Western Recorder,* Aug. 30, 1988, p. 4.

74. Ibid.

report noted, "members of the [evaluation] committee cannot recall ever knowing a faculty so despondent."[75] Southeastern administrators and trustees pledged themselves to cooperate with the evaluation teams and maintain their commitment to the SBC as well. Robert Crowley, the chairman of the board, stated that "We want to cooperate in all reasonable matters to keep accreditation in conjunction with the mandate of the Southern Baptist Convention. . . . That mandate calls for institutions and agencies of the convention enthusiastically to support the doctrinal statement entitled the Baptist Faith and Message of 1963."[76] For the fundamentalist majority on the SEBTS board of trustees, the Baptist Faith and Message statement on the nature of Scripture was an inerrantist position.

In the spring of 1989, the Southeastern trustees elected L. Russ Bush, an associate professor of philosophy at Southwestern Seminary, as the new academic dean. Bush, a prominent inerrantist, was selected by President Lewis Drummond after at least two unanimous faculty votes opposing his nomination. Faculty members insisted that any of a number of other nominees presented by the president were acceptable to them, but Bush nonetheless received the approval of the president and trustees, further dividing the institution. Chairman Crowley commented that the opposition of the faculty was "no big news. They don't want somebody with conservative theology. . . . It didn't interfere with trustees with [the election of president] Drummond and it won't interfere with Bush."[77] The trustees also approved a response to the accreditation agencies that laid the blame for the school's troubles on the previous administration of Randall Lolley. Lolley, the board charged, had been unable to control the faculty and refused to accept the diversity of views as represented by the board.[78]

Meanwhile, enrollment at the seminary dropped from 1,125 students in 1985 to around 500 students in 1989. To many moderates, the Southeastern ordeal was proof of the ultimate results of fundamentalist domination, a nightmare of institutional upheaval and mistrust, and their inability to do anything about it. Many fundamentalists seemed embarrassed by the events at the seminary. Others simply viewed it as evidence of the radical measures needed to remove the "cancer" of

75. Puckett, "Accrediting Committee Cites Problems at Southeastern."
76. Marv Knox, "Southeastern Officials Pledge Cooperation, Commitment," *Baptist True Union*, Jan. 5, 1989, p. 6.
77. "SEBTS Dean Controversial," *SBC Today* (Mar. 1989), p. 1; and "Seminary Faculty Opposes Southwestern Theologian," *Fort Worth Star-Telegram*, Feb. 2, 1989.
78. Connie Davis, "SEBTS Confirms Bush, Accreditation Reports," *Baptist and Reflector*, Mar. 22, 1989, pp. 1 and 5.

liberalism. Students lost all the way around. It was perhaps the most tragic illustration of the fragmentation of the denomination.

Social Issues and The Controversy

As The Controversy developed it effected almost every facet of denominational life. The issue of inerrancy became but one element in an ever-widening effort to reinterpret and restructure Southern Baptist responses to politics, ethics, and other social issues. Increasingly the new fundamentalist majority has moved the SBC closer to the agenda of the new religious-political right. By 1986, Paige Patterson was insisting, "We want an open, pro-life position in all of our institutions and agencies, dealing with both abortion and euthanasia. We want to be pro-family, pro-prayer anywhere."[79] He suggested that "the convention's actual posture is far more conservative than most of its [bureaucratic] leadership" on political and theological issues. Concerning fundamentalists' efforts to promote a specific social agenda Patterson observed, "I think it'll go over nearly as well as the inerrancy thing."[80] Correct theology was closely related to correct politics. From the beginning of The Controversy fundamentalists expressed concern over what they interpreted as the liberal stance taken by several convention agencies, particularly the Christian Life Commission and the Baptist Joint Committee on Public Affairs, the agencies with particular responsibility for addressing the public square of American social and political issues.

The CLC is an agency of the Southern Baptist Convention, while the BJC is a Washington-based lobby that represents the political concerns of numerous Baptist groups, including the SBC. The CLC has frequently been at the center of controversy in the SBC. During the 1960s its public stands on behalf of integration and the civil rights movement angered many Southern Baptists. More recently, fundamentalists criticized what they saw as the agency's failure to be more outspoken against abortion and in favor of "traditional family values" and other concerns associated with the new religious right. When Foy Valentine retired as executive director of the CLC in 1986, he was replaced by another moderate, Larry Baker, then dean at Midwestern Seminary. Fundamentalists on the CLC board, although they were not a majority, charged that

---

79. Brad Owens, "Patterson Thrusts Social Agenda into Fray," *Baptist Messenger*, June 26, 1986, p. 4.
80. Ibid.

they were shut out of the process leading to Baker's election. Baker's days were numbered from the beginning of his term. After surviving one trustee attempt at his removal, Baker resigned in June 1988, after a tenure of only sixteen months. He was succeeded by Richard Land, former academic vice president of Criswell College and the administrative assistant to Texas Republican Governor William Clements with particular responsibility for "traditional family values" and other church-state issues.[81] Land was elected in September 1988 by a vote of 23-2.

Land's views on social issues were no doubt consistent with those of the fundamentalist majority in the convention. They include a strong concern for pro-life issues and racial justice. He noted that "I oppose abortion except where the mother's physical life is in extreme danger." That position, he said, "puts me completely in line with resolutions [opposing abortion] passed by the convention in the last decade."[82] Here again, convention resolutions were seen as guidelines for agency leadership. Land also acknowledged his support for capital punishment "as part of the biblically mandated authority of the civil magistrates."[83] Concerning women's ordination, Land wrote that while both man and woman are created in God's image and have "eternal souls," there are "scriptural distinctions in role assignment and official position." He continued, "as I Timothy 2:11-15 and Ephesians 5:22-24 clearly indicate, the woman is to be in subordination to the man in the structure of the church as an organized body and in the family as a team in the household." Thus the New Testament "forbids" women to function in a "teaching-ruling office or ordination to the ministry or ruling authority."[84] Land's appointment as head of the CLC was a major indication that the new majority was in control.

Long before The Controversy began, the Baptist Joint Committee on Public Affairs was a favorite target of fundamentalist criticism, much of it directed toward the BJC's feisty and outspoken executive director James Dunn. Many fundamentalists were upset with the organization's opposition to a school prayer amendment, tuition tax credits to parochial schools, and director Dunn's relationship to various "liberal" causes, especially People for the American Way, an organization founded by TV producer Norman Lear to counteract new right political activities. Others felt that Southern Baptists should have their own agency that

81. Dan Martin, "Land to Be Recommended to Head CLC," *Baptist Standard*, Sept. 14, 1988, p. 3.

82. Dan Martin, "Nominee Vows Pro-Life, Racial Justice Stands," *Baptist Standard*, Sept. 14, 1988, p. 3.

83. Ibid.

84. Ibid.

represented SBC political views more unilaterally. In response to this the Executive Committee of the SBC approved organizing a Public Affairs Committee for dealing with political issues and monitoring the work of the BJC. Not an official agency of the convention, the PAC existed at the discretion of the Executive Committee. The PAC was technically a standing committee of the SBC and therefore not entitled to staff, program, or budget.

Throughout the 1980s the convention debated funding for the BJC and the continuing SBC participation in the body composed of various Baptist groups. Moderates worked to secure alternative funding for the agency should SBC funds be cut off. The PAC in the meantime continued to assert its role as the rightful interpreter of SBC political attitudes, even sending out materials urging the appointment of Judge Robert Bork to the Supreme Court. Traditionally, SBC agencies had refused to give official endorsements to political candidates or appointees.

The 1987 meeting of the SBC voted to continue the PAC as part of the BJC, but gave its members authority to act on those SBC resolutions or motions regarding church-state issues upon which there was not agreement with the BJC or which the BJC did not support. Thus the PAC could speak out on issues that reflected the right-wing sentiments of the SBC fundamentalist leadership.

At its February 1989 meeting the Executive Committee approved the creation of a new SBC agency called the Religious Liberty Commission, which would provide an exclusive Southern Baptist lobby in Washington. The Executive Committee also moved to alter but not end the SBC relationship with the Baptist Joint Committee.[85] Action on the new commission was postponed until the 1990 meeting of the SBC. By late 1989, however, the Executive Committee had decided not to recommend that a new commission be established. Some fundamentalist agency heads opposed using ever-depleting funds for setting up a new agency.

These developments again confronted moderates with a dilemma. How much dismantling of the convention were they willing to tolerate? Were they willing to find alternative ways to fund the old relationship with the BJC and permit it to represent moderate SBC interests in the nation's capitol? Would they be willing to accept the more rightward pronouncements of the new Religious Liberty Commission as increasingly representative of Southern Baptist political views? Such actions further perpetuated fragmentation.

---

85. Dan Martin, "SBC Executive Committee to Consider Creation of 'Alternative' Commission," *The Christian Index*, Jan. 19, 1989, p. 1.

The struggle between the Baptist Joint Committee and the Public Affairs Committee again served to illustrate a fundamentalist desire to direct the denomination toward positions more compatible with the agenda of the new religious-political right. It also indicated something of the difficulty fundamentalists faced in severing ties with those agencies long associated with the SBC. Unable to break those institutional relationships without creating major furor, the fundamentalist leadership moved to construct a new agency that would gradually take institutional and financial precedence over the Baptist Joint Committee and its representation of the SBC. While moderates pledged to continue funding the BJC, PAC members claimed to represent the majority opinion in the SBC regarding church-state issues. As one Executive Committee trustee observed in 1988, the "Baptist Joint Committee has been pursuing a more liberal agenda than is compatible with the SBC and, therefore, something must be done. We're going to see if there's an apparatus to accomplish our purposes apart from the BJCPA."[86]

The SBC and the New Religious-Political Right

Questions regarding the relationship between the SBC fundamentalists and the new religious-political right have increased throughout the decade of The Controversy. In surveying the impact of the new religious right on the SBC, sociologist James L. Guth noted that while many prominent Southern Baptists participate in the movement, the convention itself remains "badly split by Rightist Politics."[87] He concluded that Southern Baptist advocates of the new right agenda "are not only more supportive of activism, but also participate more than their opponents."[88] This fact, Guth believed, contributed to the public perception that "ministerial activism" in the SBC is dominated by the Christian right.[89] Guth listed Jesse Helms, James Robison, Ed McAteer, Gary Jarmin, and Charles Stanley as outspoken supporters of the new right agenda. He suggested that W. A. Criswell, Adrian Rogers, and Bailey Smith "are at least 'fellow

---

86. Dan Martin, "PAC to Make Request for $75,000 Funding," *The Christian Index*, Sept. 8, 1988, pp. 1 and 3. As this book goes to press, the SBC Executive Committee has recommended a radical cut in BJC funding along with increased funding of the CLC and the PAC as Washington lobbies. The Religious Liberty Commission is apparently dead.

87. James L. Guth, "The Politics of Preachers: Southern Baptist Ministers and Christian Right Activism," in *New Christian Politics*, ed. David G. Bromley and Anson Shupe (Macon: Mercer University Press, 1985), p. 236.

88. Ibid., p. 248.

89. Ibid.

travelers'" in the movement.[90] Responding to the suggestion that fundamentalist leadership was redirecting the denomination into a new political arena Adrian Rogers commented, "some of the things we do may seem overtly political, but to us, they are moral and spiritual issues."[91] Again, orthodoxy and politics were often inseparable.

In a documentary aired on Public Television in 1987, journalist Bill Moyers questioned Paul Pressler regarding his relationship to certain right-wing movements. Enraged at the questioning, Pressler stormed out of the interview. He subsequently led the SBC Executive Committee to pass a resolution censoring Moyers for his action and for the entire broadcast—although the Executive Committee itself was not discussed in the film and is not an official judicatory body for the SBC.

Evangelical scholar George Marsden wrote that "since the rise of the New Christian Right in politics, most of the inerrancy movement has become thoroughly allied with a national political agenda." He notes that "it is no accident" that the "fundamentalist takeover" in the SBC coincided precisely with the rise of the new religious-political right in American politics. Marsden suggested that while inerrancy was long a theme of SBC fundamentalists, "once that issue became inextricably tied to national politics, they won enough support to insure control."[92] Thus "a vast majority" of biblical inerrantists agree on such issues as opposition to abortion, support for Israel, opposition to ERA, support for school prayer, and other such agendas. Marsden wrote: "So it turns out that imposing an inerrancy test serves a twofold purpose: it ensures a Christian agency against any liberalism and it also clears the way for mobilizing support for a thoroughly right-wing political agenda."[93] Marsden warned that such practices may actually foster not a renewal of Christianity, but a "new paganism" in which worship of God and conformity to the state are inseparable.[94]

Inerrancy, therefore, is not the only issue on the fundamentalist agenda, nor is it the only question that divides forces within the SBC. As certain new right concerns continue to be promoted throughout official denominational channels the socio-political positions of the SBC may prove more divisive than "the inerrancy thing."

---

90. Ibid.
91. Thomas B. Edsall, "New Right Finally Gains Control of Huge Southern Baptist Convention," *The Washington Post*, June 14, 1986, p. A4.
92. George Marsden, "The New Paganism," *Reformed Journal* (Jan. 1988), p. 3.
93. Ibid.
94. Ibid.

SBC Subgroups: Fragmentation Becomes Formal

The Controversy between fundamentalists and moderates compelled Southern Baptists to choose between one denominational subgroup or the other. By 1979, the fundamentalist faction constituted a subgroup bent on reclaiming the SBC for a particular kind of orthodoxy and reshaping it according to a right-wing religio-political agenda. By 1989, moderates had formed numerous subgroups, the diversity of which demonstrated the problems moderates faced in creating a unified response to fundamentalism.

Many of these denominational subgroups established their own periodicals aimed at presenting their side of the story. The Peace Committee called for the abandonment or at least modification of these periodicals, but with little success. Some of these periodicals included *The Southern Baptist Journal* and *The Southern Baptist Advocate*, published by fundamentalists, and the *SBC Today* published by moderates.

As the fundamentalist subgroup came to dominate the convention, some moderates turned to a new organization, the Southern Baptist Alliance, as a means of reasserting what they believed to be the neglected principles of Baptist tradition. The Alliance officially began on February 12, 1987. Henry Crouch, a North Carolina pastor and the chairman of the new organization, insisted that "we are not a splinter group." Rather, the SBA would be "a voice of conscience within the convention." Crouch noted that the fundamentalist "takeover of the SBC has left many Southern Baptists disenfranchised . . . and we will exist as long as we feel disenfranchised."[95] Other leaders insisted that the SBA was not the beginning of a new denomination, nor was it a political group aimed at promoting moderate candidates. While its members would surely support the election of moderates as SBC president, the SBA itself was an effort to "move beyond politics" in order to provide a place for those Southern Baptists who wanted to remain in the convention but who were excluded from participation on convention boards. The organization was formed specifically as a result of the Home Mission Board decision not to fund churches served by women pastors, the continuing effort to cut funds for the Baptist Joint Committee, and the "disenfranchisement now taking place through the office of the [SBC] president."[96]

The membership of the SBA was open to individuals and congre-

---

95. "Southern Baptist Alliance Forms to Counter Threat," *Baptist and Reflector*, Feb. 18, 1987, p. 3.
    96. Ibid.

gations. Its constitution listed seven basic principles on which the organization was founded. These included:

> First, the freedom of the individual to read and interpret the scriptures.
> Second, the freedom of the local church to shape its own life and mission, for example, ordaining male or female for ministry.
> Third, cooperation with believers everywhere in giving full expression to the Gospel.
> Fourth, the servant role of leadership within the congregation.
> Fifth, theological education characterized by reverence for biblical authority but which respects open inquiry and responsible scholarship.
> Sixth, a proclamation of the Gospel that calls people to repentance and faith as well as to social and economic justice.
> And seventh, the principle of a free church in a free state, opposing any effort either by church or state to use the other for its own purposes.[97]

In response to the founding of the SBA, Adrian Rogers noted that he was "not surprised" by the action and insisted that its members had "every right to express themselves." Yet he denied SBA claims that they were disenfranchised. "We are not trying to force our views on them," Rogers observed, "but as president, I could not help but be loyal to the stated views of our convention in making my appointments."[98] Although he would not suggest that any group leave the denomination, Rogers noted that if moderates were "out of step with the majority, then they ought to conform to the wishes of the majority or they should seek a new majority."[99] Paige Patterson's response was predictable, acknowledging that while the Alliance might attract two to three hundred churches, "I would like to remind its leaders that that doesn't represent a substantial percentage of churches in the denomination."[100] The purge would continue, Patterson said, even if moderates were excluded. "I just don't think any of us can afford to say we will welcome those back into leadership positions who have questions about the reliability of the Bible," he declared.[101] The Grand Compromise had come to an end.

Almost simultaneous with the founding of the SBA, a group of conservative Southern Baptists formed the Genesis Commission. Based in Houston, Texas, the organization proposed to secure and fund con-

97. "Interview with Chairperson W. Henry Crouch," typescript, p. 2.
98. "Rogers, Fuller, Banks Respond to Southern Baptist Alliance," *Baptist and Reflector*, Feb. 18, 1987, p. 3.
99. Ibid.
100. Jim Jones, "Moderates Bolster Alliance Opposed to Baptist Leaders," *Fort Worth Star-Telegram*, Sept. 1, 1988, p. 28.
101. Ibid.

servative pastors who wanted to start churches in foreign countries. The initial efforts of the group focused on mission activities in Mexico. Many saw the Genesis Commission as a challenge to the Foreign Mission Board, a charge its organizers denied.

Fundamentalist support of ministries outside the Southern Baptist Convention was nothing new, however. Many churches did not hesitate to provide funding for numerous extradenominational programs that were more compatible with fundamentalist ideology. The formation of the Southern Baptist Alliance indicated that many moderate churches were now considering a similar response to the fundamentalist dominance of the SBC. The Alliance represented a new strategy for moderate response to The Controversy. The organization moved quickly to provide funding for various programs its members felt were being ignored or undermined by the new fundamentalist leadership in the SBC. These included support for mission churches with female pastors, the Baptist Joint Committee, and Habitat for Humanity, a program to provide housing for the poor. These actions made the SBA controversial for fundamentalists and moderates alike. Indeed, many moderate pastors feared to join the organization lest they appear to be schismatic. Fundamentalist activity in the convention, however, significantly aided the growth of the organization.

In 1988, when the SBC passed the controversial resolution on the priesthood of the believer, interest in the SBA increased dramatically. For many Southern Baptists that resolution became a symbol of the reinterpretation of Baptist doctrine that followed from fundamentalist control. Many people who had once ignored or shunned the SBA now looked to it as an alternative for funding and other strategies in the face of the fundamentalist takeover. By early 1989, the SBA had approved a landmark proposal to participate in the founding of a new theological seminary, based in Richmond, Virginia, in cooperation with other theological seminaries in the area.[102] Also in 1989, the Alliance began publication of *Commentary*, an alternative set of Sunday School materials for use in Baptist churches that was to be circulated through *SBC Today*. Such actions led many denominational executives to worry that the SBA was indeed having both a financial and a political impact on the convention. Fundamentalists were hard-pressed to criticize the SBA, since they had organized alternative seminaries and made use of non-SBC literature for years. By 1989, membership in the SBA had reached 29,000 and a new executive director, Stan Hastey, had been secured. Hastey, a highly

---

102. "Alliance Votes to Start New Seminary," *Baptist and Reflector*, Mar. 15, 1989, pp. 1 and 5.

respected journalist and longtime staff member at the Baptist Joint Committee, was already familiar with the effects of The Controversy on one agency of the convention.

Not all moderates welcomed the formation of the Alliance, however. In April 1987, Richard Bridges, the pastor of First Baptist Church in Bowling Green, Kentucky, and a leader of the moderate Kentucky Baptists for Missions, suggested that the SBC was divided into at least four groups. These included: (1) the Agenda Fundamentalists, as represented by Rogers, Patterson, and Pressler; (2) The Denominational Fundamentalists, who were fundamentalist in theology but who opposed the takeover movement; (3) the Denominational Moderates, as represented by Winfred Moore and others loyal to the convention; (4) the Agenda Moderates, as represented by the Alliance.[103] Each variation in stance was a mark of further fragmentation.

In December 1988 a group called "Baptists Committed to the Southern Baptist Convention" organized for the purpose of wresting political control of the SBC back from the fundamentalists. This "centrist" subgroup selected Texas pastor and moderate leader Winfred Moore as chairperson and named David Currie, a former staffer for the Christian Life Commission, as its salaried coordinator. The group noted, "With contributions down, baptisms down and unity shattered, enough is enough. Southern Baptists want and deserve a group to lead us out of this despair. . . . We support restoration of our convention, not its destruction."[104] Paul Pressler responded to the organization of the new subgroup by suggesting, "It appears to be a reorganization of the same people who for ten years have been resisting a return to biblical theology. Baptists need to be working together to promote the Cooperative Program, evangelism and missions, not starting new political organizations that will be divisive and counter-productive to the welfare of the convention."[105] After a decade of political victories fundamentalist leaders had begun to use the old language of denominational loyalty they had rejected as bureaucratic doubletalk only a few years before. The formation of new subgroups merely served to illustrate that denominational fragmentation was continuing unabated.

---

103. Richard W. Bridges, letter, Apr. 24, 1987.

104. "Coalition Chooses Coordinator, Plans to Recapture Convention," *SBC Today* (Jan. 1989). In 1990, former SBC president Jimmy Allen became chairperson of Baptists Committed.

105. Ibid.

The Spoils of Victory: Fundamentalist Changes in the SBC

By 1989, therefore, The Controversy had consumed the energy and attention of even the most optimistic Southern Baptists. No longer could it be dismissed as merely "a preachers' fight," or a brief, periodic swing of the ideological pendulum. The fundamentalist faction had achieved its original goals. They had controlled the convention presidency for a decade, electing fundamentalist presidents who did their bidding, and appointed inerrantists—most of whom were sympathetic to the takeover agenda—to convention boards of trustees. As a result, the direction of the denomination was irrevocably changed. Even a brief survey of denominational policies and procedures demonstrates the "fundamentalization" of the Southern Baptist Convention.

An Inerrantist Commentary

The Sunday School Board of the SBC developed plans for a multivolume biblical commentary that reflected an inerrantist interpretation of Scripture, written by Southern Baptist scholars who subscribed to the doctrine of biblical inerrancy. The initial proposal, made as a motion at the 1985 SBC meeting, was rejected by the Sunday School Board's evaluation committee. The committee gave as its reasons a general lack of interest in the project, the divisive climate in the convention, a market already "flooded" with new commentaries, commentary sets already published by Broadman Press, and an expenditure of over one million dollars. The report concluded that such high costs "should not be spent on a product for which the demand is relatively low."[106] The committee's recommendation was in turn rejected by the fundamentalist-dominated board of trustees, which mandated publication of the commentary. The first volume is scheduled for release in 1991. One fundamentalist trustee called it "the most significant publication of the Baptist Sunday School Board in this century."[107]

Writers for the commentary included three pastors, one layman, and professors from Criswell College, Mid-America, Southwestern, New Orleans, and Southern seminaries. That Southern Seminary professors should be included among the inerrantist writers was one of the

---

106. "Response to the Southern Baptist Convention Motion Concerning a New Bible Commentary," Broadman Committee Report, Feb. 2-4, 1987, typescript.

107. "BSSB Can't Agree on New Commentary Name," *Western Recorder,* Aug. 30, 1988, p. 5.

supreme ironies of The Controversy. Fundamentalists long claimed that the absence of inerrantists on the Southern Seminary faculty was evidence that their perspective was ignored in the denomination's oldest theological institution. Seven faculty members were initially approved as appropriately inerrantist and invited to write for the new commentary. Two were unable to fit the project into their personal writing schedule. Two others left the seminary for other denominational positions. Of the seven professors originally found acceptable, six had joined the faculty by or before 1980. This fact was in glaring contradiction to fundamentalist contentions that their ideology was not represented at the convention's mother seminary. By 1989, however, fundamentalist control of the SBC was secure and the veracity of old claims made little difference in the shape of the denomination.

Social and Political Agendas

By 1989, the SBC's Christian Life Commission had secured a fundamentalist executive director, ceased publication of at least two pamphlets on women in ministry, and placed increasing emphasis on pro-life issues. The new leadership also attempted to distance itself from charges of racism related to remarks by a CLC trustee regarding Martin Luther King, Jr., South Africa, and other racially controversial concerns.[108] The denomination also had moved to establish a new Religious Liberty Commission that would represent the more rightward political concerns of the constituency alongside or in place of the Baptist Joint Committee.

Theological Education

While there were no wholesale firings or purges on any seminary faculty, controversies and tensions were felt on every campus. Southeastern Seminary experienced the greatest conflict, and by 1989 its future seemed uncertain at best. All six seminaries experienced various types of tensions and decline: numerically, financially, and in faculty and student morale.

---

108. Marv Knox, "CLC Drops Surgeon General's AIDS Program," *Baptist Standard*, Sept. 21, 1988, p. 9. Regarding "race relations," the trustee was quoted as saying, among other things, "We have to be careful that we don't be caught up in the endorsement of— quote, 'the reverend,' unquote—Martin Luther King." He labeled King a "fraud."

Financial Crisis

By 1989 the most serious threat to the SBC was financial. In its February meeting the Executive Committee recommended a Cooperative Program budget 2.5 percent less than the operating budget for 1988-1989. The committee was forced to recognize the reality that Southern Baptists had not met the Cooperative Program budget for most of the decade, that capital needs had gone unmet, and the increase in budget receipts had failed to keep pace with inflation.[109] In a related development, state Baptist conventions were beginning to reevaluate their relationship to the national convention. Virginia Baptists passed "A Memorial" declaration at their state convention meeting in the fall of 1988 that was to be communicated to the SBC leadership. It asked the SBC to continue funding for the Baptist Joint Committee, to allow churches to "negatively designate" where they did not want offerings to go, to support open and balanced theological education, and to accept a slate of state-elected nominees to the committee on committees. Failure to respond to these issues would lead to a reevaluation of funding from the state.[110]

Local Church Conflicts

By 1989, The Controversy had found its way into local congregations as well. One 1989 survey of churches and pastors revealed a 31 percent increase in "forced terminations" of clergy over the results of a similar study produced in 1984. Statistics suggested that every month 116 Southern Baptist churches severed relationships with their pastors through "involuntary termination." Reasons included "lack of communication," "immorality," "performance dissatisfaction," "authoritarian leadership style," "power struggles," and "personality conflicts."[111] The Controversy had worked its way throughout the SBC, even to local congregations.

---

109. Jack P. Lowndes, "Committee Recommends SBC Budget Cuts," *The Christian Index,* Mar. 2, 1989.

110. Marv Knox, " 'Priesthood' Tops State Convention Concerns," *Baptist Standard,* Nov. 30, 1988, p. 8.

111. "Survey Shows 2,100 Pastors Fired During Past 18 Months," *Baptist Standard,* Nov. 30, 1988, p. 5.

The Controversy Continues

These developments indicated that fundamentalists had indeed won control of the SBC, but the denominational conflict had effected almost every area of convention life. After a decade of debate, fundamentalist leaders sought to rally support for their programs and their motives. SBC president Jerry Vines promised that his congregation would raise its three percent giving to the Cooperative Program.[112] Patriarch Pressler also sounded the call for loyalty to the Cooperative Program, a theme he had denounced as bureaucratic compromise ten years before. He urged fundamentalists to direct their efforts toward winning back SBC conservatives who agreed with them theologically, but "for some reason or other are voting on the other [moderate] side." The conservatives had chosen to affiliate with moderates because of friendships, because "they haven't listened to the evidence," because they have focused "on the mistakes we have made instead of the issues," or because they mistakenly sought "to defend the convention, not realizing the convention consists of all Southern Baptists."[113]

By 1989, The Controversy in the SBC showed no sign of abating. Ironically, certain subgroups within the convention had exchanged strategies. Fundamentalists now promote support for the Cooperative Program and urge constituents to unite around the traditional tasks of missions and evangelism. Moderates, on the other hand, talk of designating their offerings to special ministries and away from those fundamentalist-controlled agencies which they can no longer in good conscience support. While formal schism seems unlikely, informal fragmentation threatens to produce many of the same results.

112. "Vines Urges Churches to Increase CP Gifts," *Western Recorder,* Aug. 30, 1988, p. 5.

113. "Pressler Shares Perspective at Meeting Series," *Baptist True Union,* Sept. 22, 1988, pp. 1 and 5.

CHAPTER 7

The Future: Continued Fragmentation or a New Consensus

A Fragmented Denomination

"SBC NOT 'DISINTEGRATING,' SAYS JERRY VINES."[1] THAT HEADLINE DESCRIBED the situation confronting fundamentalist pastor Jerry Vines upon his election as president of the SBC in 1988. By then, institutional and ideological divisions were evident at almost every level of SBC life. Theological issues were overshadowed by immediate matters of denominational survival. Although the convention continued to avoid a formal schism, it was considerably less "intact" than Martin Marty had described it a decade earlier. While the denominational structure had not disintegrated, its constituency was undeniably, perhaps irrevocably, fragmented.

After a decade of tension, certain trends had become apparent. Statistical growth in baptisms, church memberships, and the organization of new congregations showed either minimal increases or obvious declines. Local churches were experiencing significant conflict and division. Baptist state conventions were showing the strain of factionalism in their own ranks, or in some cases actually considering financial realignments with the national denomination. Many missionary personnel expressed feelings of uncertainty about the future. The six denominational seminaries faced declining student enrollments and significant financial difficulties. One seminary, Southeastern, was threatened with the loss of its accreditation. New Baptist divinity schools at Samford and Wake Forest universities challenged the hegemony of SBC seminaries over theological education within the denomination. Numerous subgroups, each articulating its own vision

---

1. "SBC Not 'Disintegrating,' Says Jerry Vines," *Baptist Standard*, Nov. 23, 1988, p. 3.

of the Baptist heritage, gave dramatic evidence of a divided denomination.[2]

The most immediate problem, of course, came down to money. In 1989, for the first time in its history, the SBC Executive Committee recommended a zero-growth budget for the denomination. Many national agencies and state conventions instituted financial cutbacks because of declining revenues. The Home Mission Board was forced to eliminate staff and programs in the face of large budget deficits. Many churches, fundamentalist and moderate, accepted the idea of "negative designations," thereby refusing to contribute to certain programs, sending money only to agencies they judged theologically or ethically acceptable. Institutional difficulties were merely symptoms of a deeper spiritual malaise characterized by theological confusion and uncertainty as to the real mission of the denomination. By 1989, much of the old denominational consensus had broken down, but leaders were unable to establish a new center around which to unite the fragmented constituency.

Fundamentalists, successful in their efforts at gaining control of the convention, seemed unable to reestablish a stable basis for unity among a variety of single-issue subgroups, many committed to propelling the denomination even further toward the theological and political right. Efforts at narrowing the dogmatic parameters of the SBC beyond "the inerrancy thing," as Paige Patterson once called it, merely heightened the sense of alienation and division. Indeed, by 1989 there was some scant indication that fundamentalists themselves were beginning to fragment over certain programs and policies. Moderates, once the financial and institutional backbone of the denomination but now largely excluded from trustee appointments and other leadership positions, were reassessing their participation in convention life. Unable to agree on their role in the future of the convention, moderates remained factionalized on matters of both intent and strategy.

The Southern Baptist synthesis of denominational cooperation,

---

2. Bob Terry, "Financial Woes and SBC Priorities," *Word and Way,* Jan. 21, 1988, p. 2; Erich Bridges, "101st Offering May Bring Total to $1 Billion," *Baptist Standard,* Nov. 30, 1988; Connie Davis, "SEBTS Confirms Bush, Accreditation Reports," *Baptist and Reflector,* Mar. 22, 1989, pp. 1 and 5; Joe Westbury, "Lewis Opposes New Agency, Seminary," *Baptist and Reflector,* Mar. 22, 1989, p. 5; Jim Lowery, "Stalled SBC Growth to Be Focus of Leaders to Facilitate Outreach," *Western Recorder,* Dec. 5, 1989, p. 1; "National SBC Budget Ends Fiscal Year Below Goal, Inflation," *Florida Baptist Witness,* Oct. 27, 1988, p. 6; Joe Westbury, "Upturn in Baptism Totals Projected for '88," *Baptist Standard,* Dec. 7, 1988, p. 3; and Joe Westbury, "Baptisms Rise Slightly tho 6,210 Churches Have None," *Western Recorder,* Dec. 12, 1989, p. 1. These are but a few of the articles that reflect on recent statistical and financial changes in the SBC.

whatever it may have been, was fragile from the beginning. Theological diversity, rabid individualism, and congregational autonomy— always potential sources of rupture—were held in check by the powerful forces of southern culture, Southern Baptist denominational programs, and a degree of theological ambiguity. Ambiguity allowed the denomination to define itself in terms of dogmas that, while singularly Baptist, were still general enough to permit a certain theological flexibility in the churches. In selecting the New Hampshire Confession of Faith as a guide for its official doctrinal statement, the SBC accepted what is often called a "modified Calvinist" approach to theology. Its concepts were broad enough to embrace a variety of orthodox interpretations regarding Scripture, atonement, election, predestination, and eschatology. By refusing to define dogma narrowly, the denomination was able to maintain a constituency comprised of numerous theological traditions.

Denominationalists, concerned with world evangelization, organizational stability, and maintaining the unity needed to achieve those ends, developed a convention system that was rhetorically sectarian and programmatically establishment in its response to cultural, ecclesiastical, and political issues. Subgroups on the right and left were incorporated into denominational life but were not permitted to dominate it lest they upset the Grand Compromise on which convention unity was built. Denominational leaders were theologically conservative but organizationally pragmatic in their efforts to maintain unity, promote programs, and increase statistics. By convincing the constituency that numerical and financial success was somehow evidence of divine blessing, denominationalists were able to unite a diverse people in an enterprise of evangelistic witness and missionary endeavor.

The sense of Southern Baptistness was also shaped by powerful myths that provided a sense of unity and motivation. These myths incorporated elements of southern and Baptist senses of regionalism, triumphalism, orthodoxy, and world conquest of the gospel. In the decades immediately following the Civil War they provided an important source of stability and identity for a defeated people. Such myths suggested that the South and its people would indeed be vindicated, spiritually if not politically. The once-defeated region and its churches would rise again, achieving a greater spiritual victory than ever before. In the minds of many, the success of the denomination was evidence of the truth of its doctrine and the effectiveness of its methods. Through faithful service and unified witness Southern Baptists believed that, almost single-handedly, they could fulfill the Great Commission (Matt.

28:19-20) and hasten the coming of the kingdom. They were indeed God's "only hope" for the salvation of humanity.[3]

Conflicting attitudes toward pluralism and modernity as well as politics and authority could not be ignored forever, however. The protective cocoons of cultural and denominational solidarity could not endure indefinitely. As the statistics became less impressive and the constituency less southern, as participation in denominational programs became less uniform and the old myths no longer provided a sense of identity, the time was ripe for remythologizing Southern Baptist identity.

The "New" SBC

Fundamentalists led the way in remythologizing the Southern Baptist heritage. Their theology was authoritative and orthodox, easily preached and understood. Their rhetoric was suitably populist, able to touch the hearts and rally the support of the masses. They were articulate opponents of modernity, warning that only through the affirmation of biblical inerrancy and other fundamentalist dogmas could the convention retain its evangelical zeal and fulfill its divine mandate. Fundamentalists insisted that theirs was the tradition of both the founders and the contemporary majority of Bible-believing Southern Baptists.

At the same time, fundamentalists were surprisingly modern in their political organization and their recognition that the old SBC coalition was disappearing. In fact, the fundamentalists seemed exceptionally modern in their realization that the old sources of denominational unity no longer applied, and they were quick to apply multimedia methods for securing denominational control. Many moderates, on the other hand, continued to cling to the old style of denominational politics, fruitlessly attempting to thwart a mobilized opposition with anachronistic denominational machinery, while still claiming to represent the "conservative middle."

The fundamentalists eventually mounted an attempt to move the middle further to the right. They discovered the institutional Achilles' heel that denominational protectionists had overlooked: the appointive

3. Kenneth Bailey, *Southern White Protestantism in the Twentieth Century* (New York: Harper & Row, 1964), pp. 153-54; Linda Mays Givens, "A Programmed Piety: Education for Spirituality in Southern Baptist Study Course Literature, 1908-1986" (unpublished Ed.D. dissertation, Southern Baptist Theological Seminary, 1988); and Robert Norman Nash, Jr., "The Influence of American Myth on Southern Baptist Foreign Missions, 1845-1945" (unpublished Ph.D. dissertation, Southern Baptist Theological Seminary, 1989).

powers of the SBC presidency. Through control of that office they began their decade-long effort to change the course of the SBC. In the process, the fundamentalists fostered a sense of ideological conviction that created a new coalition of true believers with a crusading mentality directed against the destructive forces of pluralism, modernity, and liberalism. In fact, what the fundamentalists created was a new tradition by which they adapted the past to their particular vision of the present.

Remythologizing the SBC: The Fundamentalist Agenda

In short, the fundamentalists set themselves to the task of remythologizing the SBC. They would redefine it from a denomination united around certain basic Baptist doctrines, broadly interpreted, to a denomination defined almost exclusively on the basis of narrow fundamentalist dogma. Their theological agenda, rhetorical skills, and political methods helped them gain control of convention leadership and begin a process of redefining the very character of the SBC itself.

How did the fundamentalists foist their agenda on the SBC? First, they successfully redefined the use of Scripture in SBC life. They made the theory of biblical inerrancy the only acceptable dogma for defining the nature of Holy Scripture. No longer was it permissible merely to affirm Scripture as authoritative for the church and the individual. Rather, Scripture was authoritative only because it was inerrant. As Adrian Rogers declared, either the Bible is "infallible or it's fallible; it is inerrant or it is errant."[4] If it was wrong on any details of science or history, it could be wrong on redemption. Fundamentalists insisted that equivocation on any text put the Christian on a "slippery slope" that ultimately undermined the veracity of all Scripture. To fundamentalists, the use of the historical-critical method and the influence of neoorthodoxy in SBC seminaries was proof that students were being led astray. Any attempt by the moderates to explain their position on biblical authority was judged to be a denial of the "total trustworthiness" of the Bible.

At the same time, fundamentalists faced the embarrassing prospect of having to account for the existence of various theories of inerrancy. As The Controversy deepened, it became apparent that fundamentalists could not always agree among themselves on the meaning of biblical inerrancy. Publicly, at least, most resorted to a basic literalism that had characterized popular Southern Baptist hermeneutics since the

4. James C. Hefley, *The Truth in Crisis* (Dallas: Criterion Publications, 1986), p. 87.

days when it was used to defend slavery. Similarly, while denouncing neoorthodox theology and its impact on the moderates, fundamentalists hesitated to admit their own affinity with another theological system, Scottish Common Sense Realism, a highly rationalistic, propositional approach to theology.[5]

Second, the fundamentalists directed their attacks toward a particular group of enemies whom they believed were destroying the denomination. Prominent on the list were seminary professors who rejected the theory of inerrancy, as well as those pastors and denominational bureaucrats who entertained compromise in the name of unity. Professors and bureaucrats were caricatured almost *en masse* as elitists, far removed from the people, more concerned with perpetuating programs and preserving their positions than in standing for truth. While denouncing this alleged elitism, fundamentalists promoted a view of ministerial authority that threatened to undermine the role of the laity and to obscure the doctrine of the priesthood of all believers. After a decade of controversy it appeared that fundamentalists had simply substituted their own bureaucracy for that of the former denominationalists.

Third, fundamentalists insisted that they had long been excluded from leadership in the SBC and that their views were not reflected on the faculties of the seminaries. In the early stages of The Controversy fundamentalists demanded "parity," equal representation in denominational agencies. Later, as they gained majorities on boards of trustees, it appeared that only those who held inerrantist views would be employed by convention agencies. Unanimity, not parity, seemed the real agenda. In fact, numerous efforts were made to fire those agency heads who did not conform to the demands of inerrantist trustees.

The charge that fundamentalists were not represented appropriately on boards of trustees was more easily made than documented. Prior to 1979, fundamentalists had frequently been elected to the presidency of the SBC, and the denominational boards of trustees reflected the diversity of the SBC itself. Most of the people on those boards held solidly conservative sentiments. Many were no doubt inerrantists in their view of the Scriptures, but that particular criterion was simply not a prerequisite for appointment. Fundamentalist pastors often chose, for various reasons, not to be active in denominational affairs. Some readily

---

5. George Marsden, *Fundamentalism and American Culture: The Shaping of Twentieth-Century Evangelicalism, 1870-1925* (New York: Oxford, 1980); Robeson B. James, ed., *The Unfettered Word* (Waco: Word, 1987); and Duane A. Garrett and Richard R. Melick, Jr., eds., *Authority and Interpretation* (Grand Rapids: Baker, 1987). These books deal with the issue of inerrancy from various perspectives.

acknowledged that they had chosen not to participate in local, state, and national convention affairs until the movement began in 1979.

The question of having inerrantists represented on seminary faculties is also more complex than fundamentalist claims indicate. While affirmation of the authority of Holy Scripture had always been an essential element in the process of securing faculty members, adherence to a specific theory of inerrancy was not required. Nonetheless, seminary faculties generally reflected varying degrees of conservatism regarding the nature of Scripture. For the future, the real question seemed to be whether seminary trustees would permit the use of the historical-critical method at all and whether faculty who would not affirm an inerrantist viewpoint— even though they were strongly committed to biblical authority—would continue to be hired at the seminaries. As we have seen, the fact that a significant number of Southern Seminary faculty—many of whom were hired before The Controversy began—were invited to write for the new "inerrancy" commentary illustrates that certain fundamentalist claims regarding the lack of "parity" were overstated. Fundamentalists demanded parity on seminary faculties, but refused to observe it when it came to naming moderates to denominational boards of trustees.

Fourth, fundamentalists promised to maintain the numerical growth of the convention, charging that if the SBC continued down the path of liberalism, it would experience the same decline as the mainline denominations such as the Methodists and the Presbyterians. In their condemnation of the mainline liberals, fundamentalists failed to see that a denomination can decline as easily from the right as from the left. Indeed, the declines in denominational statistics became more, not less, pronounced as The Controversy deepened and fundamentalist dominance became more intense.

Fifth, the fundamentalists were well aware of the power of populism in the SBC. They promised to take power out of the hands of bureaucrats and restore it to the people—pastors and laity. They claimed to represent the real SBC, the people who paid the salaries and funded the programs. Theirs was a people's movement that would restore the true SBC to its continued triumph as God's "only hope" for world evangelization. The populist reasoning goes something like this: a majority of Southern Baptists believe in inerrancy as we define it. In fact, the only real Southern Baptists are those who believe in errancy. But the elitist majorities on denominational boards of trustees were not inerrantist or were not willing to enforce their inerrantist convictions on the church's institutions. We must therefore elect and appoint to positions of leadership in the SBC only those Southern Baptists who hold our views of inerrancy. This is not a matter for compromise but a matter of conviction.

Naturally, the fundamentalists characterize those who oppose their movement either as liberals who want to retain power or as misguided conservatives who have been duped by the liberals. If it takes political methods to return power to "the people," the fundamentalists explain it is only a response to the political labyrinth created by the bureaucrats. Political means are necessary to achieve orthodox ends.

Sixth, fundamentalists set the agenda from the pulpit, particularly the prominent pulpits of megachurches and convention-wide forums. They display an array of orators, many skilled in the use of media and widely known through their syndicated television preaching. Whatever the moderates might fault in the fundamentalists, few would deny that they are gifted communicators. These preachers were well-placed to set the agenda for defining convention problems. They touted the growth of inerrantist churches at a time when membership in liberal churches was dwindling. Inerrancy and evangelism were almost synonymous. The Methodists, Presbyterians, and other liberal denominations were declining because they had rejected inerrancy. That same fate awaited the SBC. Compromisers and heretics had to be defeated and deposed if the denomination was to be saved.

Finally, the fundamentalist movement in the SBC paralleled a broader movement in American society personified in the presidency of Ronald Reagan. It is not insignificant that the rightward drift of the SBC occurred at the same time as the rightward drift of America itself. Paul Pressler's political insights and right-wing contacts served him well in his efforts to establish control of the SBC.[6]

Why the Moderates Lost

No one can deny that the moderates lost control of the convention. Throughout the decade-long controversy they were unable to stay the fundamentalist drive for denominational dominance. Several reasons account for this failure. First, the so-called moderate coalition was virtually no coalition at all. Its members lacked consensus and direction, particularly in the first five years of The Controversy. During those early years the moderate faction was often unable to agree on a strategy or on a specific candidate for the convention presidency. They were Southern

---

6. Paul Pressler interview with Gary North, "Firestorm tapes," audio cassette. There is some indication that political tactics are dividing fundamentalists. See David K. Montoya, "Trading Principles for Power in the SBC," *The Christian Century*, Jan. 17, 1990, p. 39.

Baptists of varying theological, regional, and political sentiments whose only common bond was their disapproval of fundamentalist tactics.

Second, most moderates misread the times and the future. Many promoted the old methods for dealing with denominational controversy: let the controversy run its course. Do not confront or antagonize the opposition publicly. Bring opponents into the denominational bureaucracy and there they would be pacified and ultimately give up their ideological quest. By relying on the old formula moderates lost valuable time in confronting fundamentalist methods and ideology. In some ways, the same methods by which the moderates had established their place in convention life proved to be their undoing.

Third, many moderates refused to acknowledge that The Controversy did indeed have theological inferences. They tried to avoid theological debate by insisting that the conflict was strictly a matter of denominational politics. Thus they were not able to, or chose not to, articulate a theological response to the fundamentalists. This kept them constantly on the theological defensive and reinforced fundamentalist claims that moderates lacked conviction of belief. When the moderates did take up the challenge, their responses often sounded shrill, thus reinforcing the fundamentalist insistence that moderates were interested only in self-preservation and maintaining the status quo.

Fourth, moderates often promoted the programmatic and corporate identity of the denomination, thereby contributing to the impersonal, bureaucratic image that the fundamentalists exploited. This led many to overlook or underestimate the power of populism in the convention. By minimizing the importance of rhetoric many moderates lost the necessary forum for promoting their vision of the future for the SBC. Denominational leaders were good at directing systems and organizations but less effective in their use of populist rhetoric.

Fifth, a significant number of people sympathetic to the moderate cause refused to get involved in The Controversy. They seemed to hope that it would somehow go away without their having to choose sides. Some did not agree with the fundamentalist political agenda but were reluctant to oppose it lest they be branded as liberal. Many believed that the convention would self correct before the fundamentalists went too far in controlling the SBC. Others hoped that the silent majorities of the laity or the Woman's Missionary Union would eventually wake up and save the convention. Some did not want to alienate certain fundamentalist segments of their constituency in the local churches. Others genuinely sought to maintain neutrality in order to reshape whatever remained of the SBC when The Controversy ran its course. Still others chose not to invest time and energy in the unending conflict with fundamentalists. But by keeping their distance, they tacitly authorized that denominational decisions be made for them by their adversaries.

The moderates were in a sense the Democratic party of the Southern Baptist Convention. They were a coalition of diverse subgroups unable to agree on a common vision for the denomination or evoke the focused ideological intensity that characterized the fundamentalist camp. Their vision of the SBC was based on old methods and political alignments that could no longer muster a denominational consensus. The inability of many moderates to recognize or accept that reality helps explain their impotence in the face of the fundamentalist rise to power.

The Southern Baptist Convention: Scenarios for the Future

Over its first 130 years, the Southern Baptist Convention evolved into an amazing coalition that accommodated a great deal of theological diversity in the service of extensive missionary action. The coalition finally failed, however, as the sources of programmatic and regional stability eventually gave way. It is surprising that the denomination remained intact as long as it did, given its heritage of individualism, local autonomy, and theological diversity. With such powerful incentives to move in different directions, denominational fragmentation was no doubt inevitable. The retrograde nature of The Controversy between moderates and fundamentalists merely hastened the demise of the old coalition.

Indeed, the fragmentation of the SBC is in many respects another indication of the decline in denominational support throughout American Protestantism. A growing number of Christians no longer perceive their primary religious identity in terms of loyalty to a specific denomination. In their insightful analysis of mainline American religion, sociologists Wade Clark Roof and William McKinney conclude that "denominations will persist as organizations but they will be less able to command permanent loyalty."[7] They suggest that in modern America "what matters is less the shared experiences and affirmations of a community of like-minded believers and more a person's own spiritual journey and quest in search of an acceptable and fulfilling belief system."[8] Their studies indicate that a significant amount of denomi-

---

7. Wade Clark Roof and William McKinney, *American Mainline Religion* (New Brunswick: Rutgers University Press, 1987), p. 249.
8. Ibid., p. 67.

national "switching" occurs within both liberal and fundamentalist groups in the nation. They thus observe that, "Less and less bound to an inherited faith, an individual is in a position of 'shopping around' in a consumer market of religious alternatives and can 'pick and choose' among aspects of belief and tradition."[9] While Roof and McKinney insist that conservative-evangelical groups will continue to grow, their study does not examine the impact of extended controversy on an evangelical denomination such as the SBC.

What then is the future for America's largest Protestant denomination in the continuing and volatile struggle? Various scenarios are possible; as scenarios, I propose them here merely speculatively.

Scenario One: The Hostile Takeover

In a sense, the denomination has experienced something akin to the hostile takeover of a corporation. A new management has taken control and is intent upon placing its people in leadership positions. With the new leadership comes the elevation of a new subgroup from within the old coalition. Thus one possibility for the future is that the fundamentalists will simply replace one constituency with another, transforming the SBC into an even more identifiably fundamentalist denomination. To a large extent that has already occurred, at least on the national level of denominational life. Several agencies, including the Christian Life Commission and the Home Mission Board, illustrate the success of the takeover. Given enough time, with increasing control of boards of trustees, that takeover will become more complete. Those who disapprove of fundamentalist ideology and methodology will simply move elsewhere, conform to the changes, or disengage from their respective denominational commitments. Others, such as Jerry Falwell and various other independent fundamentalist Baptists, pleased with the fundamentalist orientation of the SBC, might choose to join or become more closely related to the denomination. Denominational losses might be overcome by adding new fundamentalist constituencies. Dissenters would be worn down and forced out or otherwise brought into line, and the fundamentalization of the SBC would be achieved. Whatever financial difficulties ensue could be solved by restructuring denominational funding, eliminating identifiably moderate programs, and reorganizing the convention to carry out a clear-cut fundamentalist agenda. Denominations can choose to change themselves. Many Southern Baptists might

9. Ibid.

be comfortable with a more clearly fundamentalist denomination. Others might find ways to accommodate such a shift.

Scenario Two: The Controversy Continues

Another scenario involves the possibility that The Controversy continues unabated, with moderates achieving occasional victories on national and state levels and fundamentalists unable to achieve total victory over their opposition: a deadlock. Moderates might choose to remain within the convention and withhold funding in such a way as to create financial problems to confront the controlling fundamentalists. Fundamentalists may discover that they have gained control of the convention at a time when denominational loyalties are difficult to sustain on both the left *and* the right. Some of their constituents are already moving toward Pentecostalism, or toward other less bellicose evangelical denominations. Fundamentalists are discovering that denomination bashing is much easier than denomination building, and that it comes at a cost. Some of the trustees they have appointed are restless over the slowness of the takeover movement and want the denomination to move more radically toward the right.

Thus The Controversy could result in a stalemate between opposing forces in which neither group is able to secure absolute victory and control. This could further complicate the denomination's efforts at ministry by continuing to divert energy and attention away from the mission of the church in evangelism and Christian action. The effects of such a statement are already evident throughout the SBC, extending the conflicts and exacerbating an already tense situation.

Scenario Three: Schism!

The possibility exists that the Southern Baptist Convention could be permanently split. Some moderates might decide to establish a new denomination or promote alliances with the American Baptist Churches, USA, the National Baptists, or other Baptist groups. Indeed, a schism in the SBC might lead eventually to the formation of a new Baptist denomination incorporating black and white denominations into a new constituency, reconciling divisions that predate the Civil War. On the other hand, if the moderates in the SBC succeed in regaining control of the convention presidency, fundamentalists might choose to leave the denomination, perhaps to form a new coalition with such independent

Baptists as Jerry Falwell and others. Although full-blown schism seems unlikely in the near future, it should not be ruled out, particularly if tensions continue to mount and one single ideological agenda continues to dominate SBC policies.

Scenario Four: A New Coalition

The most positive—but least likely—scenario projects the coming together of a new coalition of subgroups within the SBC determined to move beyond The Controversy and redirect the denomination toward a higher calling in witness and mission. This coalition would once again recognize and accommodate the presence of diverse approaches to theology and practice in the convention while affirming a common dedication to biblical authority, evangelism, and missionary endeavor. The new coalition would move to depoliticize the SBC Pastors' Conference, presidency, and boards of trustees. It would work to appoint people holding diverse theological and political sentiments—fundamentalist, moderate, and nonaligned as well as men and women, clergy and laity, whites and nonwhites—to denominational leadership. Instead of trying to create "parity" on each seminary faculty, it might shape seminaries that are discernibly fundamentalist, moderate, or "middle," each responsible to specific subgroups of the convention. Certain agencies, such as the Home and Foreign Mission Boards, might be funded cooperatively while others—seminaries, the Christian Life Commission, and the Baptist Joint Committee—might be funded by specific donations. Fundamentalist and moderate candidates could be elected alternately for two-year terms. New strategies for evangelism could be developed for responding to the pluralism of American culture.

This approach would require compromise on both sides and a willingness to permit diversity, even disagreement, for the sake of ministry and common witness. It would require a return to theological definitions that are discernibly, unashamedly Baptist but open enough to permit a confessional flexibility. It would encourage a contemporary remythologization of what it means to be Baptist in a changing South, a changing nation, and a changing world. It might even create a new criteria for evaluating denominational success based less on statistics, buildings, and size than on spiritual vitality, theological integrity, community, and sacrificial service. Regrettably, this scenario seems increasingly improbable given the depth of the fissure running through SBC life.

Organizational Inertia—Theological Confusion

Whatever the future holds, it is clear that The Controversy has resulted in organizational disunity and theological confusion at every level of SBC life. Debates, divisions, and political intrigues have distracted the denomination from ministry, impeding its response to the pressing needs of the nation and the world. While the convention might succeed in avoiding a major schism, it will certainly continue to experience significant financial and numerical decline, the fallout of a controversy that shows no sign of resolution. Programs will continue to be cut in response to monetary exigency and fundamentalist ideology. Perhaps a de facto schism has already occurred, as many members have left and many churches and individuals have decided to limit their involvement in denominational life. Valuable time and energy has been lost, victims of the continual theological debate and partisan dissension. Indeed, Southern Baptist leaders seem unable to formulate a denominational identity that conveys to their constituency a sense of openness, trust, and common endeavor. As never before, the decision to become or remain a Southern Baptist requires choosing theological and political sides in The Controversy. Diversity and dialogue are replaced by programmed discourse, polemicism, and intimidation. A. K. H. Boyd's parody of the familiar hymn poignantly describes the SBC: "We are all divided, several bodies we, small in hope and doctrine, less in charity."[10]

In spite of their claim to have solidified the doctrinal basis of the SBC, the fundamentalists have intensified the theological identity crisis of the denomination. An insistence on doctrinal certainty obscured the continuing confusion among both fundamentalists and moderates regarding the nature of Scripture, the meaning and morphology of conversion, evangelism, mission, ministerial authority, the priesthood of all believers, theological education, and the nature of the church.

Most basically, perhaps, denominationalists right and left remain confused as to the meaning of the Baptist heritage itself. Contradictory interpretations of the Baptist vision abound. The fear of heresy or schism, pluralism or totalitarianism permeates the denomination and its churches. Unity seems impossible but separation seems unthinkable. Intrigue and inertia triumph. Southern Baptists approach the twenty-first century having squandered much of their spiritual

---

10. A. K. H. Boyd, cited in Andrew L. Drummond, *German Protestantism Since Luther* (London: The Epworth Press, 1951), p. 35.

vitality and their considerable resources on a controversy in which they turned on themselves rather than confront a complex world. Like W. H. Auden's "Double Man," the Southern Baptist Convention is "perched on some great arête, where if we do not move we fall. Yet movement is heretical, since over its ironic rocks no route is truly orthodox."[11]

11. W. H. Auden, *The Double Man* (New York: Random House, 1941), p. 47.